HEART OF DARKNESS, "THE MAN WHO WOULD BE KING," AND OTHER WORKS ON EMPIRE

A Longman Cultural Edition

Joseph Conrad and Rudyard Kipling

HEART OF DARKNESS, "THE MAN WHO WOULD BE KING," AND OTHER WORKS ON EMPIRE

Edited by

David Damrosch

Columbia University

New York   Boston   San Francisco
London   Toronto   Sydney   Tokyo   Singapore   Madrid
Mexico City   Munich   Paris   Cape Town   Hong Kong   Montreal

Editor-in-Chief: Joseph P. Terry
Development Editor: Christine Halsey
Executive Marketing Manager: Ann Stypuloski
Production Coordinator: Virginia Riker
Project Coordination, Text Design, and Electronic Page Makeup: Grapevine
    Publishing Services, Inc.
Cover Designer/Manager: John Callahan
Manufacturing Buyer: Lucy Hebard
Printer and Binder: R R Donnelley and Sons Company / Harrisonburg
Cover Printer: Phoenix Color Corporation

Cover Image: Imperial Federation. *Map of the World Showing the Extent of the
British Empire in 1886* (detail)

The selections from Ghalib are taken from Ralph Russell and Khurdishul Islam,
eds., *The Oxford India Ghalib: Life, Letters, and Ghazals.* Oxford University Press,
2003. Reprinted by permission of Oxford University Press India, New Delhi.

Library of Congress Cataloging-in-Publication Data
    Joseph Conrad and Rudyard Kipling, Heart of darkness, "The man who would
be king" and other works on empire / edited by David Damrosch.
        p. cm. — (A Longman cultural edition)
        ISBN 0-321-36467-8 (alk. paper)
        1. English fiction—19th century—History and criticism. 2. Imperialism in liter-
ature. 3. Colonialism in literature. 4. Conrad, Joseph, 1857–1924 Heart of darkness. 5. Kipling, Rudyard, 1865–1936 Man who would be king. I. Damrosch,
David. II. Series.

PR868.I54J67 2006
823'.809358—dc22
                                                                            2006005780

Please visit our Web site at www.ablongman.com

ISBN: 0-321-36467-8

2 3 4 5 6 7 8 9 10—DOH—09 08 07 06

Contents

List of Illustrations

About Longman Cultural Editions

Reading always seems to vibrate with the transformation of the day—now, yesterday, and centuries ago, when the presses first put printed language into wide circulation. Correspondingly, literary culture has always been a matter of change: of new practices confronting established traditions; of texts transforming under the pressure of new techniques of reading and new perspectives of understanding; of canons shifting and expanding; of informing traditions getting reviewed and renewed, recast and reformed by emerging cultural interests and concerns; of culture, too, as a variable "text"—a reading. Inspired by the innovative *Longman Anthology of British Literature,* Longman Cultural Editions respond creatively to the changes, past and recent, by presenting key texts in contexts that illuminate the lively intersections of literature, tradition, and culture. A principal work is made more interesting by materials that place it in relation to its past, present, and future, enabling us to see how it may be reworking traditional debates and practices, how it appears amid the conversations and controversies of its own historical moment, how it gains new significances in subsequent eras of reading and reaction. Readers new to the work will discover attractive paths for exploration, while those more experienced will encounter fresh perspectives and provocative juxtapositions.

Longman Cultural Editions serve not only several kinds of readers but also (appropriately) their several contexts, from various courses of study to independent adventure. Handsomely produced and affordably priced, our volumes offer appealing companions to *The Longman Anthology of British Literature,* in some cases enriching and expanding units originally developed for the *Anthology*, and in other cases presenting this wealth for the first time. The logic and composition of the contexts vary across the series. The constants are the complete text of an important literary work, reliably edited, headed by an inviting introduction, and supplemented by helpful annotation; a table of dates to track its composition, publication, and public reception in relation to biographical, cultural, and historical events; and a guide for further inquiry and study. With these common measures and uncommon assets, Longman Cultural Editions encourage your literary pleasures with resources for lively reflection and adventurous inquiry.

SUSAN J. WOLFSON
General Editor
Professor of English
Princeton University

About This Edition

In many ways, Joseph Conrad and Rudyard Kipling set the terms for modern literary treatments of empire. They have deeply influenced most later writing in English that deals with the ambitions, complexities, and failures of imperial projects of cultural influence and political control. Any number of English, American, South Asian, and African authors—from Saul Bellow to Salman Rushdie—have worked with and against the models pioneered by Conrad and Kipling in the late Victorian era. Conrad's *Heart of Darkness* and Kipling's best-known poems and tales are now deeply established in world literature, and it can be hard to realize just how revolutionary both writers were. This Longman Cultural Edition is intended to show the literary and historical context within which—and against which—both Conrad and Kipling wrote their seminal early masterpieces in the late 1880s and the 1890s.

Rudyard Kipling burst onto the scene with ten volumes of stories and poems while he was still in his twenties; Henry James called him "the infant monster." James was astonished and a little jealous that Kipling could write so much and so well at such an early age. Both in verse and in prose, Kipling displayed an uncanny ear for the rhythms and nuances of everyday speech, ranging widely across dialects and social classes. His poems show his ability to enter deeply into the minds of the rank-and-file soldiers and lower-level administrators who were entrusted with the daily work of empire, and who were confronted with radically unfamiliar places, cultures, and conflicts. In his later years Kipling became an increasingly enthusiastic—even strident—advocate of empire, but in his major early works he took a far more measured and nuanced stance, exploring the limits of English understanding as well as the resolve and courage that ordinary people could muster in extraordinary situations.

Along with James Joyce, Kipling was the greatest master in his generation of the short story in English. The two stories of his included in this volume blend comedy and tragedy to unfold explosive issues—an interracial love affair in "Without Benefit of Clergy," featuring a strong Indian heroine and a deeply conflicted English hero; and a disastrous expedition of conquest in "The Man Who Would Be King."

These stories are followed by a section called "Contexts: Empire and Its Discontents," presenting some of the popular writing on empire in Kipling's time. The comic poets Edward Lear, Hilaire Belloc, and W. S. Gilbert typically treated the people of colonial regions as comically childlike, confused and confusing. Kipling took up these writers' conventions and radically deepened the range and impact of such verse, even as he continued to write in a lively, accessible style that won him many readers.

The colonies were seen as places of lurking danger as well as comic confusion, as at any moment the childlike natives could morph into fearsome and ruthless opponents. Several Contexts selections show English and Indian reactions to anti-colonial struggles in India and Afghanistan. First are selections relating to the rebellion or "Mutiny" of 1857, in which British rule in India was profoundly shaken—an episode seen rather differently in Indian perspective, in selections from the great Urdu poet Ghalib and his royal patron, Bahadur Shah. Last come two eyewitness reports of the Afghan War of 1879–1880, one by a soldier and then one by a reporter from the same newspaper for which Kipling was working when he wrote his great story "The Man Who Would Be King," based on the British experience in Afghanistan.

The dangers of colonial adventure have never been more harrowingly portrayed than in Joseph Conrad's great novella *Heart of Darkness*, published first in *Blackwood's Magazine* in 1899 and then in book form in 1902 (our text). This compelling, infinitely ambiguous work has been seen by many as a devastating critique of imperial rhetoric and ambition, and by others as so reliant on racist stereotypes of Africa that it reinforces the very imperialism that Conrad meant to attack. "Contexts: The Scramble for Africa" provides materials that help readers understand the literary options—and the political stakes—that were involved when Conrad wrote his narrative, eight years after he'd ventured up the Congo River himself.

A selection from the influential memoir of the early African-American abolitionist Olaudah Equiano shows some ways in which the horror of slavery was reported more than a century before Conrad's time, while two selections from the journalist-adventurer Henry Morton Stanley illustrate the language and tactics of the gung-ho imperialism that Conrad set out to undermine. Stanley was employed in the Congo by King Leopold of Belgium, who ran the colony from 1885 to 1908 as his personal property. Horrific abuses developed at the hands of Leopold's employees as they sought to extract rubber and ivory by the work of native laborers whom they effectively enslaved. In his diary Conrad recorded his first reactions to the Congo during his 1890 visit. The shocking report to Parliament by Conrad's friend Roger Casement alerted a broad public to the true conditions in the Congo and led to Leopold's loss of control over his private kingdom.

In various modes and with varying sympathies, writers sought to convey the shifting uncertainties of cultural contact and conflict in the Victorian age of imperial expansion. Looking at Conrad and Kipling together and in this lively context, we can newly appreciate their creative brilliance as artists deeply engaged in rendering real-world situations. We can also freshly see their commonalities as well as their differences, appreciating the seriousness in Kipling's light verse and the dark comedy in Conrad's telling of his tragic tale.

Several friends and colleagues have contributed in various ways to the shaping of this edition. As general editor for the Longman Cultural Editions, Susan Wolfson has been any contributor's model of good guidance and thoughtful feedback. At Longman, Joe Terry and Ann Stypuloski have been as wonderfully supportive of this volume as of the entire series in which it appears. At Columbia, Felicity Palmer gave excellent assistance in tracking down contextual materials and information for notes. Heather Henderson and William Sharpe have kindly given permission for the use here of their selections from Henry Morton Stanley's *Through the Dark Continent* and the annotations they wrote for it in our *Longman Anthology of British Literature*. Harish Trivedi took time from his busy schedule in Delhi to produce the first translations in English of the poems included here by Bahadur Shah. Finally, over the course of two decades, Edward Said—a great admirer of Conrad and, more selectively, of Kipling—taught me how to teach these writers today.

DAVID DAMROSCH
Columbia University

Max Beerbohm, *Mr. Rudyard Kipling takes a bloomin' day aht, on the blasted 'eath, along with Britannia, 'is gurl* (1904). Beerbohm's caricature shows Kipling dressed in a cheap, flashy suit, a figure of childish imperialism equipped with a fake Roman helmet and a noise-maker, while his sweetheart wears his bowler hat. The caption's parody of Cockney speech identifies Kipling with the rank-and-file soldiers he celebrated in poems such as "Tommy" and "Mandalay."

Introduction

The nineteenth century was an age of nationalism and an age of empire. In some regions, a rising nationalism meant the dismantling of old empires, most notably in South America, where lands that had been Spanish and Portuguese colonies for three hundred years began to assert their independence and then gradually achieved it. Elsewhere, though, other European powers relentlessly pressed to gain influence and control over much of the rest of the world. Imperial Russia extended its sway in central Asia and in the Balkan regions long controlled by the declining Ottoman Empire; France developed major colonial holdings in Africa, the Caribbean, and Indochina, and even King Leopold of Belgium gained control over the Congo, a region almost eighty times the size of his own small country.

The greatest of all imperial powers in the nineteenth century was England, which came to control a quarter of the entire earth's surface, by far the largest empire ever known in history. Even that figure understates England's reach, for the British Navy ruled the seas following the defeat of Napoleon's forces early in the century. By 1886, a British trade group called the Imperial Federation could publish a world map anchored by a figure of Britannia sitting at ease on the entire globe. As can be seen from the portion shown on the cover of this volume, the map highlights Britain's colonies in light red and also shows the major shipping routes that knit the seven seas into a vast delivery network. Across this network the British imported raw materials from the colonies and exported a thousand kinds of commodities, from cloth and machine guns to Bibles and popular novels.

The steady expansion of British imperial control posed enormous challenges, and created new opportunities, for poets, novelists, and travel writers. The public was eager for tales of imperial romance and adventure, and readers were fascinated and confused by the welter of peoples, languages, histories, and cultures that British troops, traders, and missionaries were now encountering. Already in the eighteenth century, a popular genre had emerged of "oriental tales," often highly fanciful in nature and written by people with little or no direct experience abroad. Foreign cultures often served just as colorful backdrops for sentimental or melodramatic plots. More philosophical writers might use tales of distant lands as allegories or mirrors of European customs and concerns (Jonathan Swift's *Gulliver's Travels* is a famous example). In the 1880s and 1890s, two great writers began writing from firsthand knowledge about the colonial experience. Born outside England and with wide experience in differing countries, Rudyard Kipling and then Joseph Conrad began to create extraordinary works that probed the anxieties and the opportunities of empire.

They came to their creative projects from very different backgrounds and viewed their work in radically different ways. Kipling achieved a precocious early success and remained an immensely popular poet and writer of tales, publishing in mass-circulation magazines and then collecting his work in bestselling books. From the beginning, he was fascinated to convey the flavor of life and speech of the soldiers and lower-level administrators who carried out the daily work of empire, a work he viewed as an essential civilizing mission. Conrad, by contrast, started writing only after years of wandering the oceans as a sailor and ship's captain, and he held deeply skeptical views about human motives and possibilities. He also made exceptional demands on his readers, weaving strangely dense and often extravagant fictions. During their later years and for decades after their deaths, Conrad and Kipling were often regarded almost as direct opposites: Kipling the hearty, popular imperialist, Conrad the troubled, complex anti-imperialist. There was some truth to this, particularly when Kipling's imperial enthusiasms grew and hardened in his later years. Yet Kipling's earlier works—which included much of his best writing—never simply endorsed the imperial project but probed its tensions and contradictions, and his many years of life in India gave him an insider's view possessed by few other European writers of his day, Conrad included. For his part, Conrad always hoped to reach a broad audience and eventually came to write bestsellers of his own; throughout his career, he built his complex fictions out of adventure tales and sailors' yarns. Both writers also based their fictions on their own experiences, as a look at their lives will show.

Conrad's Life and Works

One of the greatest English novelists, Joseph Conrad seriously began to learn English at the age of twenty-one. He was already embarked on decades of world travel that would shape his fiction once he finally decided, in 1894, to become a full-time writer. By then, he had long lived in exile from his native Poland—a country no longer even present on the map at that time, carved up between Russia and the Austro-Hungarian Empire. Born Józef Teodor Konrad Korzeniowski in 1857, he was the son of a noble-born Polish poet and patriot, Apollo Korzeniowski, whose ardent nationalism led to his arrest by the Russian government in 1861. He was exiled to a bleak northern Russian village, accompanied by four-year-old Józef and his mother, Eva. Ill with tuberculosis, Eva died there in 1865; also ill, Apollo was allowed to return to Cracow, where he died in 1869 when his son was twelve. Józef was raised thereafter by his cultured, cosmopolitan uncle Tadeusz Bobrowski, but he was bored and restless in school in Cracow, and his uncle sent him to Switzerland with a private tutor. Before long, the tutor resigned in frustration, and sixteen-year-old Józef slipped away to Marseilles and joined the French merchant navy.

He spent the next twenty years as a sailor and eventually ship captain, working first for the French merchant marine and then for British companies. His ships took him to the eastern Mediterranean, Indonesia, China, Thailand, the Philippines, South America, the West Indies, and Africa. These voyages allowed him to see firsthand the unsettling effects of the rising tide of European imperial expansion. He even became actively involved in political conflict in 1878, when he and several friends bought a ship to smuggle guns into Spain on behalf of a claimant to the throne. This effort collapsed, and Conrad was wounded not long after, either in a duel (as he claimed) or else (as his uncle believed) in a suicide attempt.

Heavily in debt, Conrad left France and joined the British merchant marine, where he served for the next sixteen years.

In London in 1889 for several months between assignments, he began *Almayer's Folly*, a novel closely based on some of his South Seas experiences, but he interrupted this project in 1890 to fulfill a childhood dream of sailing up the Congo River. Four months later he returned to England, beset with fever and a deepening tragic sense of the imperial enterprise and of life overall. "Before the Congo," he later wrote, "I was a mere animal." He became active in the efforts led by the Irish diplomat Roger Casement to expose the cruelty of imperial practices in the Congo, and in his fiction he explored the slippage of idealism into corruption, in language and practice alike.

In 1894 Conrad's life changed in decisive ways. His uncle died, and Conrad decided to settle permanently in England; he Anglicized his name as "Joseph Conrad," and later married an English-woman, Jessie George. He also took a temporary break, which proved to be permanent, from sailing, and completed *Almayer's Folly*, which soon found a publisher. Determined to make a living as a writer, he began a second novel while the first was still in press, and he soon drew the notice of some of England's leading writers, including Bernard Shaw and H. G. Wells. These new English friends regarded Conrad with some bemusement, as a master of English prose and yet still an exotic foreigner. In a memoir, Wells described him driving a carriage rapidly along a country lane, urging his puzzled horses on with imperious commands in Polish. The public at large was slower to recognize the excellence of his work. *Heart of Darkness* attracted little attention when it was published in *Blackwood's Magazine* in 1899, and Conrad's publisher didn't even bother to name it in the title when it was published in book form in *Youth: A Narrative, and Two Other Stories* (1902). Over the next decade, *Lord Jim*, *Nostromo*, and *The Secret Agent* (now regarded as masterpieces) sold poorly, and as late as 1910 Conrad still considered returning to sea. His tales of the sea and of imperial and political intrigue gradually won more attention, and he became a bestselling writer with his novels *Chance* (1913) and *Victory* (1915). World War I only deepened his pessimism about modern life, but he continued to pursue his artistic vocation with undiminished intensity until his death in 1924.

Kipling's Life and Works

Eight years younger than Conrad, Kipling began writing professionally at the early age of sixteen. He was born in 1865 in Bombay, to cultured English parents. His father was an artist and scholar who became curator of the museum at Lahore in northern India, and two of his mother's sisters married prominent English painters. Although the Kiplings weren't well-to-do, they moved in upper-class circles both in India and in England; a cousin, Stanley Baldwin, became British Prime Minister. After an idyllic early childhood in India, Kipling was sent back to England at age six for schooling. After five years of misery with foster parents, he was sent to a second-rate boarding school at Westward Ho, a village on the far western coast of England. He returned to India in 1882 and found work as a journalist, first at a small newspaper in Lahore called the *Civil and Military Gazette*, and then at a major paper in Allahabad, *The Pioneer*. He loved his work, and his assignments enabled him to hone his powers of observation and his keen ear for the many varieties of dialect and language spoken throughout northern India; as a child, in fact, he'd been at least as fluent in Hindi (thanks to his nurses and nannies) as in English.

Kipling began writing comic verse and stories for his newspapers, and at the age of twenty-one he published his first book of verse, *Departmental Ditties* (1886). Several of the poems in this volume are from that collection, as well as from *Barrack-Room Ballads* (1892). These early poems already show how closely attuned Kipling was to the modes of speech and thought of the empire's soldiers and administrators. Kipling was perfectly comfortable as a member of the imperial class; he relished a journalistic assignment to Simla, a Himalayan mountain resort that the British used as a summer seat of government, where he was told that a requirement of his assignment would be to cut a fine figure on the dance floor (no doubt an excellent place to pick up tidbits of gossip and news). Yet even Kipling's early "departmental ditties" are alive to the problems of mutual incomprehension and outright corruption that constantly shadowed British efforts to impose their vision of order and progress on their Indian subjects.

Even as he gave sympathetic voice to the viewpoints of soldiers such as his emblematic "Tommy" or the wistful speaker of "Mandalay," Kipling wasn't simply endorsing their jingoistic and often racist views. Instead, he was trying to get inside the minds of ordinary people confronted with extraordinary situations for which their limited education and experience at home had left them unprepared. When Oxford-educated writer and artist Max Beerbohm drew his satirical portrait of Kipling going out for a walk "on the blasted 'eath, along with Britannia, 'is gurl" (see p. xiv), he was registering upper-class surprise at Kipling's fascination with working-class people. The very title of Kipling's collection *Barrack-Room Ballads* looks back to William Wordsworth's revolutionary portrayals of obscure rural people in his *Lyrical Ballads* (1798–1805). Like Wordsworth, Kipling strove "to adopt the very language of men," emphasizing conversational speech instead of elaborate poetic diction.

When Kipling went beyond the barrack-room, his stories typically didn't rise too far from everyday reality, and tales such as "Without Benefit of Clergy" portray people on the lower and middle rungs of the administrative scale. Even the exquisitely refined Oscar Wilde recognized and admired what Kipling was up to:

> He who would stir us now by fiction must either give us an entirely new background or reveal to us the soul of man in its innermost workings. The first is for the moment being done for us by Mr. Rudyard Kipling. As one turns over the pages of his *Plain Tales from the Hills*, one feels as if one were seated under a palm-tree reading life by superb flashes of vulgarity. The bright colours of the bazaars dazzle one's eyes. The jaded, second-rate Anglo-Indians are in exquisite incongruity with their surroundings. The mere lack of style in the story-teller gives an odd journalistic realism to what he tells us. From the point of view of literature Mr. Kipling is a genius who drops his aspirates. From the point of view of life, he is a reporter who knows vulgarity better than any one has ever known it. Dickens knew its clothes and its comedy. Mr. Kipling knows its essence and its seriousness. He is our first authority on the second-rate, and has seen marvelous things through keyholes, and his backgrounds are real works of art. ("The Critic as Artist," 1892)

Plain Tales from the Hills, to which Wilde refers, was one of Kipling's first volumes of stories, one of six collections published from 1887 to 1889, when he returned to England—already a famous author when Conrad was tentatively beginning his first novel. Well before *Heart of Darkness* was written, Kipling had published "Without Benefit of Clergy" (1891) and his most troubled exploration of imperial adventure, "The Man Who Would Be King" (1888). He had direct experience of that story's Afghanistani background, as his newspaper had sent him three years earlier as a special correspondent to Rawalpindi near the Afghan border, to cover the new Indian Viceroy's ceremonial reception of the Amir of Afghanistan. Kipling took a side trip to the Khyber Pass (between India and Afghanistan), where local tribesmen shot at him. Writing the story while working as correspondent and assistant editor at *The Pioneer*, Kipling reflects this situation, as a Kipling-like editor describes his encounter with two drifters who set out to conquer the Afghan-like country of "Kafiristan." However much Kipling was committed to the mission of empire, the stories given here explore the depth of cultural interactions and the ambiguity of the imperial adventure, as he saw it close at hand.

Following these early successes, Kipling settled in England. Always restless, he lived for a period in Vermont after marrying an American wife, Caroline Balestier. He also made long visits to South Africa, where he became a close friend of the diamond magnate and colonial statesman Cecil Rhodes. While Kipling never revisited India after 1892, India continued to figure periodically in his work, most notably in his delightful novel *Kim* (1901). In 1907 Kipling became the first Englishman to receive the Nobel Prize in literature, and up until World War I a wide public avidly read his poems and stories. Often he contributed topical poems on public occasions. Three such poems are included here. "Recessional," written for Queen Victoria's Diamond Jubilee, is a surprisingly muted celebration of empire in the sixtieth year of Victoria's reign. "The White Man's Burden"—a phrase that has become infamous as an imperialist motto—was addressed to the United States after its defeat of Spain in the Philippines in 1898. "Ulster, 1912" shows solidarity with northern Irish Protestants who feared being abandoned by the British government that had settled their ancestors in Catholic Ireland.

Kipling's reading public declined after World War I, and for decades after his death in 1936 his later, assertive imperialism cast its shadow over his early writing. In recent years, though, this early work has been seen afresh, newly appreciated for its innovative language and its close and sympathetic attention to the real lives of the Anglo-Indian British who did the work of empire, and to the lives of the Indians who were its usually unwilling subjects. Conrad, in turn, has come to be seen as closer in outlook to Kipling than his early readers would have supposed: both writers champion the virtues of work amid chaotic and confusing situations, and both show us colonial conditions through the eyes of outsiders— whether Conrad's Marlow or Kipling's Peachey Carnehan—who struggle to make sense of their experiences. Read together, Conrad and Kipling can now be seen as consummate artists who blend stark realism with elements of impressionistic ambiguity. At once lively, dark, and irresistibly compelling, their works give us an unparalleled set of approaches to the British imperial experience.

Table of Dates

1690   Job Charnock, an agent of the English East India Company, establishes a city and major port at Calcutta on the northeast coast of India. English influence rapidly begins to grow in India, and the East India Company (originally a trading business) takes on governmental functions in the regions it controls.

1772   Calcutta becomes the capital of British India under the East India Company's Governor General Warren Hastings.

1789   Olaudah Equiano publishes *The Interesting Narrative of the Life of Olaudah Equiano, or Gustavus Vassa, the African, Written by Himself.*

1818   The East India Company gains effective control of India, directly ruling many areas and accepting tribute from local rulers of about half India's territory.

1857   Józef Teodor Konrad Korzeniowski born on December 3 in the town of Berdichev in Russian-occupied Ukraine, a province of Poland. Revolt of Indian soldiers in the British army. Fighting rapidly spreads across north India, with the rebels taking control of Delhi and other cities. The British finally suppress "the Mutiny" in March 1858. Power is transferred from the private East India Company to direct British rule; Bahadur Shah II, ruler of the Islamic Mughal Empire in north India, is exiled to Burma.

1865   Rudyard Kipling born on December 30 in Lahore, northern India. Death of Conrad's mother, Eva.

1869   Death of Conrad's father, Apollo Korzeniowski. Conrad is unofficially adopted by his uncle Tadeusz Bobrowski.

1871   Kipling sent to England, boards for five years with a family.

1874   Conrad runs away to sea, joining the French merchant marine, later serving in the British merchant marine (1878–94). Voyages include trips to Venezuela, Constantinople, Australia, India, and Indonesia.

1876   Kipling attends school at United Services College in Westward Ho, Devonshire (through 1882); later fictionalizes (and romanticizes) his experiences in *Stalky & Co.* (1899).

1878   Henry Morton Stanley publishes *Through the Dark Continent*.

1879   Second Afghan War begins, following massacre of British envoy Louis Cavagnari in Kabul in September; war concludes in August 1880 with installation of new Afghan ruler by the British.

1882   Kipling begins journalistic career in India.

1884   Berlin Conference apportions European spheres of influence in Africa and grants King Leopold II of Belgium the right to possess the Congo as his personal property.

1885   King Leopold establishes the Société Anonyme pour le Commerce du Haut-Congo (Corporation for Trade in the Upper Congo), which effectively rules the "Congo Free State" until 1908.

1886   Conrad becomes a British subject while living in London between voyages.

1889   Conrad begins his first novel, *Almayer's Folly* (published 1895). Kipling moves from India to England to make his career as a writer of fiction and poetry.

1890   Conrad obtains a job as a riverboat captain for the Belgian "Société" and spends the summer months in the Congo, traveling up the Congo River. On his return downriver, he brings Georges Klein, ill with fever, who dies en route. Henry Morton Stanley publishes *In Darkest Africa*.

1892   Kipling marries Caroline Balestier, daughter of an American publisher and writer with whom he had worked; they settle in Vermont, but Kipling feels out of place and they return to England in 1894.

1893   Kipling publishes *The Jungle Book*; sequel follows in 1895.

1896   Conrad marries Jessie George. They have two sons, Borys (born 1898) and John Alexander (born 1906).

1899   Conrad's *Heart of Darkness* appears in *Blackwood's Magazine*.

1901   Kipling, *Kim*. Death of Queen Victoria.

1902   *Heart of Darkness* published in book form together with Conrad's novella *Youth*. Kipling publishes *Just So Stories*; buys a house in the English town of Burwash, Sussex, where he lives until his death.

1904   Conrad, *Nostromo*.

1907   Kipling awarded Nobel Prize for Literature. Conrad publishes *The Secret Agent*.

1908   Following extensive agitation in the wake of Roger Casement's reports on conditions in the Congo, King Leopold is forced to relinquish control of the Congo.

1913   Conrad becomes a bestselling author with his novel *Chance*.

1914   Outbreak of World War I (through 1918).

1919   Conrad settles near Canterbury, England.

1924   Conrad dies on August 3.

1936   Kipling dies in London, January 18.

1947   India achieves independence from England.

Rudyard Kipling

Poems and Stories

Rudyard Kipling

ণ্ডুর্ত

A Tale of Two Cities

Playing on the title of Dickens's novel about London and Paris during the French revolution, Kipling contrasts two centers of British rule in India: Calcutta, settled in 1690 by Job Charnock as a trading port for the British East India Company; and Simla, a resort town in the Himalayas, which the British developed as a center of government during the hot summer months.

Where the sober-colored cultivator smiles
        On his *byles*[1];
Where the cholera, the cyclone, and the crow
        Come and go;
Where the merchant deals in indigo and tea,   5
        Hides and *ghi*[2];
Where the Babu[3] drops inflammatory hints
        In his prints;
Stands a City—Charnock chose it—packed away
        Near a Bay—   10
By the Sewage rendered fetid, by the sewer
        Made impure,
By the Sunderbunds[4] unwholesome, by the swamp
        Moist and damp;

[1]Oxen or bullocks.
[2]Clarified butter.
[3]Generally, an Indian gentleman; here, a civil servant working for the British.
[4]A swampy forest extending across southern Bangladesh and India's West Bengal State.

And the City and the Viceroy, as we see,   15
    Don't agree.

Once, two hundered years ago, the trader came
    Meek and tame.
Where his timid foot first halted, there he stayed,
    Till mere trade   20
Grew to Empire, and he sent his armies forth
    South and North
Till the country from Peshawur to Ceylon[5]
    Was his own.
Thus the midday halt of Charnock—more's the pity!—   25
    Grew a City.
As the fungus sprouts chaotic from its bed,
    So it spread—
Chance-directed, chance-erected, laid and built
    On the silt—   30
Palace, byre,[6] hovel—poverty and pride—
    Side by side;
And, above the packed and pestilential town,
    Death looked down.

But the Rulers in that City by the Sea   35
    Turned to flee—
Fled, with each returning spring-tide from its ills
    To the Hills.
From the clammy fogs of morning, from the blaze
    Of old days,   40
From the sickness of the noontide, from the heat,
    Beat retreat;
For the country from Peshawur to Ceylon
    Was their own.
But the Merchant risked the perils of the Plain   45
    For his gain.
Now the resting-place of Charnock, 'neath the palms,
    Asks an alms,

---

[5]The far north to the far south.
[6]Barn.

And the burden of its lamentation is,
    Briefly, this: 50
"Because for certain months, we boil and stew,
    So should you.
Cast the Viceroy and his Council, to perspire
    In our fire!"
And for answer to the argument, in vain   55
    We explain
That an amateur Saint Lawrence cannot cry:—
    "*All* must fry!"[7]
That the Merchant risks the perils of the Plain
    For his gain.   60
Nor can Rulers rule a house that men grow rich in,
    From its kitchen.

Let the Babu drop inflammatory hints
    In his prints;
And mature—consistent soul—his plan for stealing   65
    To Darjeeling[8]:
Let the Merchant seek, who makes his silver pile,
    England's isle;
Let the City Charnock pitched on—evil day!—
    Go Her way.   70
Though the argosies[9] of Asia at Her doors
    Heap their stores,
Though Her enterprise and energy secure
    Income sure,
Though "out-station orders punctually obeyed"   75
    Swell Her trade—
Still, for rule, administration, and the rest,
    Simla's best.

---

[7]Saint Lawrence was killed by the Romans during a time of persecution in the third century. While being tortured on a gridiron, he is said to have remarked to his torturers: "I am cooked on that side; turn me over, and eat."

[8]A cool region in the Himalayan foothills.

[9]Merchant ships.

The Last Department

Twelve hundred million men are spread
About this Earth, and I and You
Wonder, when You and I are dead,
"What will those luckless millions do?"

"None whole or clean," we cry, "or free from stain
Of favour." Wait awhile, till we attain
   The Last Department where nor fraud nor fools,
Nor grade nor greed, shall trouble us again.

Fear, Favour, or Affection—what are these   5
To the grim Head who claims our services?
   I never knew a wife or interest yet
Delay that *pukka*[1] step, miscalled "decease";

When leave, long overdue, none can deny;
When idleness of all Eternity   10
   Becomes our furlough, and the marigold
Our thriftless, bullion-minting Treasury

Transferred to the Eternal Settlement,
Each in his strait,[2] wood-scantled office pent,
   No longer Brown reverses Smith's appeals,   15
Or Jones records his Minute[3] of Dissent.

And One, long since a pillar of the Court,
As mud between the beams thereof is wrought;
   And One who wrote on phosphates for the crops
Is subject-matter of his own Report.   20

These be the glorious ends whereto we pass—
Let Him who Is, go call on Him who Was;

[1]Permanent. From a Hindi word meaning "cooked, ripe, mature."
[2]Narrow.
[3]Memorandum.

And He shall see the *malliel* steals the slab
For currie-grinder,[4] and for goats the grass.

A breath of wind, a Border bullet's flight,   25
A draught of water, or a horse's fright—
   The droning of the fat *Sheristada*[5]
Ceases, the punkah[6] stops, and falls the night

For you or Me. Do those who live decline
The step that offers, or their work resign?   30
   Trust me, To-day's Most Indispensables,
Five hundred men can take your place or mine.

The Widow at Windsor[1]

'Ave you 'eard o' the Widow at Windsor
   With a hairy gold crown on 'er 'ead?
She 'as ships on the foam—she 'as millions at 'ome,
   An' she pays us poor beggars in red.[2]
      (Ow, poor beggars in red!)   5
There's 'er nick on the cavalry 'orses,[3]
   There's 'er mark on the medical stores—
An' 'er troopers you'll find with a fair wind be'ind
   That takes us to various wars.
      (Poor beggars!—barbarious wars!)   10
         Then 'ere's to the Widow at Windsor,
            An' 'ere's to the stores an' the guns,
         The men an' the 'orses what makes up the forces
            O' Missis Victorier's sons.
            (Poor beggars! Victorier's sons!)   15

---

[4]The cemetery gardener takes the tombstone to grind spices on.

[5]Clerk of the court.

[6]Large room-cooling fan.

---

[1]Queen Victoria, whose beloved husband Prince Albert died in 1861, leaving her a widow at age 42 with nine children. She mourned him for the remaining 40 years of her life while living at her royal residence, Windsor Castle.

[2]Army uniforms; blood (the uniforms were red to camouflage blood).

[3]Army horses had a notch on the hoof to mark them as government property.

Walk wide o' the Widow at Windsor,
  For 'alf o' Creation she owns:
We 'ave bought 'er the same with the sword an' the flame,
  An' we've salted it down with our bones.
    (Poor beggars!—it's blue with our bones!)   20
Hands off o' the sons o' the Widow,
  Hands off o' the goods in 'er shop,
For the Kings must come down an' the Emperors frown
  When the Widow at Windsor says "Stop"!
    (Poor beggars!—we're sent to say "Stop"!)   25
        Then 'ere's to the Lodge o' the Widow,[4]
          From the Pole to the Tropics it runs—
            To the Lodge that we tile with the rank an' the file,
              An' open in form with the guns.
              (Poor beggars!—it's always they guns!)   30

We 'ave 'eard o' the Widow at Windsor,
  It's safest to let 'er alone:
For 'er sentries we stand by the sea an' the land
  Wherever the bugles are blown.
    (Poor beggars!—an' don't we get blown!)   35
Take 'old o' the Wings o' the Mornin',[5]
  An' flop round the earth till you're dead;
But you won't get away from the tune that they play[6]
  To the bloomin' old rag over'ead.
    (Poor beggars!—it's 'ot over'ead!)   40
        Then 'ere's to the sons o' the Widow,
          Wherever, 'owever they roam.
            'Ere's all they desire, an' if they require
              A speedy return to their 'ome.
              (Poor beggars!—they'll never see 'ome!)   45

---

[4]The speaker compares the Empire to a Freemason's Lodge. Compare Kipling's use of this symbolism in "The Man Who Would Be King," p. 46.
[5]"If I take the wings of the morning, and dwell in the uttermost parts of the sea, / even there Thy hand shall lead me" (Psalm 139:9–10).
[6]"God Save the Queen," the British anthem.

Tommy

I went into a public-'ouse to get a pint o' beer,
The publican 'e up an' sez, "We serve no red-coats here."
The girls be'ind the bar they laughed an' giggled fit to die,
I outs into the street again an' to myself sez I:
    O it's Tommy this, an' Tommy that, an' "Tommy, go away";
    But it's "Thank you, Mister Atkins," when the band begins
        to play,—
    The band begins to play, my boys, the band begins to play,
    O it's "Thank you, Mister Atkins," when the band begins
        to play.

I went into a theatre as sober as could be,
They gave a drunk civilian room, but 'adn't none for me;   10
They sent me to the gallery or round the music-'alls,
But when it comes to fightin', Lord! they'll shove me in the stalls!
    For it's Tommy this, an' Tommy that, an' "Tommy, wait
        outside";
    But it's "Special train for Atkins" when the trooper's on the
        tide,—
    The troopship's on the tide, my boys, the troopship's on the
        tide,   15
    O it's "Special train for Atkins" when the trooper's on the
        tide.

Yes, makin' mock o' uniforms that guard you while you sleep
Is cheaper than them uniforms, an' they're starvation cheap;
An' hustlin' drunken soldiers when they're goin' large a bit
Is five times better business than paradin' in full kit.[1]   20
    Then it's Tommy this, an' Tommy that, an' "Tommy, 'ow's
        yer soul?"
    But it's "Thin red line of 'eroes" when the drums begin to
        roll,—
    The drums begin to roll, my boys, the drums begin to roll,
    O it's "Thin red line of 'eroes" when the drums begin to roll.

---

[1]Uniform and gear.

We aren't no thin red 'eroes, nor we aren't no blackguards too,   25
But single men in barricks, most remarkable like you;
An' if sometimes our conduck isn't all your fancy paints,
Why, single men in barricks don't grow into plaster saints;
> While it's Tommy this, an' Tommy that, an' "Tommy, fall
> be'ind,"
> But it's "Please to walk in front, sir," when there's trouble
> in the wind,—   30
> There's trouble in the wind, my boys, there's trouble in the
> wind,
> O it's "Please to walk in front, sir," when there's trouble in
> the wind.

You talk o' better food for us, an' schools, an' fires, an' all:
We'll wait for extry rations if you treat us rational.
Don't mess about the cook-room slops, but prove it to our face   35
The Widow's Uniform is not the soldier-man's disgrace.
> For it's Tommy this, an' Tommy that, an' "Chuck him out,
> the brute!"
> But it's "Saviour of 'is country" when the guns begin to shoot;
> An' it's Tommy this, an' Tommy that, an' anything you please;
> An' Tommy ain't a bloomin' fool—you bet that Tommy sees!

The Young British Soldier

When the 'arf-made recruity goes out to the East
'E acts like a babe an' 'e drinks like a beast,
An' 'e wonders because 'e is frequent deceased
> Ere 'e's fit for to serve as a soldier.
> > Serve, serve, serve as a soldier,   5
> > Serve, serve, serve as a soldier,
> > Serve, serve, serve as a soldier,
> > > So-oldier *of* the Queen!

Now all you recruities what's drafted to-day,
You shut up your rag-box an' 'ark to my lay,   10
An' I'll sing you a soldier as far as I may:
> A soldier what's fit for a soldier.
> > Fit, fit, fit for a soldier . . .

First mind you steer clear o' the grog-sellers' huts,
For they sell you Fixed Bay'nets that rots out your guts—   15
Ay, drink that 'ud eat the live steel from your butts—
    An' it's bad for the young British soldier.
      Bad, bad, bad for the soldier . . .

When the cholera comes—as it will past a doubt—
Keep out of the wet and don't go on the shout,[1]   20
For the sickness gets in as the liquor dies out,
    An' it crumples the young British soldier.
      Crum-, crum-, crumples the soldier . . .

But the worst o' your foes is the sun over'ead:
You *must* wear your 'elmet for all that is said: 25
If 'e finds you uncovered 'e'll knock you down dead,
    An' you'll die like a fool of a soldier.
      Fool, fool, fool of a soldier . . .

If you're cast for fatigue by a sergeant unkind,
Don't grouse like a woman nor crack on nor blind;   30
Be handy and civil, and then you will find
    That it's beer for the young British soldier.
      Beer, beer, beer for the soldier . . .

Now, if you must marry, take care she is old—
A troop-sergeant's widow's the nicest I'm told,   35
For beauty won't help if your rations is cold,
    Nor love ain't enough for a soldier.
      'Nough, 'nough, 'nough for a soldier . . .

If the wife should go wrong with a comrade, be loath
To shoot when you catch 'em—you'll swing, on my oath!—   40
Make 'im take 'er and keep 'er: that's Hell for them both,
    An' you're shut o' the curse of a soldier.
      Curse, curse, curse of a soldier . . .

When first under fire an' you're wishful to duck,
Don't look nor take 'eed at the man that is struck,   45

[1]Get drunk. Periodic cholera epidemics claimed many English as well as native lives in India.

Be thankful you're livin', and trust to your luck
    And march to your front like a soldier.
        Front, front, front like a soldier . . .

When 'arf of your bullets fly wide in the ditch,
Don't call your Martini[2] a cross-eyed old bitch;   50
She's human as you are—you treat her as sich,
    An' she'll fight for the young British soldier.
        Fight, fight, fight for the soldier . . .

When shakin' their bustles like ladies so fine,
The guns o' the enemy wheel into line,   55
Shoot low at the limbers an' don't mind the shine,
    For noise never startles the soldier.
        Start-, start-, startles the soldier . . .

If your officer's dead and the sergeants look white,
Remember it's ruin to run from a fight: 60
So take open order, lie down, and sit tight,
    And wait for supports like a soldier.
        Wait, wait, wait like a soldier . . .

When you're wounded and left on Afghanistan's plains,
And the women come out to cut up what remains,   65
Jest roll to your rifle and blow out your brains
    An' go to your Gawd like a soldier.
        Go, go, go like a soldier,
        Go, go, go like a soldier,
        Go, go, go like a soldier,   70
        So-oldier *of* the Queen!

Fuzzy-Wuzzy

(Soudan Expeditionary Force)

This poem refers to the Sudan campaign of 1883–85, during which British forces tried to put down an uprising of Sudanese militants known as Mahdists. A British force was sent to relieve General

[2]Rifle.

Charles George Gordon, governor of the Sudan, whose garrison in Khartoum was besieged by the Mahdists; the relief force faced strong resistance en route and arrived outside Khartoum on January 28, 1885, two days after the city had fallen to the Mahdi Muhammed Ahmad and Gordon had been killed.

We've fought with many men acrost the seas,
   An' some of 'em was brave an' some was not:
The Paythan an' the Zulu an' Burmese[1];
   But the Fuzzy was the finest o' the lot.
We never got a ha'porth's change of 'im: 5
   'E squatted in the scrub an' 'ocked our 'orses,
'E cut our sentries up at Sua*kim*,
   An' 'e played the cat an' banjo with our forces.
      So 'ere's *to* you, Fuzzy-Wuzzy, at your 'ome in the Soudan;
      You're a pore benighted 'eathen but a first-class fightin' man;
      We gives you your certificate, an' if you want it signed
      We'll come an' 'ave a romp with you whenever you're
        inclined.

We took our chanst among the Khyber 'ills,
   The Boers knocked us silly at a mile,
The Burman give us Irriwaddy chills,   15
   An' a Zulu *impi*[2] dished us up in style:
But all we ever got from such as they
   Was pop to what the Fuzzy made us swaller;
We 'eld our bloomin' own, the papers say,
   But man for man the Fuzzy knocked us 'oller.   20
      Then 'ere's *to* you, Fuzzy-Wuzzy, an' the missis and the kid;
      Our orders was to break you, an' of course we went an' did.
      We sloshed you with Martinis,[3] an' it wasn't 'ardly fair;
      But for all the odds agin' you, Fuzzy-Wuz, you broke the
        square.[4]

[1]Previous imperial wars in Afghanistan, South Africa, and Burma.
[2]Warrior.
[3]Rifles.
[4]The ordered ranks of the British attack force.

'E 'asn't got no papers of 'is own,   25
   'E 'asn't got no medals nor rewards,
So we must certify the skill 'e's shown
   In usin' of 'is long two-'anded swords:
When 'e's 'oppin' in an' out among the bush
   With 'is coffin-'eaded shield an' shovel-spear,   30
An 'appy day with Fuzzy on the rush
   Will last an 'ealthy Tommy for a year.
      So 'ere's *to* you, Fuzzy-Wuzzy, an' your friends which are no
        more,
      If we 'adn't lost some messmates we would 'elp you to deplore;
      But give an' take's the gospel, an' we'll call the bargain fair,
      For if you 'ave lost more than us, you crumpled up the square!

'E rushes at the smoke when we let drive,
   An', before we know, 'e's 'ackin' at our 'ead;
'E's all 'ot sand an' ginger when alive,
   An' 'e's generally shammin' when 'e's dead.   40
'E's a daisy, 'e's a ducky, 'e's a lamb!
   'E's a injia-rubber idiot on the spree,
'E's the on'y thing that doesn't give a damn
   For a Regiment o' British Infantree!
      So 'ere's *to* you, Fuzzy-Wuzzy, at your 'ome in the Soudan;
      You're a pore benighted 'eathen but a first-class fightin' man;
      An' 'ere's *to* you, Fuzzy-Wuzzy, with your 'ayrick 'ead of 'air—
      You big black boundin' beggar—for you broke a British square!

Gunga Din[1]

You may talk o' gin and beer
When you're quartered safe out 'ere,
An' you're sent to penny-fights an' Aldershot it[2];
But when it comes to slaughter

---

[1]Gunga Din's name suggests both the Indian landscape ("Gunga" is from the river Ganges) and his Islamic faithfulness: "Din" (rhymes with "seen") means "faith" in Arabic.

[2]The speaker is home in England, addressing recruits at the training camp in the town of Aldershot.

You will do your work on water,   5
An' you'll lick the bloomin' boots of 'im that's got it.
Now in Injia's sunny clime,
Where I used to spend my time
A-servin' of 'Er Majesty the Queen,
Of all them blackfaced crew   10
The finest man I knew
Was our regimental bhisti,[3] Gunga Din.
     He was "Din! Din! Din!
  You limpin' lump o' brick-dust, Gunga Din!
     Hi! slippery *hitherao*![4]   15
     Water, get it! *Panee lao*[5]
  You squidgy-nosed old idol, Gunga Din."

The uniform 'e wore
Was nothin' much before,
An' rather less than 'arf o' that be'ind,   20
For a piece o' twisty rag
An' a goatskin water-bag
Was all the field-equipment 'e could find.
When the sweatin' troop-train lay
In a sidin' through the day,   25
Where the 'eat would make your bloomin' eyebrows crawl,
We shouted "Harry By!"[6]
Till our throats were bricky-dry,
Then we wopped 'im 'cause 'e couldn't serve us all.
     It was "Din! Din! Din!   30
  You 'eathen, where the mischief 'ave you been?
     You put some *juldee*[7] in it
     Or I'll *marrow*[8] you this minute
  If you don't fill up my helmet, Gunga Din!"

[3]Water carrier.
[4]Come here.
[5]Water, quickly.
[6]Corruption of Hindi "Hari bhai," "Hey, brother."
[7]Speed.
[8]Hit.

'E would dot an' carry one   35
Till the longest day was done;
An' 'e didn't seem to know the use o' fear.
If we charged or broke or cut,
You could bet your bloomin' nut,
'E'd be waitin' fifty paces right flank rear.   40
With 'is *mussick*[9] on 'is back,
'E would skip with our attack,
An' watch us till the bugles made "Retire,"
An' for all 'is dirty 'ide
'E was white, clear white, inside   45
When 'e went to tend the wounded under fire!
   It was "Din! Din! Din!"
  With the bullets kickin' dust-spots on the green.
    When the cartridges ran out,
    You could hear the front-files shout,   50
  "Hi! ammunition-mules an' Gunga Din!"

I shan't forgit the night
When I dropped be'ind the fight
With a bullet where my belt-plate should 'a' been.
I was chokin' mad with thirst,   55
An' the man that spied me first
Was our good old grinnin', gruntin' Gunga Din.
'E lifted up my 'ead,
An' he plugged me where I bled,
An' 'e guv me 'arf-a-pint o' water-green: 60
It was crawlin' and it stunk,
But of all the drinks I've drunk,
I'm gratefullest to one from Gunga Din.
   It was "Din! Din! Din!
  'Ere's a beggar with a bullet through 'is spleen;   65
    'E's chawin' up the ground,
    An' 'e's kickin' all around:
  For Gawd's sake git the water, Gunga Din!"

[9]Water bag.

'E carried me away
To where a dooli[10] lay,   70
An' a bullet come an' drilled the beggar clean.
'E put me safe inside,
An' just before 'e died,
"I 'ope you liked your drink," sez Gunga Din.
So I'll meet 'im later on   75
At the place where 'e is gone—
Where it's always double drill and no canteen;
'E'll be squattin' on the coals
Givin' drink to poor damned souls,
An' I'll get a swig in hell from Gunga Din!   80
      Yes, Din! Din! Din!
    You Lazarushian-leather[11] Gunga Din!
      Though I've belted you and flayed you,
      By the livin' Gawd that made you,
    You're a better man than I am, Gunga Din!   85

Mandalay

By the old Moulmein Pagoda,[1] lookin' eastward to the sea,
There's a Burma girl a-settin', and I know she thinks o' me;
For the wind is in the palm-trees, and the temple-bells they say:
"Come you back, you British soldier; come you back to Mandalay!"
    Come you back to Mandalay,   5
    Where the old Flotilla lay:
    Can't you 'ear their paddles chunkin' from Rangoon to
      Mandalay?
    On the road to Mandalay,
    Where the flyin'-fishes play,
    An' the dawn comes up like thunder outer China 'crost the
      Bay!   10

---

[10]Stretcher.

[11]An invented word, combining "Russian leather" with Lazarus, the beggar in Jesus's parable (Luke 16) who goes to heaven while a rich man who ignored him must burn in hell, begging for water.

---

[1]The Kyaikthanlan pagoda, erected in 875 in the river port town of Moulmein (now Mawlamyine), Burma.

'Er petticoat was yaller an' 'er little cap was green,
An' 'er name was Supi-yaw-lat—jes' the same as Theebaw's Queen,[2]
An' I seed her first a-smokin' of a whackin' white cheroot,
An' a-wastin' Christian kisses on an 'eathen idol's foot:
  Bloomin' idol made o'mud—   15
  Wot they called the Great Gawd Budd[3]—
  Plucky lot she cared for idols when I kissed 'er where she stud!
  On the road to Mandalay . . .

When the mist was on the rice-fields an' the sun was droppin' slow,
She'd git 'er little banjo an' she'd sing "*Kulla-lo-lo!*"   20
With 'er arm upon my shoulder an' 'er cheek agin' my cheek
We useter watch the steamers an' the *hathis*[4] pilin' teak.
  Elephints a-pilin' teak
  In the sludgy, squdgy creek,
  Where the silence 'ung that 'eavy you was 'arf afraid to
   speak!   25
  On the road to Mandalay . . .

But that's all shove be'ind me—long ago an' fur away,
An' there ain't no 'busses runnin' from the Bank to Mandalay;
An' I'm learnin' 'ere in London what the ten-year soldier tells:
"If you've 'eard the East a-callin', you won't never 'eed naught
  else."   30
  No! you won't 'eed nothin' else
  But them spicy garlic smells,
  An' the sunshine an' the palm-trees an' the tinkly temple-bells;
  On the road to Mandalay . . .

I am sick o' wastin' leather on these gritty pavin'-stones,   35
An' the blasted Henglish drizzle wakes the fever in my bones;
Tho' I walks with fifty 'ousemaids outer Chelsea to the Strand,
An' they talks a lot o' lovin', but wot do they understand?
  Beefy face an' grubby 'and—

---

[2]Thibaw Min, the last king of Burma, reigned 1875–85. In 1886 Burma was annexed by the British. His queen Supayalat had a reputation for cruelty and involvement in courtly intrigues.
[3]Corruption of "Buddha."
[4]Working elephants.

Law! wot do they understand? 40
I've a neater, sweeter maiden in a cleaner, greener land!
On the road to Mandalay . . .

Ship me somewheres east of Suez, where the best is like the worst,
Where there aren't no Ten Commandments an' a man can raise a
   thirst;
For the temple-bells are callin', an' it's there that I would be— 45
By the old Moulmein Pagoda, looking lazy at the sea;
   On the road to Mandalay,
   Where the old Flotilla lay,
   With our sick beneath the awnings when we went to
   Mandalay!
   On the road to Mandalay, 50
   Where the flyin'-fishes play,
      An' the dawn comes up like thunder outer China 'crost the
      Bay!

Recessional

(A Victorian Ode)

1897

*A recessional is the closing hymn in a church service. Kipling wrote
this cautionary poem for Queen Victoria's Diamond Jubilee in 1897,
the sixtieth anniversary of her reign.*

God of our fathers, known of old,
   Lord of our far-flung battle line,
Beneath whose awful[1] hand we hold
   Dominion over palm and pine—
Lord God of Hosts, be with us yet, 5
Lest we forget—lest we forget![2]

---

[1] Awe-inspiring.
[2] "Then beware lest thou forget the Lord, who brought thee forth out of the land of
Egypt" (Deuteronomy 6:21).

The tumult and the shouting dies;
    The Captains and the Kings depart;
Still stands Thine ancient sacrifice,
    An humble and a contrite heart.[3]   10
Lord God of Hosts, be with us yet,
Lest we forget—lest we forget!

Far-called our navies melt away;
    On dune and headland sinks the fire[4];
Lo, all our pomp of yesterday   15
    Is one with Nineveh and Tyre![5]
Judge of the Nations, spare us yet,
Lest we forget—lest we forget!

If, drunk with sight of power, we loose
    Wild tongues that have not Thee in awe,   20
Such boastings as the Gentiles use,
    Or lesser breeds without the Law[6]—
Lord God of Hosts, be with us yet,
Lest we forget—lest we forget!

For heathen heart that puts her trust   25
    In reeking tube and iron shard—
All valiant dust that builds on dust,
    And guarding calls not Thee to guard.
For frantic boast and foolish word,
Thy Mercy on Thy People, Lord!   30

[3]Paraphrasing Psalm 51:17.
[4]Bonfires had been lit around England in honor of the Jubilee.
[5]Pagan cities destroyed by God in punishment for their sins, in the view of the biblical prophets.
[6]In the Bible, the Gentiles are pagans who lack God's Law and live by the law of nature.

The White Man's Burden

1899

(The United States and the Philippine Islands)

In 1898 the United States fought and won the Spanish-American war. One of the terms of the peace treaty was the handover of the Philippines, formerly a Spanish colony—an annexation that marked the emergence of the United States as an imperial power. "The White Man's Burden" was Kipling's reflection on the obligations of this new status.

Take up the White Man's burden—
Send forth the best ye breed—
Go bind your sons to exile
To serve your captives' need;
To wait in heavy harness,   5
On fluttered folk and wild—
Your new-caught, sullen peoples,
Half-devil and half-child.

Take up the White Man's Burden—
In patience to abide,   10
To veil the threat of terror
And check the show of pride;
By open speech and simple,
An hundred times made plain,
To seek another's profit,   15
And work another's gain.

Take up the White Man's burden—
The savage wars of peace—
Fill full the mouth of Famine
And bid the sickness cease;   20
And when your goal is nearest
The end for others sought,
Watch Sloth and heathen Folly
Bring all your hope to nought.

Take up the White Man's burden—   25
No tawdry rule of kings,
But toil of serf and sweeper—
The tale of common things.
The ports ye shall not enter,
The roads ye shall not tread,   30
Go make them with your living,
And mark them with your dead.

Take up the White Man's burden—
And reap his old reward:
The blame of those ye better,   35
The hate of those ye guard—
The cry of hosts ye humour
(Ah, slowly!) toward the light:—
"Why brought ye us from bondage,
Our loved Egyptian night?"[1]   40

Take up the White Man's burden—
Ye dare not stoop to less—
Nor call too loud on Freedom
To cloak your weariness;
By all ye cry or whisper,   45
By all ye leave or do,
The silent, sullen peoples
Shall weigh your Gods and you.

Take up the White Man's burden—
Have done with childish days—   50
The lightly proffered laurel,
The easy, ungrudged praise.
Comes now, to search your manhood
Through all the thankless years,
Cold, edged with dear-bought wisdom,   55
The judgment of your peers!

[1]In the Book of Exodus, the Israelites repeatedly complain when they must wander
through the harsh Arabian desert after Moses has freed them from slavery in Egypt.

Ulster

1912

In 1912 a bill was introduced into Parliament proposing Home Rule in Ireland. Many in the Protestant majority in Northern Ireland regarded this plan as a betrayal of British protection, leaving them to be dominated by the far more numerous Irish Catholics. On "Ulster Day," September 28, 1912, hundreds of thousands of men signed the Ulster Covenant, declaring their loyalty to King George V and their rejection of Home Rule.

("Their webs shall not become garments, neither shall
they cover themselves with their works: their works
are works of iniquity and the act of violence is in
their hands."

—*Isaiah* 59:6)

The dark eleventh hour
Draws on and sees us sold
To every evil power
We fought against of old.
Rebellion, rapine, hate,   5
Oppression, wrong and greed
Are loosed to rule our fate,
By England's act and deed.

The Faith in which we stand,
The laws we made and guard,   10
Our honour, lives, and land
Are given for reward
To Murder done by night,
To Treason taught by day,
To folly, sloth, and spite,   15
And we are thrust away.

The blood our fathers spilt,
Our love, our toils, our pains,
Are counted us for guilt,

And only bind our chains.   20
Before an Empire's eyes
The traitor claims his price.
What need of further lies?
We are the sacrifice.

We asked no more than leave   25
To reap where we had sown,
Through good and ill to cleave
To our own flag and throne.
Now England's shot and steel
Beneath that flag must show   30
How loyal hearts should kneel
To England's oldest foe.

We know the war prepared
On every peaceful home,
We know the hells declared   35
For such as serve not Rome[1]—
The terror, threats, and dread
In market, hearth, and field—
We know, when all is said.
We perish if we yield.   40

Believe, we dare not boast,
Believe, we do not fear
We stand to pay the cost
In all that men hold dear.
What answer from the North?   45
One Law, one Land, one Throne
If England drive us forth
We shall not fall alone!

---

[1]Reflecting fears of Protestant northern Irish that independence would bring oppression by the Catholic majority of Ireland.

Without Benefit of Clergy[1]

Before my Spring I garnered Autumn's gain,
  Out of her time my field was white with grain,
The year gave up her secrets to my woe.
  Forced and deflowered each sick season lay,
In mystery of increase and decay;
  I saw the sunset ere men saw the day,
Who am too wise in that I should not know.

—*Bitter Waters.*[2]

1

"But if it be a girl?"

"Lord of my life, it cannot be. I have prayed for so many nights, and sent gifts to Sheikh Badl's shrine so often, that I know God will give us a son—a man-child that shall grow into a man. Think of this and be glad. My mother shall be his mother till I can take him again, and the mullah of the Pattan mosque shall cast his nativity[3]—God send he be born in an auspicious hour!—and then, and then thou wilt never weary of me, thy slave."

"Since when hast thou been a slave, my queen?"

"Since the beginning—till this mercy came to me. How could I be sure of thy love when I knew that I had been bought with silver?"

"Nay, that was the dowry. I paid it to thy mother."

"And she has buried it, and sits upon it all day long like a hen. What talk is yours of dower! I was bought as though I had been a Lucknow dancing-girl[4] instead of a child."

"Art thou sorry for the sale?"

"I have sorrowed; but to-day I am glad. Thou wilt never cease to love me now?—answer, my king."

"Never—never. No."

"Not even though the *mem-log*—the white women of thy own blood—love thee? And remember, I have watched them driving in the evening; they are very fair."

[1]Kipling is ironically adapting a Church term (referring to clergymen's legal immunity) to mean "without a formal church marriage."

[2]Kipling's own poem.

[3]A horoscope based on the day and time of the child's birth.

[4]Prostitute.

"I have seen fire-balloons[5] by the hundred. I have seen the moon, and—then I saw no more fire-balloons."

Ameera clapped her hands and laughed. "Very good talk," she said. Then with an assumption of great stateliness, "It is enough. Thou hast my permission to depart,—if thou wilt."

The man did not move. He was sitting on a low red-lacquered couch in a room furnished only with a blue and white floor-cloth, some rugs, and a very complete collection of native cushions. At his feet sat a woman of sixteen, and she was all but all the world in his eyes. By every rule and law she should have been otherwise, for he was an Englishman, and she a Mussulman's daughter bought two years before from her mother, who, being left without money, would have sold Ameera shrieking to the Prince of Darkness if the price had been sufficient.

It was a contract entered into with a light heart; but even before the girl had reached her bloom she came to fill the greater portion of John Holden's life. For her, and the withered hag her mother, he had taken a little house overlooking the great red-walled city, and found,—when the marigolds had sprung up by the well in the court-yard, and Ameera had established herself according to her own ideas of comfort, and her mother had ceased grumbling at the inadequacy of the cooking-places, the distance from the daily market, and at matters of house-keeping in general,—that the house was to him his home. Any one could enter his bachelor's bungalow by day or night, and the life that he led there was an unlovely one. In the house in the city his feet only could pass beyond the outer courtyard to the women's rooms; and when the big wooden gate was bolted behind him he was king in his own territory, with Ameera for queen. And there was going to be added to this kingdom a third person whose arrival Holden felt inclined to resent. It interfered with his perfect happiness. It disarranged the orderly peace of the house that was his own. But Ameera was wild with delight at the thought of it, and her mother not less so. The love of a man, and particularly a white man, was at the best an inconstant affair, but it might, both women argued, be held fast by a baby's hands. "And then," Ameera would always say, "then he will never care for the white *mem-log*. I hate them all—I hate them all."

[5]Hot-air balloons.

"He will go back to his own people in time," said the mother; "but by the blessing of God that time is yet afar off."

Holden sat silent on the couch thinking of the future, and his thoughts were not pleasant. The drawbacks of a double life are manifold. The Government, with singular care, had ordered him out of the station for a fortnight on special duty in the place of a man who was watching by the bedside of a sick wife. The verbal notification of the transfer had been edged by a cheerful remark that Holden ought to think himself lucky in being a bachelor and a free man. He came to break the news to Ameera.

"It is not good," she said slowly, "but it is not all bad. There is my mother here, and no harm will come to me—unless indeed I die of pure joy. Go thou to thy work and think no troublesome thoughts. When the days are done I believe . . . nay, I am sure. And—and then I shall lay *him* in thy arms, and thou wilt love me for ever. The train goes to-night, at midnight is it not? Go now, and do not let thy heart be heavy by cause of me. But thou wilt not delay in returning? Thou wilt not stay on the road to talk to the bold white *mem-log*. Come back to me swiftly, my life."

As he left the courtyard to reach his horse that was tethered to the gate-post, Holden spoke to the white-haired old watchman who guarded the house, and bade him under certain contingencies despatch the filled-up telegraph-form that Holden gave him. It was all that could be done, and with the sensations of a man who has attended his own funeral Holden went away by the night mail to his exile. Every hour of the day he dreaded the arrival of the telegram, and every hour of the night he pictured to himself the death of Ameera. In consequence his work for the State was not of first-rate quality, nor was his temper towards his colleagues of the most amiable. The fortnight ended without a sign from his home, and, torn to pieces by his anxieties, Holden returned to be swallowed up for two precious hours by a dinner at the club, wherein he heard, as a man hears in a swoon, voices telling him how execrably he had performed the other man's duties, and how he had endeared himself to all his associates. Then he fled on horseback through the night with his heart in his mouth. There was no answer at first to his blows on the gate, and he had just wheeled his horse round to kick it in when Pir Khan appeared with a lantern and held his stirrup.

"Has aught occurred?" said Holden.

"The news does not come from my mouth, Protector of the Poor, but—" He held out his shaking hand as befitted the bearer of good news who is entitled to a reward.

Holden hurried through the courtyard. A light burned in the upper room. His horse neighed in the gateway, and he heard a shrill little wail that sent all the blood into the apple of his throat. It was a new voice, but it did not prove that Ameera was alive.

"Who is there?" he called up the narrow brick staircase.

There was a cry of delight from Ameera, and then the voice of the mother, tremulous with old age and pride—"We be two women and—the—man—thy—son."

On the threshold of the room Holden stepped on a naked dagger, that was laid there to avert ill-luck, and it broke at the hilt under his impatient heel.

"God is great!" cooed Ameera in the half-light. "Thou hast taken his misfortunes on thy head."

"Ay, but how is it with thee, life of my life? Old woman, how is it with her?"

"She has forgotten her sufferings for joy that the child is born. There is no harm; but speak softly," said the mother.

"It only needed thy presence to make me all well," said Ameera. "My king, thou hast been very long away. What gifts hast thou for me? Ah, ah! It is I that bring gifts this time. Look, my life, look. Was there ever such a babe? Nay, I am too weak even to clear my arm from him."

"Rest then, and do not talk. I am here, *bachari* (little woman)."

"Well said, for there is a bond and a heel-rope (*peecharee*) between us now that nothing can break. Look—canst thou see in this light? He is without spot or blemish. Never was such a man-child. *Ya illah!*[6] he shall be a pundit—no, a trooper of the Queen. And, my life, dost thou love me as well as ever, though I am faint and sick and worn? Answer truly."

"Yea. I love as I have loved, with all my soul. Lie still, pearl, and rest."

"Then do not go. Sit by my side here—so. Mother, the lord of this house needs a cushion. Bring it." There was an almost imperceptible movement on the part of the new life that lay in the hollow

[6]By God.

of Ameera's arm. "Aho!" she said, her voice breaking with love. "The babe is a champion from his birth. He is kicking me in the side with mighty kicks. Was there ever such a babe! And he is ours to us—thine and mine. Put thy hand on his head, but carefully, for he is very young, and men are unskilled in such matters."

Very cautiously Holden touched with the tips of his fingers the downy head.

"He is of the Faith," said Ameera; "for lying here in the night-watches I whispered the call to prayer and the profession of faith[7] into his ears. And it is most marvellous that he was born upon a Friday,[8] as I was born. Be careful of him, my life; but he can almost grip with his hands."

Holden found one helpless little hand that closed feebly on his finger. And the clutch ran through his body till it settled about his heart. Till then his sole thought had been for Ameera. He began to realise that there was some one else in the world, but he could not feel that it was a veritable son with a soul. He sat down to think, and Ameera dozed lightly.

"Get hence, *sahib*,"[9] said her mother under her breath. "It is not good that she should find you here on waking. She must be still."

"I go," said Holden submissively. "Here be rupees. See that my *baba* gets fat and finds all that he needs."

The chink of the silver roused Ameera. "I am his mother, and no hireling," she said weakly. "Shall I look to him more or less for the sake of money? Mother, give it back. I have borne my lord a son."

The deep sleep of weakness came upon her almost before the sentence was completed. Holden went down to the courtyard very softly with his heart at ease. Pir Khan, the old watchman, was chuckling with delight. "This house is now complete," he said, and without further comment thrust into Holden's hands the hilt of a sabre worn many years ago when he, Pir Khan, served the Queen in the police. The bleat of a tethered goat came from the well-kerb.

"There be two," said Pir Khan, "two goats of the best. I bought them, and they cost much money; and since there is no birth-party

---

[7]The foundation of Islamic belief: "There is no God but God [Allah], and Muhammad is His Prophet."

[8]The Muslim holy day.

[9]Master.

assembled their flesh will be all mine. Strike craftily, *sahib!* 'Tis an ill-balanced sabre at the best. Wait till they raise their heads from cropping the marigolds."

"And why?" said Holden, bewildered.

"For the birth-sacrifice. What else? Otherwise the child being unguarded from fate may die. The Protector of the Poor knows the fitting words to be said."

Holden had learned them once with little thought that he would ever speak them in earnest. The touch of the cold sabre-hilt in his palm turned suddenly to the clinging grip of the child up-stairs—the child that was his own son—and a dread of loss filled him.

"Strike!" said Pir Khan. "Never life came into the world but life was paid for it. See, the goats have raised their heads. Now! With a drawing cut!"

Hardly knowing what he did, Holden cut twice as he muttered the Mahomedan prayer that runs: "Almighty! In place of this my son I offer life for life, blood for blood, head for head, bone for bone, hair for hair, skin for skin." The waiting horse snorted and bounded in his pickets at the smell of the raw blood that spirted over Holden's riding-boots.

"Well smitten!" said Pir Khan wiping the sabre. "A swordsman was lost in thee. Go with a light heart, Heaven-born. I am thy servant, and the servant of thy son. May the Presence live a thousand years and . . . the flesh of the goats is all mine?" Pir Khan drew back richer by a month's pay. Holden swung himself into the saddle and rode off through the low-hanging wood-smoke of the evening. He was full of riotous exultation, alternating with a vast vague tenderness directed towards no particular object, that made him choke as he bent over the neck of his uneasy horse. "I never felt like this in my life," he thought. "I'll go to the club and pull myself together."

A game of pool was beginning, and the room was full of men. Holden entered, eager to get to the light and the company of his fellows, singing at the top of his voice—

In Baltimore a-walking, a lady I did meet!

"Did you?" said the club-secretary from his corner. "Did she happen to tell you that your boots were wringing wet? Great goodness, man, it's blood!"

"Bosh!" said Holden, picking his cue from the rack. "May I cut in? It's dew. I've been riding through high crops. My faith! my boots are in a mess though!

And if it be a girl she shall wear a wedding-ring,
And if it be a boy he shall fight for his king,
With his dirk, and his cap, and his little jacket blue,
He shall walk the quarter-deck—"

"Yellow on blue—green next player," said the marker monotonously.

"*He shall walk the quarter-deck,*—Am I green, marker? *He shall walk the quarter-deck,*—eh! that's a bad shot,—*As his daddy used to do!*"

"I don't see that you have anything to crow about," said a zealous junior civilian acidly. "The Government is not exactly pleased with your work when you relieved Sanders."

"Does that mean a wigging[10] from headquarters?" said Holden with an abstracted smile. "I think I can stand it."

The talk beat up round the ever-fresh subject of each man's work, and steadied Holden till it was time to go to his dark empty bungalow, where his butler received him as one who knew all his affairs. Holden remained awake for the greater part of the night, and his dreams were pleasant ones.

2

"How old is he now?"

"*Ya illah!* What a man's question! He is all but six weeks old; and on this night I go up to the house-top with thee, my life, to count the stars. For that is auspicious. And he was born on a Friday under the sign of the Sun, and it has been told to me that he will outlive us both and get wealth. Can we wish for aught better, beloved?"

"There is nothing better. Let us go up to the roof, and thou shalt count the stars—but a few only, for the sky is heavy with cloud."

"The winter rains are late, and maybe they come out of season. Come, before all the stars are hid. I have put on my richest jewels."

---

[10]Scolding.

"Thou hast forgotten the best of all."

"*Ai!* Ours. He comes also. He has never yet seen the skies."

Ameera climbed the narrow staircase that led to the flat roof. The child, placid and unwinking, lay in the hollow of her right arm, gorgeous in silver-fringed muslin with a small skull-cap on his head. Ameera wore all that she valued most. The diamond nose-stud that takes the place of the Western patch[11] in drawing attention to the curve of the nostril, the gold ornament in the centre of the forehead studded with tallow-drop emeralds and flawed rubies, the heavy circlet of beaten gold that was fastened round her neck by the softness of the pure metal, and the chinking curb-patterned silver anklets hanging low over the rosy ankle-bone. She was dressed in jade-green muslin as befitted a daughter of the Faith,[12] and from shoulder to elbow and elbow to wrist ran bracelets of silver tied with floss silk, frail glass bangles slipped over the wrist in proof of the slenderness of the hand, and certain heavy gold bracelets that had no part in her country's ornaments, but, since they were Holden's gift and fastened with a cunning European snap, delighted her immensely.

They sat down by the low white parapet of the roof, overlooking the city and its lights.

"They are happy down there," said Ameera. "But I do not think that they are as happy as we. Nor do I think the white *mem-log* are as happy. And thou?"

"I know they are not."

"How dost thou know?"

"They give their children over to the nurses."

"I have never seen that," said Ameera with a sigh, "nor do I wish to see. *Ahi!*"—she dropped her head on Holden's shoulder,— "I have counted forty stars, and I am tired. Look at the child, love of my life, he is counting too."

The baby was staring with round eyes at the dark of the heavens. Ameera placed him in Holden's arms, and he lay there without a cry.

"What shall we call him among ourselves?" she said. "Look! Art thou ever tired of looking? He carries thy very eyes. But the mouth—"

[11]Beauty spot.
[12]Green is a symbol of Islam.

"Is thine, most dear. Who should know better than I?"

"'Tis such a feeble mouth. Oh, so small! And yet it holds my heart between its lips. Give him to me now. He has been too long away."

"Nay, let him lie; he has not yet begun to cry."

"When he cries thou wilt give him back—eh? What a man of mankind thou art! If he cried he were only the dearer to me. But, my life, what little name shall we give him?"

The small body lay close to Holden's heart. It was utterly helpless and very soft. He scarcely dared to breathe for fear of crushing it. The caged green parrot that is regarded as a sort of guardian-spirit in most native households moved on its perch and fluttered a drowsy wing.

"There is the answer," said Holden. "Mian Mittu has spoken. He shall be the parrot. When he is ready he will talk mightily and run about. Mian Mittu is the parrot in thy—in the Mussulman tongue, is it not?"

"Why put me so far off?" said Ameera fretfully. "Let it be like unto some English name—but not wholly. For he is mine."

"Then call him Tota, for that is likest English."

"Ay, Tota, and that is still the parrot. Forgive me, my lord, for a minute ago, but in truth he is too little to wear all the weight of Mian Mittu for name. He shall be Tota—our Tota to us. Hearest thou, oh, small one? Littlest, thou art Tota." She touched the child's cheek, and he waking wailed, and it was necessary to return him to his mother, who soothed him with the wonderful rhyme of *Aré koko, Faré koko!* which says—

"Oh crow! Go crow! Baby's sleeping sound,
And the wild plums grow in the jungle, only a penny a pound.
Only a penny a pound, *baba*, only a penny a pound."

Reassured many times as to the price of those plums, Tota cuddled himself down to sleep. The two sleek, white well-bullocks in the courtyard were steadily chewing the cud of their evening meal; old Pir Khan squatted at the head of Holden's horse, his police sabre across his knees, pulling drowsily at a big water-pipe that croaked like a bull-frog in a pond. Ameera's mother sat spinning in the lower verandah, and the wooden gate was shut and barred. The music of a marriage-procession came to the roof above the gentle hum of the city, and a string of flying-foxes crossed the face of the low moon.

"I have prayed," said Ameera after a long pause, "I have prayed for two things. First, that I may die in thy stead if thy death is demanded, and in the second, that I may die in the place of the child. I have prayed to the Prophet and to Beebee Miriam.[13] Thinkest thou either will hear?"

"From thy lips who would not hear the lightest word?"

"I asked for straight talk, and thou hast given me sweet talk. Will my prayers be heard?"

"How can I say? God is very good."

"Of that I am not sure. Listen now. When I die, or the child dies, what is thy fate? Living, thou wilt return to the bold white *mem-log*, for kind calls to kind."

"Not always."

"With a woman, no; with a man it is otherwise. Thou wilt in this life, later on, go back to thine own folk. That I could almost endure, for I should be dead. But in thy very death thou wilt be taken away to a strange place and a paradise that I do not know."

"Will it be paradise?"

"Surely, for who would harm thee? But we two—I and the child—shall be elsewhere, and we cannot come to thee, nor canst thou come to us. In the old days, before the child was born, I did not think of these things; but now I think of them always. It is very hard talk."

"It will fall as it will fall. To-morrow we do not know, but to-day and love we know well. Surely we are happy now."

"So happy that it were well to make our happiness assured. And thy Beebee Miriam should listen to me; for she is also a woman. But then she would envy me! It is not seemly for men to worship a woman."

Holden laughed aloud at Ameera's little spasm of jealousy.

"Is it not seemly? Why didst thou not turn me from worship of thee, then?"

"Thou a worshipper! And of me? My king, for all thy sweet words, well I know that I am thy servant and thy slave, and the dust under thy feet. And I would not have it otherwise. See!"

[13]The Virgin Mary, known as Miriam in the Qur'an.

Before Holden could prevent her she stooped forward and touched his feet; recovering herself with a little laugh she hugged Tota closer to her bosom. Then, almost savagely—

"Is it true that the bold white *mem-log* live for three times the length of my life? Is it true that they make their marriages not before they are old women?"

"They marry as do others—when they are women."

"That I know, but they wed when they are twenty-five. Is that true?"

"That is true."

"*Ya illah!* At twenty-five! Who would of his own will take a wife even of eighteen? She is a woman—aging every hour. Twenty-five! I shall be an old woman at that age, and—Those *mem-log* remain young for ever. How I hate them!"

"What have they to do with us?"

"I cannot tell. I know only that there may now be alive on this earth a woman ten years older than I who may come to thee and take thy love ten years after I am an old woman, gray-headed, and the nurse of Tota's son. That is unjust and evil. They should die too."

"Now, for all thy years thou art a child, and shalt be picked up and carried down the staircase."

"Tota! Have a care for Tota, my lord! Thou at least art as foolish as any babe!" Ameera tucked Tota out of harm's way in the hollow of her neck, and was carried downstairs laughing in Holden's arms, while Tota opened his eyes and smiled after the manner of the lesser angels.

He was a silent infant, and, almost before Holden could realise that he was in the world, developed into a small gold-coloured little god and unquestioned despot of the house overlooking the city. Those were months of absolute happiness to Holden and Ameera—happiness withdrawn from the world, shut in behind the wooden gate that Pir Khan guarded. By day Holden did his work with an immense pity for such as were not so fortunate as himself, and a sympathy for small children that amazed and amused many mothers at the little station-gatherings. At nightfall he returned to Ameera,—Ameera, full of the wondrous doings of Tota; how he had been seen to clap his hands together and move his fingers with intention and purpose—which was manifestly a miracle—how later, he had of his own initiative crawled out of his low bedstead on to the floor and swayed on both feet for the space of three breaths.

"And they were long breaths, for my heart stood still with delight," said Ameera.

Then Tota took the beasts into his councils—the well-bullocks, the little gray squirrels, the mongoose that lived in a hole near the well, and especially Mian Mittu, the parrot, whose tail he grievously pulled, and Mian Mittu screamed till Ameera and Holden arrived.

"Oh villain! Child of strength! This to thy brother on the house-top! *Tobah, tobah!* Fie! Fie! But I know a charm to make him wise as Suleiman and Aflatoun.[14] Now look," said Ameera. She drew from an embroidered bag a handful of almonds. "See! we count seven. In the name of God!"

She placed Mian Mittu, very angry and rumpled, on the top of his cage, and seating herself between the babe and the bird she cracked and peeled an almond less white than her teeth. "This is a true charm, my life, and do not laugh. See! I give the parrot one-half and Tota the other." Mian Mittu with careful beak took his share from between Ameera's lips, and she kissed the other half into the mouth of the child, who ate it slowly with wondering eyes. "This I will do each day of seven, and without doubt he who is ours will be a bold speaker and wise. Eh, Tota, what wilt thou be when thou art a man and I am gray-headed?" Tota tucked his fat legs into adorable creases. He could crawl, but he was not going to waste the spring of his youth in idle speech. He wanted Mian Mittu's tail to tweak.

When he was advanced to the dignity of a silver belt—which, with a magic square engraved on silver and hung round his neck, made up the greater part of his clothing—he staggered on a perilous journey down the garden to Pir Khan, and proffered him all his jewels in exchange for one little ride on Holden's horse, having seen his mother's mother chaffering with pedlars in the verandah. Pir Khan wept and set the untried feet on his own gray head in sign of fealty, and brought the bold adventurer to his mother's arms, vowing that Tota would be a leader of men ere his beard was grown.

One hot evening, while he sat on the roof between his father and mother watching the never ending warfare of the kites that the

[14]Proverbially wise men in Islamic tradition.

city boys flew, he demanded a kite of his own with Pir Khan to fly it, because he had a fear of dealing with anything larger than himself, and when Holden called him a "spark,"[15] he rose to his feet and answered slowly in defence of his new-found individuality, "*Hum'park nahin hai. Hum admi hai* [I am no spark, but a man]."

The protest made Holden choke and devote himself very seriously to a consideration of Tota's future. He need hardly have taken the trouble. The delight of that life was too perfect to endure. Therefore it was taken away as many things are taken away in India—suddenly and without warning. The little lord of the house, as Pir Khan called him, grew sorrowful and complained of pains who had never known the meaning of pain. Ameera, wild with terror, watched him through the night, and in the dawning of the second day the life was shaken out of him by fever—the seasonal autumn fever. It seemed altogether impossible that he could die, and neither Ameera nor Holden at first believed the evidence of the little body on the bedstead. Then Ameera beat her head against the wall and would have flung herself down the well in the garden had Holden not restrained her by main force.

One mercy only was granted to Holden. He rode to his office in broad daylight and found waiting him an unusually heavy mail that demanded concentrated attention and hard work. He was not, however, alive to this kindness of the gods.

3

The first shock of a bullet is no more than a brisk pinch. The wrecked body does not send in its protest to the soul till ten or fifteen seconds later. Holden realised his pain slowly, exactly as he had realised his happiness, and with the same imperious necessity for hiding all trace of it. In the beginning he only felt that there had been a loss, and that Ameera needed comforting, where she sat with her head on her knees shivering as Mian Mittu from the house-top called, *Tota! Tota! Tota!* Later all his world and the daily life of it rose up to hurt him. It was an outrage that any one of the children at the band-stand in the evening should be alive and clamorous, when his own child lay dead. It was more than mere pain when one of them touched him, and stories told by over-fond

[15]British slang for a bold young man.

fathers of their children's latest performances cut him to the quick. He could not declare his pain. He had neither help, comfort, nor sympathy; and Ameera at the end of each weary day would lead him through the hell of self-questioning reproach which is reserved for those who have lost a child, and believe that with a little—just a little more care—it might have been saved.

"Perhaps," Ameera would say, "I did not take sufficient heed. Did I, or did I not? The sun on the roof that day when he played so long alone and I was—*ahi!* braiding my hair—it may be that the sun then bred the fever. If I had warned him from the sun he might have lived. But, oh my life, say that I am guiltless! Thou knowest that I loved him as I love thee. Say that there is no blame on me, or I shall die—I shall die!"

"There is no blame,—before God, none. It was written, and how could we do aught to save? What has been, has been. Let it go, beloved."

"He was all my heart to me. How can I let the thought go when my arm tells me every night that he is not here? *Ahi! Ahi!* Oh, Tota, come back to me—come back again, and let us be all together as it was before!"

"Peace, peace! For thine own sake, and for mine also, if thou lovest me—rest."

"By this I know thou dost not care; and how shouldst thou? The white men have hearts of stone and souls of iron. Oh, that I had married a man of mine own people—though he beat me—and had never eaten the bread of an alien!"

"Am I an alien—mother of my son?"

"What else—*Sahib?* . . . Oh, forgive me—forgive! The death has driven me mad. Thou art the life of my heart, and the light of my eyes, and the breath of my life, and—and I have put thee from me, though it was but for a moment. If thou goest away, to whom shall I look for help? Do not be angry. Indeed, it was the pain that spoke and not thy slave."

"I know, I know. We be two who were three. The greater need therefore that we should be one."

They were sitting on the roof as of custom. The night was a warm one in early spring, and sheet-lightning was dancing on the horizon to a broken tune played by far-off thunder. Ameera settled herself in Holden's arms.

"The dry earth is lowing like a cow for the rain, and I—I am afraid. It was not like this when we counted the stars. But thou lovest me as much as before, though a bond is taken away? Answer!"

"I love more because a new bond has come out of the sorrow that we have eaten together, and that thou knowest."

"Yea, I knew," said Ameera in a very small whisper. "But it is good to hear thee say so, my life, who art so strong to help. I will be a child no more, but a woman and an aid to thee. Listen! Give me my *sitar* and I will sing bravely."

She took the light silver-studded *sitar* and began a song of the great hero Rajah Rasalu. The hand failed on the strings, the tune halted, checked, and at a low note turned off to the poor little nursery-rhyme about the wicked crow—

"And the wild plums grow in the jungle, only a penny a pound.
Only a penny a pound, *baba*—only. . . ."

Then came the tears, and the piteous rebellion against fate till she slept, moaning a little in her sleep, with the right arm thrown clear of the body as though it protected something that was not there. It was after this night that life became a little easier for Holden. The ever-present pain of loss drove him into his work, and the work repaid him by filling up his mind for nine or ten hours a day. Ameera sat alone in the house and brooded, but grew happier when she understood that Holden was more at ease, according to the custom of women. They touched happiness again, but this time with caution.

"It was because we loved Tota that he died. The jealousy of God was upon us," said Ameera. "I have hung up a large black jar before our window to turn the evil eye from us, and we must make no protestations of delight, but go softly underneath the stars, lest God find us out. Is that not good talk, worthless one?"

She had shifted the accent on the word that means "beloved," in proof of the sincerity of her purpose. But the kiss that followed the new christening was a thing that any deity might have envied. They went about henceforward saying, "It is naught, it is naught"; and hoping that all the Powers heard.

The Powers were busy on other things. They had allowed thirty million people four years of plenty, wherein men fed well and the crops were certain, and the birth-rate rose year by year; the districts reported a purely agricultural population varying from nine hundred to two thousand to the square mile of the overburdened earth; and the Member for Lower Tooting,[16] wandering about India in top-hat and frock-coat, talked largely of the benefits of British rule, and suggested as the one thing needful the establishment of a duly qualified electoral system and a general bestowal of the franchise. His long-suffering hosts smiled and made him welcome, and when he paused to admire, with pretty picked words, the blossom of the blood-red *dhak*-tree that had flowered untimely for a sign of what was coming, they smiled more than ever.

It was the Deputy Commissioner of Kot-Kumharsen, staying at the club for a day, who lightly told a tale that made Holden's blood run cold as he overheard the end.

"He won't bother any one any more. Never saw a man so astonished in my life. By Jove, I thought he meant to ask a question in the House about it. Fellow-passenger in his ship—dined next him—bowled over by cholera and died in eighteen hours. You needn't laugh, you fellows. The Member for Lower Tooting is awfully angry about it; but he's more scared. I think he's going to take his enlightened self out of India."

"I'd give a good deal if he were knocked over. It might keep a few vestrymen of his kidney to their own parish. But what's this about cholera? It's full early for anything of that kind," said the warden of an unprofitable salt-lick.

"Don't know," said the Deputy Commissioner reflectively. "We've got locusts with us. There's sporadic cholera all along the north—at least we're calling it sporadic for decency's sake. The spring crops are short in five districts, and nobody seems to know where the rains are. It's nearly March now. I don't want to scare anybody, but it seems to me that Nature's going to audit her accounts with a big red pencil this summer."

"Just when I wanted to take leave, too!" said a voice across the room.

"There won't be much leave this year, but there ought to be a great deal of promotion. I've come in to persuade the Government to put my pet canal on the list of famine-relief works. It's an ill-wind that blows no good. I shall get that canal finished at last."

[16]A provincial member of the British Parliament, in India on a fact-finding junket.

"Is it the old programme then," said Holden; "famine, fever, and cholera?"

"Oh no. Only local scarcity and an unusual prevalence of seasonal sickness. You'll find it all in the reports if you live till next year. You're a lucky chap. *You* haven't got a wife to send out of harm's way. The hill-stations ought to be full of women this year."

"I think you're inclined to exaggerate the talk in the *bazars*," said a young civilian in the Secretariat. "Now I have observed—"

"I daresay you have," said the Deputy Commissioner, "but you've a great deal more to observe, my son. In the meantime, I wish to observe to you—" and he drew him aside to discuss the construction of the canal that was so dear to his heart. Holden went to his bungalow and began to understand that he was not alone in the world, and also that he was afraid for the sake of another,—which is the most soul-satisfying fear known to man.

Two months later, as the Deputy had foretold, Nature began to audit her accounts with a red pencil. On the heels of the spring-reapings came a cry for bread, and the Government, which had decreed that no man should die of want, sent wheat. Then came the cholera from all four quarters of the compass. It struck a pilgrim-gathering of half a million at a sacred shrine. Many died at the feet of their god; the others broke and ran over the face of the land carrying the pestilence with them. It smote a walled city and killed two hundred a day. The people crowded the trains, hanging on to the footboards and squatting on the roofs of the carriages, and the cholera followed them, for at each station they dragged out the dead and the dying. They died by the roadside, and the horses of the Englishmen shied at the corpses in the grass. The rains did not come, and the earth turned to iron lest man should escape death by hiding in her. The English sent their wives away to the hills and went about their work, coming forward as they were bidden to fill the gaps in the fighting-line. Holden, sick with fear of losing his chiefest treasure on earth, had done his best to persuade Ameera to go away with her mother to the Himalayas.

"Why should I go?" said she one evening on the roof.

"There is sickness, and people are dying, and all the white *mem-log* have gone."

"All of them?"

"All—unless perhaps there remain some old scald-head who vexes her husband's heart by running risk of death."

"Nay; who stays is my sister, and thou must not abuse her, for I will be a scald-head too. I am glad all the bold *mem-log* are gone."

"Do I speak to a woman or a babe? Go to the hills, and I will see to it that thou goest like a queen's daughter. Think, child. In a red-lacquered bullock cart, veiled and curtained, with brass peacocks upon the pole and red cloth hangings. I will send two orderlies for guard and—"

"Peace! Thou art the babe in speaking thus. What use are those toys to me? *He* would have patted the bullocks and played with the housings. For his sake, perhaps,—thou hast made me very English—I might have gone. Now, I will not. Let the *mem-log* run."

"Their husbands are sending them, beloved."

"Very good talk. Since when hast thou been my husband to tell me what to do? I have but borne thee a son. Thou art only all the desire of my soul to me. How shall I depart when I know that if evil befall thee by the breadth of so much as my littlest finger-nail—is that not small?—I should be aware of it though I were in paradise. And here, this summer thou mayest die—*ai, janee,* die! and in dying they might call to tend thee a white woman, and she would rob me in the last of thy love!"

"But love is not born in a moment or on a death-bed!"

"What dost thou know of love, stoneheart? She would take thy thanks at least and, by God and the Prophet and Beebee Miriam the mother of thy Prophet,[17] that I will never endure. My lord and my love, let there be no more foolish talk of going away. Where thou art, I am. It is enough." She put an arm round his neck and a hand on his mouth.

There are not many happinesses so complete as those that are snatched under the shadow of the sword. They sat together and laughed, calling each other openly by every pet name that could move the wrath of the gods. The city below them was locked up in its own torments. Sulphur fires blazed in the streets; the conches in the Hindu temples screamed and bellowed, for the gods were inattentive in those days. There was a service in the great Mahomedan

[17]The Qur'an views Jesus as one of a series of prophets leading up to the Prophet of Islam, Muhammad.

shrine, and the call to prayer from the minarets was almost unceasing. They heard the wailing in the houses of the dead, and once the shriek of a mother who had lost a child and was calling for its return. In the gray dawn they saw the dead borne out through the city gates, each litter with its own little knot of mourners. Wherefore they kissed each other and shivered.

It was a red and heavy audit, for the land was very sick and needed a little breathing-space ere the torrent of cheap life should flood it anew. The children of immature fathers and undeveloped mothers made no resistance. They were cowed and sat still, waiting till the sword should be sheathed in November if it were so willed. There were gaps among the English, but the gaps were filled. The work of superintending famine-relief, cholera-sheds, medicine-distribution, and what little sanitation was possible, went forward because it was so ordered.

Holden had been told to keep himself in readiness to move to replace the next man who should fall. There were twelve hours in each day when he could not see Ameera, and she might die in three. He was considering what his pain would be if he could not see her for three months, or if she died out of his sight. He was absolutely certain that her death would be demanded—so certain, that when he looked up from the telegram and saw Pir Khan breathless in the doorway, he laughed aloud. "And?" said he,—

"When there is a cry in the night and the spirit flutters into the throat, who has a charm that will restore? Come swiftly, Heaven-born! It is the black cholera."

Holden galloped to his home. The sky was heavy with clouds, for the long-deferred rains were near and the heat was stifling. Ameera's mother met him in the courtyard, whimpering, "She is dying. She is nursing herself into death. She is all but dead. What shall I do, *sahib?*"

Ameera was lying in the room in which Tota had been born. She made no sign when Holden entered, because the human soul is a very lonely thing and, when it is getting ready to go away, hides itself in a misty borderland where the living may not follow. The black cholera does its work quietly and without explanation. Ameera was being thrust out of life as though the Angel of Death had himself put his hand upon her. The quick breathing seemed to show that she was either afraid or in pain, but neither eyes nor mouth gave any answer to Holden's kisses. There was nothing to be said or done. Holden could only wait and suffer. The first drops of the rain began to fall on the roof and he could hear shouts of joy in the parched city.

The soul came back a little and the lips moved. Holden bent down to listen. "Keep nothing of mine," said Ameera. "Take no hair from my head. *She* would make thee burn it later on. That flame I should feel. Lower! Stoop lower! Remember only that I was thine and bore thee a son. Though thou wed a white woman to-morrow, the pleasure of receiving in thy arms thy first son is taken from thee for ever. Remember me when thy son is born—the one that shall carry thy name before all men. His misfortunes be on my head. I bear witness—I bear witness"—the lips were forming the words on his ear—"that there is no God but—thee, beloved!"

Then she died. Holden sat still, and all thought was taken from him,—till he heard Ameera's mother lift the curtain.

"Is she dead, *sahib*?"

"She is dead."

"Then I will mourn, and afterwards take an inventory of the furniture in this house. For that will be mine. The *sahib* does not mean to resume it? It is so little, so very little, *sahib*, and I am an old woman. I would like to lie softly."

"For the mercy of God be silent a while. Go out and mourn where I cannot hear."

"*Sahib*, she will be buried in four hours."

"I know the custom. I shall go ere she is taken away. That matter is in thy hands. Look to it, that the bed on which—on which she lies—"

"Aha! That beautiful red-lacquered bed. I have long desired—"

"That the bed is left here untouched for my disposal. All else in the house is thine. Hire a cart, take everything, go hence, and before sunrise let there be nothing in this house but that which I have ordered thee to respect."

"I am an old woman. I would stay at least for the days of mourning, and the rains have just broken. Whither shall I go?"

"What is that to me? My order is that there is a going. The house-gear is worth a thousand rupees and my orderly shall bring thee a hundred rupees to-night."

"That is very little. Think of the cart-hire."

"It shall be nothing unless thou goest, and with speed. O woman, get hence and leave me with my dead!"

The mother shuffled down the staircase, and in her anxiety to take stock of the house-fittings forgot to mourn. Holden stayed by Ameera's side and the rain roared on the roof. He could not think connectedly by reason of the noise, though he made many attempts to do so. Then four sheeted ghosts glided dripping into the room and stared at him through their veils. They were the washers of the dead. Holden left the room and went out to his horse. He had come in a dead, stifling calm through ankle-deep dust. He found the courtyard a rain-lashed pond alive with frogs; a torrent of yellow water ran under the gate, and a roaring wind drove the bolts of the rain like buckshot against the mud-walls. Pir Khan was shivering in his little hut by the gate, and the horse was stamping uneasily in the water.

"I have been told the *sahib's* order," said Pir Khan. "It is well. This house is now desolate. I go also, for my monkey-face would be a reminder of that which has been. Concerning the bed, I will bring that to thy house yonder in the morning; but remember, *sahib*, it will be to thee a knife turning in a green wound. I go upon a pilgrimage, and I will take no money. I have grown fat in the protection of the Presence whose sorrow is my sorrow. For the last time I hold his stirrup."

He touched Holden's foot with both hands and the horse sprang out into the road, where the creaking bamboos were whipping the sky and all the frogs were chuckling. Holden could not see for the rain in his face. He put his hands before his eyes and muttered—

"Oh you brute! You utter brute!"

The news of his trouble was already in his bungalow. He read the knowledge in his butler's eyes when Ahmed Khan brought in food, and for the first and last time in his life laid a hand upon his master's shoulder, saying, "Eat, *sahib*, eat. Meat is good against sorrow. I also have known. Moreover the shadows come and go, *sahib*; the shadows come and go. These be curried eggs."

Holden could neither eat nor sleep. The heavens sent down eight inches of rain in that night and washed the earth clean. The waters tore down walls, broke roads, and scoured open the shallow graves on the Mahomedan burying-ground. All next day it rained, and Holden sat still in his house considering his sorrow. On the morning of the third day he received a telegram which said only, "Ricketts, Myndonie. Dying. Holden relieve. Immediate." Then he thought that before he departed he would look at the house wherein he had been master and lord. There was a break in the weather, and the rank earth steamed with vapour.

He found that the rains had torn down the mud pillars of the gateway, and the heavy wooden gate that had guarded his life hung lazily from one hinge. There was grass three inches high in the courtyard; Pir Khan's lodge was empty, and the sodden thatch sagged between the beams. A gray squirrel was in possession of the verandah, as if the house had been untenanted for thirty years instead of three days. Ameera's mother had removed everything except some mildewed matting. The *tick-tick* of the little scorpions as they hurried across the floor was the only sound in the house. Ameera's room and the other one where Tota had lived were heavy with mildew; and the narrow staircase leading to the roof was streaked and stained with rainborne mud. Holden saw all these things, and came out again to meet in the road Durga Dass, his landlord,—portly, affable, clothed in white muslin, and driving a Cee-spring buggy. He was overlooking his property to see how the roofs stood the stress of the first rains.

"I have heard," said he, "you will not take this place any more, *sahib*?"

"What are you going to do with it?"

"Perhaps I shall let it again."

"Then I will keep it on while I am away."

Durga Dass was silent for some time. "You shall not take it on, *sahib*," he said. "When I was a young man I also—, but to-day I am a member of the Municipality. Ho! Ho! No. When the birds have gone what need to keep the nest? I will have it pulled down— the timber will sell for something always. It shall be pulled down, and the Municipality shall make a road across, as they desire, from the burning-ghaut[18] to the city wall, so that no man may say where this house stood."

---

[18]Place where Hindus cremate their dead.

The Man Who Would Be King

Brother to a Prince and fellow to a beggar if he be found worthy.[1]

The law, as quoted, lays down a fair conduct of life, and one not easy to follow. I have been fellow to a beggar again and again under circumstances which prevented either of us finding out whether the other was worthy. I have still to be brother to a Prince, though I once came near to kinship with what might have been a veritable King, and was promised the reversion[2] of a Kingdom—army, law-courts, revenue, and policy all complete. But, today, I greatly fear that my King is dead, and if I want a crown I must go hunt it for myself.

The beginning of everything was in a railway train upon the road to Mhow from Ajmir.[3] There had been a Deficit in the Budget, which necessitated travelling, not Second-class, which is only half as dear as First-class, but by Intermediate, which is very awful indeed. There are no cushions in the Intermediate class, and the population are either Intermediate, which is Eurasian, or native, which for a long night journey is nasty, or Loafer, which is amusing though intoxicated. Intermediates do not buy from refreshment-rooms. They carry their food in bundles and pots, and buy sweets from the native sweetmeat-sellers, and drink the road-side water. That is why in the hot weather Intermediates are taken out of the carriages dead, and in all weathers are most properly looked down upon.

My particular Intermediate happened to be empty till I reached Nasirabad, when a big black-browed gentleman in shirt-sleeves entered, and, following the custom of Intermediates, passed the time of day. He was a wanderer and a vagabond like myself, but with an educated taste for whisky. He told tales of things he had seen and done, of out-of-the-way corners of the Empire into which he had penetrated, and of adventures in which he risked his life for a few days' food.

"If India was filled with men like you and me, not knowing more than the crows where they'd get their next day's rations, it isn't

---

[1]This verse (echoing the last lines of the Masonic verse "Banquet Night") refers to the principles of Freemasonry, particularly the obligation to mutual aid among members.

[2]Inheritance.

[3]Mhow is a town and British military base in central India. Ajmir was the capital of Rajputana Province (now Rajasthan State) in northwestern India.

seventy millions of revenue the land would be paying—it's seven hundred millions," said he; and as I looked at his mouth and chin I was disposed to agree with him.

We talked politics—the politics of Loaferdom, that see things from the underside where the lath and plaster is not smoothed off— and we talked postal arrangements because my friend wanted to send a telegram back from the next station to Ajmir, the turning-off place from the Bombay to the Mhow line as you travel westward. My friend had no money beyond eight annas,[4] which he wanted for dinner, and I had no money at all, owing to the hitch in the Budget before mentioned. Further, I was going into a wilderness where, though I should resume touch with the Treasury, there were no telegraph offices. I was, therefore, unable to help him in any way.

"We might threaten a Station-master, and make him send a wire on tick,"[5] said my friend, "but that'd mean inquiries for you and for me, and *I've* got my hands full these days. Did you say you are travelling back along this line within any days?"

"Within ten," I said.

"Can't you make it eight?" said he. "Mine is rather urgent business."

"I can send your telegram within ten days if that will serve you," I said.

"I couldn't trust the wire to fetch him now I think of it. It's this way. He leaves Delhi on the 23rd for Bombay. That means he'll be running through Ajmir about the night of the 23rd."

"But I'm going into the Indian Desert," I explained.

"Well *and* good," said he. "You'll be changing at Marwar Junction to get into Jodhpore territory—you must do that—and he'll be coming through Marwar Junction in the early morning of the 24th by the Bombay Mail. Can you be at Marwar Junction on that time? 'Twon't be inconveniencing you because I know that there's precious few pickings to be got out of these Central Indian States—even though you pretend to be correspondent of the *Backwoodsman*."

"Have you ever tried that trick?" I asked.

"Again and again, but the Residents[6] find you out, and then you get escorted to the Border before you've time to get your knife into

[4]Small coins.

[5]With charges reversed.

[6]Local British officials.

them. But about my friend here. I *must* give him a word o' mouth to tell him what's come to me or else he won't know where to go. I would take it more than kind of you if you was to come out of Central India in time to catch him at Marwar Junction, and say to him: 'He has gone South for the week.' He'll know what that means. He's a big man with a red beard, and a great swell he is. You'll find him sleeping like a gentleman with all his luggage round him in a Second-class compartment. But don't you be afraid. Slip down the window, and say: 'He has gone South for the week,' and he'll tumble. It's only cutting your time of stay in those parts by two days. I ask you as a stranger—going to the West," he said with emphasis.

"Where have *you* come from?" said I.

"From the East," said he, "and I am hoping that you will give him the message on the Square—for the sake of my Mother as well as your own."

Englishmen are not usually softened by appeals to the memory of their mothers, but for certain reasons, which will be fully apparent, I saw fit to agree.

"It's more than a little matter," said he, "and that's why I asked you to do it—and now I know that I can depend on you doing it. A Second-class carriage at Marwar Junction, and a red-haired man asleep in it. You'll be sure to remember. I get out at the next station, and I must hold on there till he comes or sends me what I want."

"I'll give the message if I catch him," I said, "and for the sake of your Mother as well as mine I'll give you a word of advice. Don't try to run the Central Indian States just now as the correspondent of the *Backwoodsman*. There's a real one knocking about here, and it might lead to trouble."

"Thank you," said he simply, "and when will the swine be gone? I can't starve because he's ruining my work. I wanted to get hold of the Degumber Rajah[7] down here about his father's widow, and give him a jump."

"What did he do to his father's widow, then?"

"Filled her up with red pepper and slippered her to death as she hung from a beam. I found that out myself, and I'm the only man that would dare going into the State to get hush-money for it. They'll try to poison me, same as they did in Chortumna when I

---

[7]Rajahs of Degumber and Chortumna, fictitious titles for notoriously corrupt rajahs of the time.

went on the loot there. But you'll give the man at Marwar Junction my message?"

He got out at a little roadside station, and I reflected. I had heard, more than once, of men personating correspondents of newspapers and bleeding small Native States with threats of exposure, but I had never met any of the caste before. They led a hard life, and generally die with great suddenness. The Native States have a wholesome horror of English newspapers which may throw light on their peculiar methods of government, and do their best to choke correspondents with champagne, or drive them out of their mind with four-in-hand barouches.[8] They do not understand that nobody cares a straw for the internal administration of Native States so long as oppression and crime are kept within decent limits, and the ruler is not drugged, drunk, or diseased from one end of the year to the other. They are the dark places of the earth, full of unimaginable cruelty, touching the Railway and the Telegraph on one side, and, on the other, the days of Harun-al-Raschid.[9] When I left the train I did business with divers Kings, and in eight days passed through many changes of life. Sometimes I wore dress-clothes and consorted with Princes and Politicals, drinking from crystal and eating from silver. Sometimes I lay out upon the ground and devoured what I could get, from a plate made of leaves, and drank the running water, and slept under the same rug[10] as my servant. It was all in the day's work.

Then I headed for the Great Indian Desert upon the proper date, as I had promised, and the night Mail set me down at Marwar Junction, where a funny, little, happy-go-lucky, native-managed railway runs to Jodhpore. The Bombay Mail from Delhi makes a short halt at Marwar. She arrived as I got in, and I had just time to hurry to her platform and go down the carriages. There was only one Second-class on the train. I slipped the window and looked down upon a flaming red beard, half covered by a railway rug. That was my man, fast asleep, and I dug him gently in the ribs. He woke with a grunt, and I saw his face in the light of the lamps. It was a great and shining face.

[8]Carriages.
[9]Caliph of medieval Baghdad, prominent in *The Thousand and One Nights.*
[10]Blanket.

"Tickets again?" said he.

"No," said I. "I am to tell you that he is gone South for the week. He has gone South for the week!"

The train had begun to move out. The red man rubbed his eyes. "He has gone South for the week," he repeated. "Now that's just like his impidence. Did he say that I was to give you anything? 'Cause I won't."

"He didn't," I said, and dropped away, and watched the red lights die out in the dark. It was horribly cold because the wind was blowing off the sands. I climbed into my own train—not an Intermediate Carriage this time—and went to sleep.

If the man with the beard had given me a rupee I should have kept it as a memento of a rather curious affair. But the consciousness of having done my duty was my only reward.

Later on I reflected that two gentlemen like my friends could not do any good if they forgathered and personated correspondents of newspapers, and might, if they black-mailed one of the little rat-trap states of Central India or Southern Rajputana, get themselves into serious difficulties. I therefore took some trouble to describe them as accurately as I could remember to people who would be interested in deporting them; and succeeded, so I was later informed, in having them headed back from the Degumber borders.

Then I became respectable, and returned to an Office where there were no Kings and no incidents outside the daily manufacture of a newspaper. A newspaper office seems to attract every conceivable sort of person, to the prejudice of discipline. Zenana-mission ladies arrive, and beg that the Editor will instantly abandon all his duties to describe a Christian prize-giving in a back-slum of a perfectly inaccessible village; Colonels who have been overpassed for command sit down and sketch the outline of a series of ten, twelve, or twenty-four leading articles on Seniority *versus* Selection; Missionaries wish to know why they have not been permitted to escape from their regular vehicles of abuse and swear at a brother-missionary under special patronage of the editorial We; stranded theatrical companies troop up to explain that they cannot pay for their advertisements, but on their return from New Zealand or Tahiti will do so with interest; inventors of patent punkah-pulling machines,[11]

---

[11]Punkahs were large fans, usually operated by hand.

carriage couplings, and unbreakable swords and axle-trees, call with specifications in their pockets and hours at their disposal; tea-companies enter and elaborate their prospectuses with the office pens; secretaries of ball-committees clamour to have the glories of their last dance more fully described; strange ladies rustle in and say, "I want a hundred lady's cards printed *at once*, please," which is manifestly part of an Editor's duty; and every dissolute ruffian that ever tramped the Grand Trunk Road[12] makes it his business to ask for employment as a proof-reader. And, all the time, the telephone-bell is ringing madly, and Kings are being killed on the Continent, and Empires are saying, "You're another," and Mister Gladstone is calling down brimstone upon the British Dominions, and the little black copy-boys are whining, "*kaa-pi chay-ha-yeh*"[13] like tired bees, and most of the paper is as blank as Modred's shield.

But that is the amusing part of the year. There are six other months when none ever comes to call, and the thermometer walks inch by inch up to the top of the glass, and the office is darkened to just above reading-light, and the press-machines are red-hot of touch, and nobody writes anything but accounts of amusements in the Hill-stations or obituary notices. Then the telephone becomes a tinkling terror, because it tells you of the sudden deaths of men and women that you knew intimately, and the prickly-heat covers you with a garment, and you sit down and write: "A slight increase of sickness is reported from the Khuda Janta Khan District. The outbreak is purely sporadic in its nature, and, thanks to the energetic efforts of the District authorities, is now almost at an end. It is, however, with deep regret we record the death, etc."

Then the sickness really breaks out, and the less recording and reporting the better for the peace of the subscribers. But the Empires and the Kings continue to divert themselves as selfishly as before, and the Foreman thinks that a daily paper really ought to come out once in twenty-four hours, and all the people at the Hill-stations in the middle of their amusements say: "Good gracious! Why can't the paper be sparkling? I'm sure there's plenty going on up here."

---

[12]The Grand Trunk Road, running over 1,500 miles from Calcutta to Peshawar, was built by the British Raj in the 19th c. upon the foundations of a 16th-c. road established by the Muslim Emperor of India, Sher Shah Suri. It features prominently in Kipling's novel *Kim*.

[13]"Copy wanted."

That is the dark half of the moon, and, as the advertisements say, "must be experienced to be appreciated."

It was in that season, and a remarkably evil season, that the paper began running the last issue of the week on Saturday night, which is to say Sunday morning, after the custom of a London paper. This was a great convenience, for immediately after the paper was put to bed, the dawn would lower the thermometer from 96° to almost 84° for half an hour, and in that chill—you have no idea how cold is 84° on the grass until you begin to pray for it—a very tired man could get off to sleep ere the heat roused him.

One Saturday night it was my pleasant duty to put the paper to bed alone. A King or courtier or a courtesan or a Community was going to die or get a new Constitution, or do something that was important on the other side of the world, and the paper was to be held open till the latest possible minute in order to catch the telegram.

It was a pitchy black night, as stifling as a June night can be, and the *loo*, the red-hot wind from the westward, was booming among the tinder-dry trees and pretending that the rain was on its heels. Now and again a spot of almost boiling water would fall on the dust with the flop of a frog, but all our weary world knew that was only pretence. It was a shade cooler in the press-room than the office, so I sat there, while the type ticked and clicked, and the night-jars hooted at the windows, and the all but naked compositors wiped the sweat from their foreheads, and called for water. The thing that was keeping us back, whatever it was, would not come off, though the *loo* dropped and the last type was set, and the whole round earth stood still in the choking heat, with its finger on its lip, to wait the event. I drowsed, and wondered whether the telegraph was a blessing, and whether this dying man, or struggling people, might be aware of the inconvenience the delay was causing. There was no special reason beyond the heat and worry to make tension, but, as the clock-hands crept up to three o'clock, and the machines spun their fly-wheels two or three times to see that all was in order before I said the word that would set them off, I could have shrieked aloud.

Then the roar and rattle of the wheels shivered the quiet into little bits. I rose to go away, but two men in white clothes stood in front of me. The first one said: "It's him!" The second said: "So it is!" And they both laughed almost as loudly as the machinery roared, and mopped their foreheads. "We seed there was a light burning across the road, and we were sleeping in that ditch there for coolness, and I said to my friend here, The office is open. Let's come along and speak to him as turned us back from the Degumber State," said the smaller of the two. He was the man I had met in the Mhow train, and his fellow was the red-bearded man of Marwar Junction. There was no mistaking the eyebrows of the one or the beard of the other.

I was not pleased, because I wished to go to sleep, not to squabble with loafers. "What do you want?" I asked.

"Half an hour's talk with you, cool and comfortable, in the office," said the red-bearded man. "We'd *like* some drink—the Contrack doesn't begin yet, Peachey, so you needn't look—but what we really want is advice. We don't want money. We ask you as a favour, because we found out you did us a bad turn about Degumber State."

I led from the press-room to the stifling office with the maps on the walls, and the red-haired man rubbed his hands. "That's something like," said he. "This was the proper shop to come to. Now, Sir, let me introduce to you Brother Peachey Carnehan, that's him, and Brother Daniel Dravot, that is *me*, and the less said about our professions the better, for we have been most things in our time. Soldier, sailor, compositor, photographer, proof-reader, street-preacher, and correspondents of the *Backwoodsman* when we thought the paper wanted one. Carnehan is sober, and so am I. Look at us first, and see that's sure. It will save you cutting into my talk. We'll take one of your cigars apiece, and you shall see us light up."

I watched the test. The men were absolutely sober, so I gave them each a tepid whisky and soda.

"Well *and* good," said Carnehan of the eyebrows, wiping the froth from his moustache. "Let me talk now, Dan. We have been all over India, mostly on foot. We have been boiler-fitters, engine-drivers, petty contractors, and all that, and we have decided that India isn't big enough for such as us."

They certainly were too big for the office. Dravot's beard seemed to fill half the room and Carnehan's shoulders the other half, as they sat on the big table. Carnehan continued: "The country isn't half worked out because they that governs it won't let you touch it. They spend all their blessed time in governing it, and you can't lift a spade, nor chip a rock, nor look for oil, nor anything like that, without all the Government saying, 'Leave it alone, and let us govern.' Therefore, such *as* it is, we will let it alone, and go away to some other place where a man isn't crowded and can come to his own. We are not little men, and there is nothing that we are afraid of except Drink, and we have signed a Contrack on that. *Therefore*, we are going away to be Kings."

"Kings in our own right," muttered Dravot.

"Yes, of course," I said. "You've been tramping in the sun, and it's a very warm night, and hadn't you better sleep over the notion? Come tomorrow."

"Neither drunk nor sunstruck," said Dravot. "We have slept over the notion half a year, and require to see Books and Atlases, and we have decided that there is only one place now in the world that two strong men can Sar-a-*whack*.[14] They call it Kafiristan. By my reckoning it's the top right-hand corner of Afghanistan, not more than three hundred miles from Peshawar. They have two-and-thirty heathen idols there, and we'll be the thirty-third and thirty-fourth. It's a mountainous country, and the women of those parts are very beautiful."

"But that is provided against in the Contrack," said Carnehan. "Neither Woman nor Liqu-or, Daniel."

"And that's all we know, except that no one has gone there, and they fight, and in any place where they fight a man who knows how to drill men can always be a King. We shall go to those parts and say to any King we find—'D'you want to vanquish your foes?' and we will show him how to drill men; for that we know better than anything else. Then we will subvert that King and seize his Throne and establish a Dy-nasty."

"You'll be cut to pieces before you're fifty miles across the Border," I said. "You have to travel through Afghanistan to get to that country. It's one mass of mountains and peaks and glaciers, and no Englishman has been through it. The people are utter brutes, and even if you reached them you couldn't do anything."

"That's more like," said Carnehan. "If you could think us a little more mad we would be more pleased. We have come to you to know about this country, to read a book about it, and to be shown maps. We want you to tell us that we are fools and to show us your books." He turned to the bookcases.

---

[14]Dravot is playing on "Sarawak," a region in Malaysia that became a British protectorate in 1888.

"Are you at all in earnest?" I said.

"A little," said Dravot sweetly. "As big a map as you have got, even if it's all blank where Kafiristan is, and any books you've got. We can read, though we aren't very educated."

I uncased the big thirty-two-miles-to-the-inch map of India, and two smaller Frontier maps, hauled down volume INF-KAN of the *Encyclopædia Britannica*, and the men consulted them.

"See here!" said Dravot, his thumb on the map. "Up to Jagdallak, Peachey and me know the road. We was there with Roberts' Army.[15] We'll have to turn off to the right at Jagdallak through Laghmann territory. Then we get among the hills—fourteen thousand feet—fifteen thousand—it will be cold work there, but it don't look very far on the map."

I handed him Wood on the *Sources of the Oxus*. Carnehan was deep in the *Encyclopædia*.

"They're a mixed lot," said Dravot reflectively; "and it won't help us to know the names of their tribes. The more tribes the more they'll fight, and the better for us. From Jagdallak to Ashang—H'mm!"

"But all the information about the country is as sketchy and inaccurate as can be," I protested. "No one knows anything about it really. Here's the file of *United Services' Institute*. Read what Bellew says."

"Blow Bellew!" said Carnehan. "Dan, they're a stinkin' lot of heathens, but this book here says they think they're related to us English."

I smoked while the men poured over Raverty, Wood, the maps, and the *Encyclopædia*.

"There is no use your waiting," said Dravot politely. "It's about four o'clock now. We'll go before six o'clock if you want to sleep, and we won't steal any of the papers. Don't you sit up. We're two harmless lunatics, and if you come tomorrow evening down to the Serai,[16] we'll say good-bye to you."

"You *are* two fools," I answered. "You'll be turned back at the Frontier or cut up the minute you set foot in Afghanistan. Do you want any money or a recommendation down-country? I can help you to the chance of work next week."

---

[15]The British force in Afghanistan during the Afghan War of 1879–80; see the selections from Major Mitford's *To Caubul with the Cavalry Brigade*, p. 107.

[16]Bazaar.

"Next week we shall be hard at work ourselves, thank you," said Dravot. "It isn't so easy being a King as it looks. When we've got our Kingdom in going order we'll let you know, and you can come up and help us to govern it."

"Would two lunatics make a contrack like that?" said Carnehan, with subdued pride, showing me a greasy half-sheet of notepaper on which was written the following. I copied it, then and there, as a curiosity—

> *This Contrack between me and you persuing witnesseth in the name of God—Amen and so forth.*
>> *(One)   That me and you will settle this matter together; i.e. to be Kings of Kafiristan.*
>> *(Two)   That you and me will not, while this matter is being settled, look at any Liquor, nor any Woman black, white, or brown, so as to get mixed up with one or the other harmful.*
>> *(Three) That we conduct ourselves with Dignity and Discretion, and if one of us gets into trouble the other will stay by him.*
> *Signed by you and me this day,*
>> *Peachey Taliaferro Carnehan*
>> *Daniel Dravot*
>> *Both Gentlemen at Large*

"There was no need for the last article," said Carnehan, blushing modestly; "but it looks regular. Now you know the sort of men that loafers are—we *are* loafers, Dan, until we get out of India—and *do* you think that we would sign a Contrack like that unless we was in earnest? We have kept away from the two things that make life worth having."

"You won't enjoy your lives much longer if you are going to try this idiotic adventure. Don't set the office on fire," I said, "and go away before nine o'clock."

I left them still poring over the maps and making notes on the back of the "Contrack." "Be sure to come down to the Serai tomorrow," were their parting words.

The Kumharsen Serai is the great four-square sink of humanity where the strings of camels and horses from the North load and unload. All the nationalities of Central Asia may be found there, and

most of the folk of India proper. Balkh and Bokhara there meet
Bengal and Bombay, and try to draw eye-teeth. You can buy
ponies, turquoises, Persian pussy-cats, saddle-bags, fat-tailed sheep
and musk in the Kumharsen Serai, and get many strange things for
nothing. In the afternoon I went down to see whether my friends
intended to keep their word or were lying there drunk.

A priest attired in fragments of ribbons and rags stalked up to
me, gravely twisting a child's paper whirligig. Behind him was his
servant bending under a load of a crate of mud toys. The two were
loading up two camels, and the inhabitants of the Serai watched
them with shrieks of laughter.

"The priest is mad," said a horse-dealer to me. "He is going up
to Kabul to sell toys to the Amir. He will either be raised to honor
or have his head cut off. He came in here this morning and has
been behaving madly ever since."

"The witless are under the protection of God," stammered a
flat-cheeked Usbeg in broken Hindi. "They foretell future events."

"Would they could have foretold that my caravan would have
been cut up by the Shinwaris almost within shadow of the Pass!"
grunted the Yusufzai agent of a Rajputana trading-house whose
goods had been diverted into the hands of other robbers just across
the Border, and whose misfortunes were the laughing-stock of the
bazaar. "Ohé, priest, whence come you and whither do you go?"

"From Roum have I come," shouted the priest, waving his
whirligig; "from Roum, blown by the breath of a hundred devils
across the sea! O thieves, robbers, liars, the blessing of Pir Khan on
pigs, dogs, and perjurers! Who will take the Protected of God to
the North to sell charms that are never still to the Amir? The
camels shall not gall, the sons shall not fall sick, and the wives shall
remain faithful while they are away, of the men who give me place
in their caravan. Who will assist me to slipper the King of the Roos
with a golden slipper with a silver heel? The protection of Pir Khan
be upon his labours!" He spread out the skirts of his gaberdine and
pirouetted between the lines of tethered horses.

"There starts a caravan from Peshawar to Kabul in twenty
days, *Huzrut*,"[17] said the Yusufzai trader. "My camels go there-
with. Do thou also go and bring us good luck."

[17]"Presence"; an honorary term of address.

"I will go even now!" shouted the priest. "I will depart upon my winged camels, and be at Peshawar in a day! Ho! Hazar Mir Khan," he yelled to his servant, "drive out the camels, but let me first mount my own."

He leaped on the back of his beast as it knelt, and, turning round to me, cried: "Come thou also, Sahib, a little along the road, and I will sell thee a charm—an amulet that shall make thee King of Kafiristan."

Then the light broke upon me, and I followed the two camels out of the Serai till we reached open road and the priest halted.

"What d'you think o' that?" said he in English. "Carnehan can't talk their patter, so I've made him my servant. He makes a handsome servant. 'Tisn't for nothing that I've been knocking about the country for fourteen years. Didn't I do that talk neat? We'll hitch on to a caravan at Peshawar till we get to Jagdallak, and then we'll see if we can get donkeys for our camels, and strike into Kafiristan. Whirligigs for the Amir, O Lor! Put your hand under the camel-bags and tell me what you feel."

I felt the butt of a Martini,[18] and another and another.

"Twenty of 'em," said Dravot placidly. "Twenty of 'em and ammunition to correspond, under the whirligigs and the mud dolls."

"Heaven help you if you are caught with those things!" I said. "A Martini is worth her weight in silver among the Pathans."[19]

"Fifteen hundred rupees of capital—every rupee we could beg, borrow, or steal—are invested on these two camels," said Dravot. "We won't get caught. We're going through the Khyber[20] with a regular caravan. Who'd touch a poor mad priest?"

"Have you got everything you want?" I asked, overcome with astonishment.

"Not yet, but we shall soon. Give us a memento of your kindness, *Brother*.[21] You did me a service, yesterday, and that time in Marwar. Half my Kingdom shall you have, as the saying is." I slipped a small charm compass from my watch-chain and handed it up to the priest.

---

[18]A high-quality rifle.

[19]An Afghan ethnic group.

[20]The Khyber Pass between India and Afghanistan.

[21]Emphasizing the word so as to hint that he recognizes him as a fellow Freemason, perhaps from the Masonic compass symbol on his watch-chain.

"Good-bye," said Dravot, giving me hand cautiously. "It's the last time we'll shake hands with an Englishman these many days. Shake hands with him, Carnehan," he cried, as the second camel passed me.

Carnehan leaned down and shook hands. Then the camels passed away along the dusty road, and I was left alone to wonder. My eye could detect no failure in disguises. The scene in the Serai proved that they were complete to the native mind. There was just the chance, therefore, that Carnehan and Dravot would be able to wander through Afghanistan without detection. But, beyond, they would find death—certain and awful death.

Ten days later a native correspondent giving me the news of the day from Peshawar, wound up his letter with: "There has been much laughter here on account of a certain mad priest who is going in his estimation to sell petty gauds and insignificant trinkets which he ascribes as great charms to H.H. the Amir of Bukhara. He passed through Peshawar and associated himself to the Second Summer caravan that goes to Kabul. The merchants are pleased because through superstition they imagine that such mad fellows bring good fortune."

The two, then, were beyond the Border. I would have prayed for them, but, that night, a real King died in Europe, and demanded an obituary notice.

*   *   *

The wheel of the world swings through the same phases again and again. Summer passed and winter thereafter, and came and passed again. The daily paper continued and I with it, and upon the third summer there fell a hot night, a night-issue, and a strained waiting for something to be telegraphed from the other side of the world, exactly as had happened before. A few great men had died in the past two years, the machines worked with more clatter, and some of the trees in the office garden were a few feet taller. But that was all the difference.

I passed over to the press-room, and went through just such a scene as I have already described. The nervous tension was stronger than it had been two years before, and I felt the heat more acutely. At three o'clock I cried, "Print off," and turned to go when there crept to my chair what was left of a man. He was bent into a circle, his head was sunk between his shoulders, and he moved his feet one over the other like a bar. I could hardly see whether he walked or crawled—this rag-wrapped, whining cripple who addressed me by name, crying that he was come back. "Can you give me a drink?" he whimpered. "For the Lord's sake give me a drink!"

I went back to the office, the man following with groans of pain, and I turned on the lamp.

"Don't you know me?" he gasped, dropping into a chair, and he turned his drawn face, surmounted by a shock of grey hair, to the light.

I looked at him intently. Once before had I seen eyebrows that met over the nose in an inch-broad black band, but for the life of me I could not tell where.

"I don't know you," I said, handing him the whisky. "What can I do for you?"

He took a gulp of the spirit raw, and shivered in spite of the suffocating heat.

"I've come back," he repeated; "and I was the King of Kafiristan—me and Dravot—crowned Kings we was! In this office we settled it—you setting there and giving us the books. I am Peachey—Peachey Taliaferro Carnehan, and you've been setting here ever since—O Lord!"

I was more than a little astonished, and expressed my feelings accordingly.

"It's true," said Carnehan, with a dry cackle, nursing his feet, which were wrapped in rags. "True as gospel. Kings we were, with crowns upon our heads—me and Dravot—poor Dan—oh, poor, poor Dan, that would never take advice, not though I begged of him!"

"Take the whisky," I said, "and take your own time. Tell me all you can recollect of everything from beginning to end. You got across the Border on your camels, Dravot dressed as a mad priest and you his servant. Do you remember that?"

"I ain't mad—yet, but I shall be that way soon. Of course I remember. Keep looking at me, or maybe my words will go all to pieces. Keep looking at me in my eyes and don't say anything."

I leaned forward and looked into his face as steadily as I could. He dropped one hand upon the table and I grasped it by the wrist. It was twisted like a bird's claw, and upon the back was a ragged red diamond-shaped scar.

"No, don't look there. Look at *me*," said Carnehan. "That comes afterwards, but for the Lord's sake don't distrack me. We left with that caravan, me and Dravot playing all sorts of antics to amuse the people we were with. Dravot used to make us laugh in the evenings when all the people was cooking their dinners—cooking their dinners, and . . . what did they do then? They lit little fires with sparks that went into Dravot's beard, and we all laughed—fit to die. Little red fires they was, going into Dravot's big red beard—so funny." His eyes left mine and he smiled foolishly.

"You went as far as Jagdallak with that caravan," I said at a venture, "after you had lit those fires. To Jagdallak, where you turned off to try to get into Kafiristan."

"No, we didn't neither. What are you talking about? We turned off before Jagdallak, because we heard the roads was good. But they wasn't good enough for our two camels—mine and Dravot's. When we left the caravan, Dravot took off all his clothes and mine too, and said we would be heathen, because the Kafirs didn't allow Mohammedans to talk to them. So we dressed betwixt and between, and such a sight as Daniel Dravot I never saw yet nor expect to see again. He burned half his beard, and slung a sheep-skin over his shoulder, and shaved his head into patterns. He shaved mine, too, and made me wear outrageous things to look like a heathen. That was in a most mountaineous country, and our camels couldn't go along any more because of the mountains. They were tall and black, and coming home I saw them fight like wild goats—there are lots of goats in Kafiristan. And these mountains, they never keep still, no more than the goats. Always fighting they are, and don't let you sleep at night."

"Take some more whisky," I said very slowly. "What did you and Daniel Dravot do when the camels could go no farther because of the rough roads that led into Kafiristan?"

"What did which do? There was a party called Peachey Taliaferro Carnehan that was with Dravot. Shall I tell you about him? He died out there in the cold. Slap from the bridge fell old Peachey, turning and twisting in the air like a penny whirligig that you can sell to the Amir—No; they was two for three ha'pence, those whirligigs, or I am much mistaken and woful sore . . . And then these camels were no use, and Peachey said to Dravot—'For the Lord's sake let's get out of this before our heads are chopped off,' and with that they killed the camels all among the mountains, not having anything in particular to eat, but first they took off the boxes with the guns and the ammunition, till two men came along driving four mules. Dravot up and dances in front of them, singing—'Sell me four mules.' Says the first man—'If you are rich enough to buy, you are rich enough to rob'; but before ever he could put his hand to his knife, Dravot breaks his neck over his knee, and the other party runs away. So Carnehan loaded the mules with the rifles that was taken off the camels, and together we starts forward into those bitter cold mountaineous parts, and never a road broader than the back of your hand."

He paused for a moment, while I asked him if he could remember the nature of the country through which he had journeyed.

"I am telling you as straight as I can, but my head isn't as good as it might be. They drove nails through it to make me hear better how Dravot died. The country was mountaineous and the mules were most contrary, and the inhabitants was dispersed and solitary. They went up and up, and down and down, and that other party, Carnehan, was imploring of Dravot not to sing and whistle so loud, for fear of bringing down the tremenjus avalanches. But Dravot says that if a King couldn't sing it wasn't worth being King, and whacked the mules over the rump, and never took no heed for ten cold days. We came to a big level valley all among the mountains, and the mules were near dead, so we killed them, not having anything in special for them or us to eat. We sat upon the boxes, and played odd and even with the cartridges that was jolted out.

"Then ten men with bows and arrows ran down that valley, chasing twenty men with bows and arrows, and the row was tremenjus. They was fair men—fairer than you or me—with yellow hair and remarkable well built. Says Dravot, unpacking the guns—'This is the beginning of the business. We'll fight for the ten men,' and with that he fires two rifles at the twenty men, and drops one of them at two hundred yards from the rock where he was sitting. The other men began to run, but Carnehan and Dravot sits on the boxes picking them off at all ranges, up and down the valley. Then we goes up to the ten men that had run across the snow too, and they fires a footy little arrow at us. Dravot he shoots above their heads and they all falls down flat. Then he walks over them and kicks them, and then he lifts them up and shakes hands all round to make them friendly like. He calls them and gives them the boxes to carry, and waves his hand for all the world as though he was King already.

They takes the boxes and him across the valley and up the hill into a pine wood on the top, where there was half-a-dozen big stone idols. Dravot he goes to the biggest—a fellow they call Imbra—and lays a rifle and a cartridge at his feet, rubbing his nose respectful with his own nose, patting him on the head, and saluting in front of it. He turns round to the men and nods his head, and says—'That's all right. I'm in the know too, and all these old jim-jams are my friends.' Then he opens his mouth and points down it, and when the first man brings him food, he says—'No'; and when the second man brings him food, he says—'No'; but when one of the old priests and the boss of the village brings him food, he says—'Yes,' very haughty, and eats it slow. That was how we came to our first village, without any trouble, just as though we had tumbled from the skies. But we tumbled from one of those damned rope-bridges, you see, and—you couldn't expect a man to laugh much after that?"

"Take some more whisky and go on," I said. "That was the first village you came into. How did you get to be King?"

"I wasn't King," said Carnehan. "Dravot he was the King, and a handsome man he looked with the gold crown on his head and all. Him and the other party stayed in that village, and every morning Dravot sat by the side of old Imbra, and the people came and worshipped. That was Dravot's order. Then a lot of men came into the valley, and Carnehan and Dravot picks them off with the rifles before they knew where they was, and runs down into the valley and up again the other side and finds another village, same as the first one, and the people all falls down flat on their faces, and Dravot says—'Now what is the trouble between you two villages?' and the people points to a woman, as fair as you or me, that was carried off, and Dravot takes her back to the first village and counts up the dead—eight there was. For each dead man Dravot pours a little milk on the ground and waves his arms like a whirligig, and 'That's all right,' says he. Then he and Carnehan takes the big boss of each village by the arm and walks them down into the valley, and shows them how to scratch a line with a spear right down the valley, and gives each a sod of turf from both sides of the line. Then all the people comes down and shouts like the devil and all, and Dravot says—'Go and dig the land, and be fruitful and multiply,'[22]

---

[22]As God commanded Adam and Eve (Genesis 1:28).

which they did, though they didn't understand. Then we asks the names of things in their lingo—bread and water and fire and idols and such, and Dravot leads the priest of each village up to the idol, and says he must sit there and judge the people, and if anything goes wrong he is to be shot.

"Next week they was all turning up the land in the village as quiet as bees and much prettier, and the priests heard all the complaints and told Dravot in dumb show what it was about. 'That's just the beginning,' says Dravot. 'They think we're Gods.' He and Carnehan picks out twenty good men and shows them how to click off a rifle, and form fours, and advance in line, and they was very pleased to do so, and clever to see the hang of it. Then he takes out his pipe and his baccy-pouch and leaves one at one village, and one at the other, and off we two goes to see what was to be done in the next valley. That was all rock, and there was a little village there, and Carnehan says—'Send 'em to the old valley to plant,' and takes 'em there, and gives 'em some land that wasn't took before. They were a poor lot, and we blooded 'em with a kid[23] before letting 'em into the new Kingdom. That was to impress the people, and then they settled down quiet, and Carnehan went back to Dravot who had got into another valley, all snow and ice and most mountaineous. There was no people there and the Army got afraid, so Dravot shoots one of them, and goes on till he finds some people in a village, and the Army explains that unless the people wants to be killed they had better not shoot their little matchlocks; for they had matchlocks. We makes friends with the priest, and I stays there alone with two of the Army, teaching the men how to drill, and a thundering big Chief comes across the snow with kettle-drums and horns twanging, because he heard there was a new God kicking about. Carnehan sights for the brown of the men half a mile across the snow and wings one of them. Then he sends a message to the Chief that, unless he wished to be killed, he must come and shake hands with me and leave his arms behind. The Chief comes alone first, and Carnehan shakes hands with him and whirls his arms about, same as Dravot used, and very much surprised that Chief was, and strokes my eyebrows. Then Carnehan goes alone to the Chief, and asks him in dumb show if he had an enemy he hated. 'I

---

[23]Sacrificed a young goat.

have,' says the Chief. So Carnehan weeds out the pick of his men, and sets the two of the Army to show them drill, and at the end of two weeks the men can manoeuvre about as well as Volunteers. So he marches with the Chief to a great big plain on the top of a mountain, and the Chief's men rushes into a village and takes it, we three Martinis firing into the brown of the enemy. So we took that village too, and I gives the Chief a rag from my coat and says, 'Occupy till I come'; which was scriptural.[24] By way of a reminder, when me and the Army was eighteen hundred yards away, I drops a bullet near him standing on the snow, and all the people falls flat on their faces. Then I sends a letter to Dravot wherever he be by land or by sea."

At the risk of throwing the creature out of train I interrupted— "How could you write a letter up yonder?"

"The letter?—Oh!—The letter! Keep looking at me between the eyes, please. It was a string-talk letter, that we'd learned the way of it from a blind beggar in the Punjab."

I remember that there had once come to the office a blind man with a knotted twig and a piece of string which he wound round the twig according to some cipher[25] of his own. He could, after the lapse of days or hours, repeat the sentence which he had reeled up. He had reduced the alphabet to eleven primitive sounds, and tried to teach me the method, but I could not understand.

"I sent that letter to Dravot," said Carnehan; "and told him to come back because this Kingdom was growing too big for me to handle, and then I struck for the first valley, to see how the priests were working. They called the village we took along with the Chief, Bashkai, and the first village we took, Er-Heb. The priests at Er-Heb was doing all right, but they had a lot of pending cases about land to show me, and some men from another village had been firing arrows at night. I went out and looked for that village, and fired four rounds at it from a thousand yards. That used all the cartridges I cared to spend, and I waited for Dravot, who had been away two or three months, and I kept my people quiet.

"One morning I heard the devil's own noise of drums and horns, and Dan Dravot marches down the hill with his Army and a

---

[24]From the instructions given by a departing nobleman to each of his servants in Jesus's parable of the talents (Luke 19:13).
[25]Code.

tail of hundreds of men, and, which was the most amazing, a great gold crown on his head. 'My Gord, Carnehan,' says Daniel, 'this is a tremenjus business, and we've got the whole country as far as it's worth having. I am the son of Alexander by Queen Semiramis,[26] and you're my younger brother and a God too! It's the biggest thing we've ever seen. I've been marching and fighting for six weeks with the Army, and every footy little village for fifty miles has come in rejoiceful; and more than that, I've got the key of the whole show, as you'll see, and I've got a crown for you! I told 'em to make two of 'em at a place called Shu, where the gold lies in the rock like suet in mutton. Gold I've seen, and turquoise I've kicked out of the cliffs, and there's garnets in the sands of the river, and here's a chunk of amber that a man brought me. Call up all the priests and, here, take your crown.'

"One of the men opens a black hair bag, and I slips the crown on. It was too small and too heavy, but I wore it for the glory. Hammered gold it was—five pound weight, like a hoop of a barrel.

"'Peachey,' says Dravot, 'we don't want to fight no more. The Craft's[27] the trick, so help me!' and he brings forward that same Chief that I left at Bashkai—Billy Fish we called him afterwards, because he was so like Billy Fish that drove the big tank-engine at Mach on the Bolan in the old days. 'Shake hands with him,' says Dravot, and I shook hands and nearly dropped, for Billy Fish gave me the Grip. I said nothing, but tried him with the Fellow Craft Grip. He answers all right, and I tried the Master's Grip, but that was a slip. 'A Fellow Craft he is!' I says to Dan, 'Does he know the word?'—'He does,' says Dan, 'and all the priests know. It's a miracle! The Chiefs and the priests can work a Fellow Craft Lodge in a way that's very like ours, and they've cut the marks on the rocks, but they don't know the Third Degree, and they've come to find out. It's Gord's Truth. I've known these long years that the Afghans knew up to the Fellow Craft Degree, but this is a miracle. A God and a Grand-Master of the Craft am I, and a Lodge in the Third Degree I will open, and we'll raise the head priests and the Chiefs of the Village.'

"'It's against all the law,' says I, 'holding a Lodge without warrant from any one; and you know we never held office in any Lodge.'

[26]Alexander the Great had conquered the region in the 4th c. B.C.E. Semiramis was a notoriously promiscuous queen of Assyria centuries before Alexander's time.

[27]Freemasonry.

"'It's a master-stroke o' policy,' says Dravot. 'It means running the country as easy as a four-wheeled bogie on a down grade. We can't stop to inquire now, or they'll turn against us. I've forty Chiefs at my heel, and passed and raised according to their merit they shall be. Billet these men on the villages, and see that we run up a Lodge of some kind. The temple of Imbra will do for the Lodge-room. The women must make aprons as you show them.[28] I'll hold a levee of Chiefs tonight and Lodge tomorrow.'

"I was fair run off my legs, but I wasn't such a fool as not to see what a pull this Craft business gave us. I showed the priests' families how to make aprons of the degrees, but for Dravot's apron the blue border and marks was made of turquoise lumps on white hide, not cloth. We took a great square stone in the temple for the Master's chair, and little stones for the officers' chairs, and painted the black pavement with white squares, and did what we could to make things regular.

"At the levee which was held that night on the hillside with big bonfires, Dravot gives out that him and me were Gods and sons of Alexander, and Past Grand-Masters in the Craft, and was come to make Kafiristan a country where every man should eat in peace and drink in quiet, and especially obey us. Then the Chiefs come round to shake hands, and they were so hairy and white and fair it was just shaking hands with old friends. We gave them names according as they was like men we had known in India—Billy Fish, Holly Dilworth, Pikky Kergan, that was Bazaar-master when I was at Mhow, and so on, and so on.

"*The* most amazing miracles was at Lodge next night. One of the old priests was watching us continuous, and I felt uneasy, for I knew we'd have to fudge the Ritual, and I didn't know what the man knew. The old priest was a stranger come in from beyond the village of Bashkai. The minute Dravot puts on that Master's apron that the girls had made for him, the priest fetches a whoop and a howl, and tries to overturn the stone that Dravot was sitting on. 'It's all up now,' I says. 'That comes of meddling with the Craft without warrant!' Dravot never winked an eye, not when ten priests took and tilted over the Grand-Master's chair—which was to say the stone of Imbra. The priests begins rubbing the bottom end of it to clear away the black dirt, and presently he shows all the other priests the Master's Mark,

[28]During rituals in their lodges, Masons would wear aprons decorated with Masonic symbols.

same as was on Dravot's apron, cut into the stone. Not even the priests of the temple of Imbra knew it was there. The old chap falls flat on his face at Dravot's feet and kisses 'em. 'Luck again,' says Dravot, across the Lodge to me; 'they say it's the Missing Mark that no one could understand the why of. We're more than safe now.' Then he bangs the butt of his gun for a gavel and says: 'By virtue of the authority vested in me by my own right hand and the help of Peachey, I declare myself Grand-Master of all Freemasonry in Kafiristan in this the Mother Lodge o' the country, and King of Kafiristan equally with Peachey!' At that he puts on his crown and I puts on mine—I was doing Senior Warden—and we opens the Lodge in most ample form. It was an amazing miracle! The priests moved in Lodge through the first two degrees almost without telling, as if the memory was coming back to them. After that, Peachey and Dravot raised such as was worthy—high priests and Chiefs of far-off villages. Billy Fish was the first, and I can tell you we scared the soul out of him. It was not in any way according to Ritual, but it served our turn. We didn't raise more than ten of the biggest men, because we didn't want to make the Degree common. And they was clamouring to be raised.

"'In another six months,' says Dravot, 'we'll hold another Communication, and see how you are working.' Then he asks them about their villages, and learns that they was fighting one against the other, and were sick and tired of it. And when they weren't doing that they was fighting with the Mohammedans. 'You can fight those when they come into our country,' says Dravot. 'Tell off every tenth man of your tribes for a Frontier guard, and send two hundred at a time to this valley to be drilled. Nobody is going to be shot or speared any more so long as he does well, and I know that you won't cheat me, because you're white people—sons of Alexander—and not like common, black Mohammedans. You are *my* people, and by God,' says he, running off into English at the end— 'I'll make a damned fine Nation of you, or I'll die in the making!'

"I can't tell all we did for the next six months, because Dravot did a lot I couldn't see the hang of, and he learned their lingo in a way I never could. My work was to help the people plough, and now and again go out with some of the Army and see what the other villages were doing, and make 'em throw rope-bridges across the ravines which cut up the country horrid. Dravot was very kind to me, but when he walked up and down in the pine wood pulling that bloody red beard of his with both fists I knew he was thinking plans I would not advise about, and I just waited for orders.

"But Dravot never showed me disrespect before the people. They were afraid of me and the Army, but they loved Dan. He was the best of friends with the priests and the Chiefs; but anyone could come across the hills with a complaint, and Dravot would hear him out fair, and call four priests together and say what was to be done. He used to call in Billy Fish from Bashkai, and Pikky Kergan from Shu, and an old Chief we called Kafuzelum—it was like enough to his real name—and hold councils with 'em when there was any fighting to be done in small villages. That was his Council of War, and the four priests of Bashkai, Shu, Khawak, and Madora was his Privy Council. Between the lot of 'em they sent me, with forty men and twenty rifles and sixty men carrying turquoises, into the Ghorband country to buy those hand-made Martini rifles, that come out of the Amir's workshops at Kabul, from one of the Amir's Herati regiments that would have sold the very teeth out of their mouths for turquoises.

"I stayed in Ghorband a month, and gave the Governor there the pick of my baskets for hush-money, and bribed the Colonel of the regiment some more, and, between the two and the tribespeople, we got more than a hundred hand-made Martinis, a hundred good Kohat Jezails that'll throw to six hundred yards, and forty man-loads of very bad ammunition for the rifles. I came back with what I had, and distributed 'em among the men that the Chiefs sent in to me to drill. Dravot was too busy to attend to those things, but the old Army that we first made helped me, and we turned out five hundred men that could drill, and two hundred that knew how to hold arms pretty straight. Even those cork-screwed, hand-made guns was a miracle to them. Dravot talked big about powder-shops and factories, walking up and down in the pine wood when the winter was coming on.

"'I won't make a Nation,' says he. 'I'll make an Empire! These men aren't niggers; they're English! Look at their eyes—look at their mouths. Look at the way they stand up. They sit on chairs in their own houses. They're the Lost Tribes,[29] or something like it, and they've grown to be English. I'll take a census in the spring if the priests don't get frightened. There must be a fair two million of 'em in these hills.

---

[29]The Lost Tribes of Israel. See p. 111 for Major Mitford's speculations on a Jewish heritage in Afghanistan. In the 19th c., "nigger" was used in England to refer insultingly to dark-skinned foreigners of any race.

The villages are full o' little children. Two million people—two hundred and fifty thousand fighting men—and all English! They only want the rifles and a little drilling. Two hundred and fifty thousand men, ready to cut in on Russia's right flank when she tries for India! Peachey, man,' he says, chewing his beard in great hunks, 'we shall be Emperors—Emperors of the Earth! Rajah Brooke[30] will be a suckling to us. I'll treat with the Viceroy on equal terms. I'll ask him to send me twelve picked English—to help us govern a bit. There's Mackray, Sergeant-pensioner at Segowli—many's the good dinner he's given me, and his wife a pair of trousers. There's Donkin, the Warder of Toung-hoo Jail; there's hundreds that I could lay my hands on if I was in India. The Viceroy shall do it for me. I'll send a man through in the spring for those men, and I'll write for a dispensation from the Grand Lodge for what I've done as Grand-Master. That—and all the Sniders[31] that'll be thrown out when the native troops in India take up the Martini. They'll be worn smooth, but they'll do for fighting in these hills. Twelve English, a hundred thousand Sniders run through the Amir's country in driblets—I'd be content with twenty thousand in one year—and we'd be an Empire. When everything was shipshape I'd hand over the crown—this crown that I'm wearing now—to Queen Victoria on my knees, and she'd say: "Rise up, Sir Daniel Dravot." Oh, it's big! It's big, I tell you! But there's so much to be done in every place—Bashkai, Khawak, Shu, and everywhere else.'

"'What is it?' I says. 'There are no more men coming in to be drilled this autumn. Look at those fat, black clouds. They're bringing the snow.'

"'It isn't that,' says Daniel, putting his hand very hard on my shoulder; 'and I don't wish to say anything that's against you, for no other living man would have followed me and made me what I am as you have done. You're a first-class Commander-in-Chief, and the people know you, but—it's a big country, and somehow you can't help me, Peachey, in the way I want to be helped.'

"'Go to your blasted priests, then!' I said, and I was sorry when I made that remark, but it did hurt me sore to find Daniel talking so superior when I'd drilled all the men, and done all he told me.

---

[30]Sir James Brooke became known as the "White Rajah of Sarawak" when he was made rajah of the Malaysian province in 1841 as a reward for his assistance in quashing rebellion there.

[31]Older style of rifle.

"'Don't let's quarrel, Peachey,' says Daniel without cursing. 'You're a King too, and the half of this Kingdom is yours; but can't you see, Peachey, we want cleverer men than us now—three or four of 'em, that we can scatter about for our Deputies. It's a hugeous great State, and I can't always tell the right thing to do, and I haven't time for all I want to do, and here's the winter coming on and all.' He put half his beard into his mouth, all red like the gold of his crown.

"'I'm sorry, Daniel,' says I. 'I've done all I could. I've drilled the men and shown the people how to stack their oats better; and I've brought in those tinware rifles from Ghorband—but I know what you're driving at. I take it Kings always feel oppressed that way.'

"'There's another thing too,' says Dravot, walking up and down. 'The winter's coming and these people won't be giving much trouble, and if they do we can't move about. I want a wife.'

"'For God's sake leave the women alone!' I says. 'We've both got all the work we can, though I *am* a fool. Remember the Contrack, and keep clear o' women.'

"'The Contrack only lasted till such time as we was Kings; and Kings we have been these months past,' says Dravot, weighting his crown in his hand. 'You go get a wife too, Peachey—a nice, strappin', plump girl that'll keep you warm in the winter. They're prettier than English girls, and we can take the pick of 'em. Boil 'em once or twice in hot water and they'll come out like chicken and ham.'

"'Don't tempt me!' I says. 'I will not have any dealings with a woman not till we are a dam' side more settled than we are now. I've been doing the work o' two men, and you've been doing the work o' three. Let's lie off a bit, and see if we can get some better tobacco from Afghan country and run in some good liquor; but no women.'

"'Who's talking o' *women?*' says Dravot. 'I said *wife*—a Queen to breed a King's son for the King. A Queen out of the strongest tribe, that'll make them your blood-brothers, and that'll lie by your side and tell you all the people thinks about you and their own affairs. That's what I mean.'

"'Do you remember that Bengali woman I kept at Mogul Serai when I was a plate-layer?' says I. 'A fat lot o' good she was to me. She taught me the lingo and one or two other things; but what happened? She ran away with the Station-master's servant and half my month's pay. Then she turned up at Dadur Junction in tow of a half-caste, and had the impidence to say I was her husband—all among the drivers in the running-shed too!'

"'We've done with that,' says Dravot; 'these women are whiter than you or me, and a Queen I will have for the winter months.'

"'For the last time o' asking, Dan, do *not*,' I says. 'It'll only bring us harm. The Bible says that Kings ain't to waste their strength on women, 'specially when they've got a new raw Kingdom to work over.'

"'For the last time of answering I will,' said Dravot, and he went away through the pine-trees looking like a big red devil, the sun being on his crown and beard and all.

"But getting a wife was not as easy as Dan thought. He put it before the Council, and there was no answer till Billy Fish said that he'd better ask the girls. Dravot damned them all around. 'What's wrong with me?' he shouts, standing by the idol Imbra. 'Am I a dog or am I not enough of a man for your wenches? Haven't I put the shadow of my hand over this country? Who stopped the last Afghan raid?' It was me really, but Dravot was too angry to remember. 'Who bought your guns? Who repaired the bridges? Who's the Grand-Master of the sign cut in the stone?' says he, and he thumped his hand on the block that he used to sit on in Lodge, and at Council, which opened like Lodge always. Billy Fish said nothing and no more did the others. 'Keep your hair on, Dan,' said I; 'and ask the girls. That's how it's done at Home, and these people are quite English.'

"'The marriage of the King is a matter of State,' says Dan, in a white-hot rage, for he could feel, I hope, that he was going against his better mind. He walked out of the Council-room, and the others sat still, looking at the ground.

"'Billy Fish,' says I to the Chief of Bashkai, 'what's the difficulty here? A straight answer to a true friend.'

"'You know,' says Billy Fish. 'How should a man tell you who knows everything? How can daughters of men marry Gods or Devils? It's not proper.'

"I remembered something like that in the Bible[32]; but if, after seeing us as long as they had, they still believed we were Gods, it wasn't for me to undeceive them.

---

[32]In Genesis 6:2, amid growing wickedness on earth before God orders the Flood, "the sons of God saw that the daughters of men were fair; and they took to wife such of them as they chose"—an improper and perhaps forced crossing of boundaries.

"'A God can do anything,' says I. 'If the King is fond of a girl he'll not let her die.'—'She'll have to,' said Billy Fish. 'There are all sorts of Gods and Devils in these mountains, and now and again a girl marries one of them and isn't seen any more. Besides, you two know the Mark cut in the stone. Only the Gods know that. We thought you were men till you showed the sign of the Master.'

"I wished then that we had explained about the loss of the genuine secrets of a Master-Mason at the first go-off; but I said nothing. All that night there was a blowing of horns in a little dark temple half-way down the hill, and I heard a girl crying fit to die. One of the priests told us that she was being prepared to marry the King.

"'I'll have no nonsense of that kind,' says Dan. 'I don't want to interfere with your customs, but I'll take my own wife.'—'The girl's a bit afraid,' says the priest. 'She thinks she's going to die, and they are a-heartening of her up down in the temple.'

"'Hearten her very tender, then,' says Dravot, 'or I'll hearten you with the butt of a gun so you'll never want to be heartened again.' He licked his lips, did Dan, and stayed up walking about more than half the night, thinking of the wife that he was going to get in the morning. I wasn't any means comfortable, for I knew that dealings with a woman in foreign parts, though you was a crowned King twenty times over, could not but be risky. I got up very early in the morning while Dravot was asleep, and I saw the priests talking together in whispers, and the Chiefs talking together too, and they looked at me out of the corners of their eyes.

"'What is up, Fish?' I say to the Bashkai man, who was wrapped up in his furs and looking splendid to behold.

"'I can't rightly say,' says he, 'but if you can make the King drop all this nonsense about marriage, you'll be doing him and me and yourself a great service.'

"'That I do believe,' says I. 'But sure, you know, Billy, as well as me, having fought against and for us, that the King and me are nothing more than two of the finest men that God Almighty ever made. Nothing more, I do assure you.'

"'That may be,' says Billy Fish, 'and yet I should be sorry if it was.' He sinks his head upon his great fur cloak for a minute and thinks. 'King,' says he, 'be you man or God or Devil, I'll stick by you today. I have twenty of my men with me, and they will follow me. We'll go to Bashkai until the storm blows over.'

"A little snow had fallen in the night, and everything was white except the greasy fat clouds that blew down and down from the north. Dravot came out with his crown on his head, swinging his arms and stamping his feet, and looking more pleased than Punch.

"'For the last time, drop it, Dan,' says I in a whisper, 'Billy Fish here says that there will be a row.'

"'A row amongst my people!' says Dravot. 'Not much, Peachey, you're a fool not to get a wife too. Where's the girl?' says he with a voice as loud as the braying of a jackass. 'Call up all the Chiefs and priests, and let the Emperor see if his wife suits him.'

"There was no need to call anyone. They were all there leaning on their guns and spears round the clearing in the centre of the pine wood. A lot of priests went down to the little temple to bring up the girl, and the horns blew fit to wake the dead. Billy Fish saunters round and gets as close to Daniel as he could, and behind him stood his twenty men with matchlocks. Not a man of them under six feet. I was next to Dravot, and behind me was twenty men of the regular Army. Up comes the girl, and a strapping wench she was, covered with silver and turquoises, but white as death, and looking back every minute at the priests.

"'She'll do,' said Dan, looking her over. 'What's to be afraid of, lass? Come and kiss me.' He puts his arm round her. She shuts her eyes, gives a bit of a squeak, and down goes her face in the side of Dan's flaming red beard.

"'The slut's bitten me!' says he, clapping his hand to his neck, and, sure enough, his hand was red with blood. Billy Fish and two of his matchlock-men catches hold of Dan by the shoulders and drags him into the Bashkai lot, while the priests howls in their lingo—'Neither God nor Devil but a man!' I was all taken aback, for a priest cut at me in front, and the Army behind began firing into the Bashkai men.

"'God A'mighty!' says Dan. 'What is the meaning o' this?'

"'Come back! Come away!' says Billy Fish. 'Ruin and Mutiny is the matter. We'll break for Bashkai if we can.'

"I tried to give some sort of orders to my men—the men of the Regular Army—but it was no use, so I fired into the brown of 'em with an English Martini and drilled three beggars in a line. The valley was full of shouting, howling creatures, and every soul was shrieking, 'Not a God or a Devil but only a man!' The Bashkai troops stuck to Billy Fish for all they were worth, but their matchlocks wasn't half as good as the Kabul breech-loaders, and four of them dropped. Dan was bellowing like a bull, for he was very wrathy; and Billy Fish had a hard job to prevent him running out at the crowd.

"'We can't stand,' says Billy Fish. 'Make a run for it down the valley! The whole place is against us.' The matchlock-men ran, and we went down the valley in spite of Dravot. He was swearing horribly and crying out he was King. The priests rolled great stones on us, and the regular Army fired hard, and there wasn't more than six men, not counting Dan, Billy Fish, and Me, that came down to the bottom of the valley alive.

"Then they stopped firing and the horns in the temple blew again. 'Come away—for God's sake come away!' says Billy Fish. 'They'll send runners out to all the villages before ever we get to Bashkai. I can protect you there, but I can't do anything now.'

"My own notion is that Dan began to go mad in his head from that hour. He stared up and down like a stuck pig. Then he was all for walking back alone and killing the priests with his bare hands; which he could have done. 'An Emperor am I,' says Daniel, 'and next year I shall be a Knight of the Queen.'

"'All right, Dan,' says I, 'but come along now while there's time.'

"'It's your fault,' says he, 'for not looking after your Army better. There was mutiny in the midst, and you didn't know—you damned engine-driving, plate-laying, missionary's-pass-hunting hound!' He sat upon a rock and called me every foul name he could lay tongue to. I was too heart-sick to care, though it was all his foolishness that brought the smash.

"'I'm sorry, Dan,' says I, 'but there's no accounting for natives. This business is our 'Fifty-Seven.[33] Maybe we'll make something out of it yet, when we've got to Bashkai.'

"'Let's get to Bashkai, then,' says Dan, 'and, by God, when I come back here again I'll sweep the valley so there isn't a bug in a blanket left!'

"We walked all that day, and all that night Dan was stumping up and down on the snow, chewing his beard and muttering to himself.

---

[33]The Revolt or Mutiny of 1857, in which British rule in India was almost overthrown.

"'There's no hope o' getting clear,' said Billy Fish. 'The priests will have sent runners to the villages to say that you are only men. Why didn't you stick on as Gods till things was more settled? I'm a dead man,' says Billy Fish, and he throws himself down on the snow and begins to pray to his Gods.

"Next morning we was in a cruel bad country—all up and down, no level ground at all, and no food either. The six Bashkai men looked at Billy Fish hungry-ways as if they wanted to ask something, but they said never a word. At noon we came to the top of a flat mountain all covered with snow, and when we climbed up into it, behold, there was an Army in position waiting in the middle!

"'The runners have been very quick,' says Billy Fish, with a little bit of a laugh. 'They are waiting for us.'

"Three or four men began to fire from the enemy's side, and a chance shot took Daniel in the calf of the leg. That brought him to his senses. He looks across the snow at the Army, and sees the rifles that we had brought into the country.

"'We're done for,' says he. 'They are Englishmen, these people—and it's my blasted nonsense that has brought you to this. Get back, Billy Fish, and take your men away; you've done what you could, and now cut for it. Carnehan,' says he, 'shake hands with me and go along with Billy. Maybe they won't kill you. I'll go and meet 'em alone. It's me that did it. Me, the King!'

"'Go!' says I. 'Go to Hell, Dan! I'm with you here. Billy Fish, you clear out, and we two will meet these folk.'

"'I'm a Chief,' says Billy Fish, quite quiet. 'I stay with you. My men can go.'

"The Bashkai fellows didn't wait for a second word, but ran off, and Dan and Me and Billy Fish walked across to where the drums were drumming and the horns were horning. It was cold—awful cold. I've got that cold in the back of my head now. There's a lump of it there."

The punkah-coolies had gone to sleep. Two kerosene lamps were blazing in the office, and the perspiration poured down my face and splashed on the blotter as I leaned forward. Carnehan was shivering, and I feared that his mind might go. I wiped my face, took a fresh grip of the piteously mangled hands, and said: "What happened after that?"

The momentary shift of my eyes had broken the clear current.

"What was you pleased to say?" whined Carnehan. "They took them without any sound. Not a little whisper all along the snow, not though the King knocked down the first man that set hand on him—not though old Peachey fired his last cartridge into the brown of 'em. Not a single solitary sound did those swines make. They just closed up tight, and I tell you their furs stunk. There was a man called Billy Fish, a good friend of us all, and they cut his throat, Sir, then and there, like a pig; and the King kicks up the bloody snow and says: 'We've had a dashed fine run for our money. What's coming next?' But Peachey, Peachey Taliaferro, I tell you, Sir, in confidence as betwixt two friends, he lost his head, Sir. No, he didn't neither. The King lost his head, so he did, all along o' one of those cunning rope-bridges. Kindly let me have the paper-cutter, Sir. It tilted this way. They marched him a mile across that snow to a rope-bridge over a ravine with a river at the bottom. You may have seen such. They prodded him behind like an ox. 'Damn your eyes!' says the King. 'D'you suppose I can't die like a gentleman?' He turns to Peachey—Peachey that was crying like a child. 'I've brought you to this, Peachey,' says he. 'Brought you out of your happy life to be killed in Kafiristan, where you was late Commander-in-Chief of the Emperor's forces. Say you forgive me, Peachey.'—'I do,' says Peachey. 'Fully and freely do I forgive you, Dan.'—'Shake hands, Peachey,' says he. 'I'm going now.' Out he goes, looking neither right nor left, and when he was plumb in the middle of those dizzy looking ropes—'Cut, you beggars,' he shouts; and they cut, and old Dan fell, turning round and round and round, twenty thousand miles, for he took half an hour to fall till he struck the water, and I could see his body caught on a rock with the gold crown close beside.

"But do you know what they did to Peachey between two pine-trees? They crucified him, Sir, as Peachey's hand will show. They used wooden pegs for his hands and his feet; and he didn't die. He hung there and screamed, and they took him down next day, and said it was a miracle that he wasn't dead. They took him down—poor old Peachey that hadn't done them any harm—that hadn't done them any—"

He rocked to and fro and wept bitterly, wiping his eyes with the back of his scarred hands and moaning like a child for some ten minutes.

"They was cruel enough to feed him up in the temple, because they said he was more of a God than old Daniel that was a man. Then they turned him out on the snow, and told him to go home, and Peachey came home in about a year, begging along the roads quite safe; for Daniel Dravot he walked before and said, 'Come along, Peachey. It's a big thing we're doing.' The mountains they danced at night, and the mountains they tried to fall on Peachey's head, but Dan he held up his hand, and Peachey came along bent double. He never let go of Dan's hand, and he never let go of Dan's head. They gave it to him as a present in the temple, to remind him not to come again, and though the crown was pure gold, and Peachey was starving, never would Peachey sell the same. You knew Dravot, Sir! You knew Right Worshipful Brother Dravot! Look at him now!"

He fumbled in the mass of rags round his bent waist; brought out a black horsehair bag embroidered with silver thread, and shook therefrom on to my table—the dried withered head of Daniel Dravot! The morning sun that had long been paling the lamps struck the red beard and blind sunken eyes; struck, too, a heavy circlet of gold studded with raw turquoises, that Carnehan placed tenderly on the battered temples.

"You be'old now," said Carnehan, "the Emperor in his 'abit as he lived—the King of Kafiristan with his crown upon his head. Poor old Daniel that was a monarch once!"

I shuddered, for, in spite of defacements manifold, I recognized the head of the man of Marwar Junction. Carnehan rose to go. I attempted to stop him. He was not fit to walk abroad. "Let me take away the whisky, and give me a little money," he gasped. "I was a King once. I'll go to the Deputy Commissioner and ask to be set in the Poorhouse till I get my health. No, thank you, I can't wait till you get a carriage for me. I've urgent private affairs—in the south—at Marwar."

He shambled out of the office and departed in the direction of the Deputy Commissioner's house. That day at noon I had occasion to go down the blinding hot Mall, and I saw a crooked man crawling along the white dust of the roadside, his hat in his hand, quavering dolorously after the fashion of street-singers at Home. There was not a soul in sight, and he was out of all possible earshot of houses. And he sang through his nose, turning his head from right to left:

"The Son of Man goes forth to war,
    A golden crown to gain;
His blood-red banner streams afar—
    Who follows in his train?"[34]

I waited to hear no more, but put the poor wretch into my carriage
and drove him off to the nearest missionary for eventual transfer to
the Asylum. He repeated the hymn twice while he was with me
whom he did not in the least recognize, and I left him singing it to
the missionary.

Two days later I inquired after his welfare of the Superintendent of the Asylum.

"He was admitted suffering from sunstroke. He died early yesterday morning," said the Superintendent. "Is it true that he was
half an hour bare-headed in the sun at mid-day?"

"Yes," said I, "but do you happen to know if he had anything
upon him by any chance when he died?"

"Not to my knowledge," said the Superintendent.

And there the matter rests.

---

[34]Based on a well-known hymn by Bishop Reginald Heber (1783–1826) in *Hymns
Ancient and Modern*, which has "kingly" rather than "golden" in line 2. Later edi-
tions of Kipling's story also corrected the first line from "The Son of Man" to "The
Son of God."

CONTEXTS

EMPIRE
AND ITS DISCONTENTS

"NEW CROWNS FOR OLD ONES!"

(ALADDIN *adapted.*)

John Tenniel, *New Crowns for Old Ones!* Published in *Punch*, 1876. Political cartoonist and illustrator John Tenniel (best known today for his illustrations to Lewis Carroll's Alice books) shows Prime Minister Benjamin Disraeli presenting Queen Victoria with an elaborate crown as Empress of India, a title he arranged for her to receive in 1876. Of Jewish parentage, Disraeli was always regarded in England as an exotic foreigner, even when he was running the country; here, he is dressed as Aladdin, granting the Queen's secret wish. The somewhat dubious Queen is exchanging her British crown for the gaudy new one, topped with the famous diamond known in Arabic as the Koh-i-Noor ("Mountain of Light"). Long possessed by the Muslim rulers of northern India, this gem was acquired in 1849 by the British when they annexed the Punjab region of India. Prominent among Queen Victoria's crown jewels, it symbolized India, "the jewel in the crown" of her empire.

Empire and
Its Discontents

The expanding reach of the British Empire in the nineteenth century sent soldiers, sailors, merchants, and missionaries around the globe, where they came into close contact with a dizzying variety of languages, cultures, and histories. These contacts posed imaginative as well as practical challenges: How could these many cultures be comprehended, much less controlled? For those who went abroad and for the British public back home, the Empire became a major source of pride, fascination, and confusion. Many writers responded with sentimental or satiric poetry and tales, and the public devoured a constant stream of travelers' accounts of visits to distant lands.

This section opens with several poems showing the Empire in popular verse during the years when Kipling grew up and began writing his own colonial stories and verse. In the immensely popular comic poems of Edward Lear and Hilaire Belloc, "India" was a vividly exotic but deeply confusing region. The natives and their outlandish customs were a constant source of interest, and so were the experiences of the British and Irish men and women who set out from England and Ireland to seek their fortunes, convert the heathen, or do the work of empire. W. S. Gilbert's *Bab Ballads* include many poems about the sailors who enabled Britannia to "rule the waves" throughout the Victorian period. As Kipling was to do more fully, Gilbert comically explored the slang and speech rhythms of lower-class enlisted men and the opportunities that empire offered them for self-sacrifice and self-invention.

Imperial settings fostered exciting tales of exploration and discovery, with natives often treated as childlike beneficiaries of European benevolence. Yet there were uneasy undertones, threats of violent resistance. The so-called "Mutiny" of 1857 in India shocked the British (and even many Indians) by revealing just how rapidly violence could break the "thin, red line" of British rule. The revolt generated anxieties across the rest of the century and began the process of struggle that culminated in Indian independence in 1947. From England, poet Christina Rossetti registered a reaction to the 1857 revolt. An eyewitness account was recorded by the great poet Ghalib, who was horrified by the violence displayed on both sides. Following his prose memoir are three poems on the revolt and its aftermath, one by Ghalib himself and two by his patron, Bahadur Shah II, the last ruler of the Muslim Mughal Empire in north India.

If India was "the jewel in the crown" of empire, neighboring Afghanistan was a prize that kept getting away, a daunting world where violence and revolt were the norm instead of the exception. Kipling's "The Man Who Would Be King" is a striking imaginative reworking of the British experience there and a cautionary tale for post-"Mutiny" British rule in India and beyond. The story looks back to the First Afghan War of 1839–42, in which more than 4,000 British troops were massacred after briefly occupying the Afghan capital. Kipling wrote his story in 1888, after the Second Afghan War of 1879–80, in which a smaller-scale massacre was avenged by a British expeditionary force. The accounts given here, one by a soldier who served in this expedition and one by a reporter embedded with the British troops, were among Kipling's sources for his phantasmagoric fiction of an imperial adventure gone haywire.

Edward Lear (1812–1888)

Born outside London as the youngest of twenty-one children, Edward Lear lived much of his life abroad. He supported himself chiefly as a painter of watercolor landscapes, and in 1846 he gave drawing lessons to Queen Victoria. Spending his later years in Italy, he traveled widely for artistic inspiration, his trips including India and Ceylon. He is best known today for the limericks and other comic poems collected in The Book of Nonsense *and several later books, which portray a surreal world of physical and psychic instability, all couched in lively language studded with odd or made-up words. "The Akond of Swat" is an entire poem generated by Lear's encounter with the opaque title phrase during his Indian travels.*

The Akond of Swat[1]

Who, or why, or which, or *what*, Is the Akond of SWAT?
Is he tall or short, or dark or fair?
Does he sit on a stool or a sofa or chair,   or SQUAT,
        The Akond of Swat?

Is he wise or foolish, young or old?
Does he drink his soup and his coffee cold,   or HOT,
        The Akond of Swat?

Does he sing or whistle, jabber or talk,
And when riding abroad does he gallop or walk,   or TROT,
        The Akond of Swat?

Does he wear a turban, a fez, or a hat?
Does he sleep on a mattress, a bed, or a mat,   or a COT,
        The Akond of Swat?

When he writes a copy in round-hand size,
Does he cross his T's and finish his I's   with a DOT,
        The Akond of Swat?

Can he write a letter concisely clear
Without a speck or a smudge or smear   or BLOT,
        The Akond of Swat?

Do his people like him extremely well?
Or do they, whenever they can, rebel,   or PLOT,
        At the Akond of Swat?

If he catches them then, either old or young,
Does he have them chopped in pieces or hung,   or SHOT,
        The Akond of Swat?

Do his people prig[2] in the lanes or park?
Or even at times, when days are dark,   GAROTTE?[3]
        O the Akond of Swat!

Does he study the wants of his own dominion?
Or doesn't he care for public opinion   a JOT,
        The Akond of Swat?

---

[1]Ruler (akond) of a small principality in northern India during the nineteenth century. "For the existence of this potentate see Indian newspapers, *passim*. The proper way to read the verses is to make an immense emphasis on the monosyllabic rhymes, which indeed ought to be shouted out by a chorus" [Lear's note].

[2]Commit robbery.

[3]Strangle people.

To amuse his mind do his people show him
Pictures, or any one's last new poem,   or WHAT,
                         For the Akond of Swat?

At night if he suddenly screams and wakes,
Do they bring him only a few small cakes,   or a LOT,
                         For the Akond of Swat?

Does he live on turnips, tea, or tripe?
Does he like his shawl to be marked with a stripe,   or a DOT,
                         The Akond of Swat?

Does he like to lie on his back in a boat
Like the lady who lived in that isle remote,   SHALLOTT,[4]
                         The Akond of Swat?

Is he quiet, or always making a fuss?
Is his steward a Swiss or a Swede or a Russ,   or a SCOT,
                         The Akond of Swat?

Does he like to sit by the calm blue wave?
Or to sleep and snore in a dark green cave,   or a GROTT,
                         The Akond of Swat?

Does he drink small beer from a silver jug?
Or a bowl? or a glass? or a cup? or a mug?   or a POT,
                         The Akond of Swat?

Does he beat his wife with a gold-topped pipe,
When she let the gooseberries grow too ripe,   or ROT,
                         The Akond of Swat?

Does he wear a white tie when he dines with friends,
And tie it neat in a bow with ends,   or a KNOT,
                         The Akond of Swat?

Does he like new cream, and hate mince-pies?
When he looks at the sun does he wink his eyes,   or NOT,
                         The Akond of Swat?

Does he teach his subjects to roast and bake?
Does he sail about on an inland lake,   in a YACHT,
                         The Akond of Swat?

Some one, or nobody, knows I wot
Who or which or why or what
                         Is the Akond of Swat!

---

[4]"The Lady of Shalott" (1832) was a famous poem by Tennyson, set in the days of King Arthur. Tennyson himself submits this place name to extravagant rhyming.

Hilaire Belloc (1870–1953)

Born in France to a French father and English mother, Hilaire Belloc studied at Oxford and became a British citizen, making a career as a historian, novelist, and poet and serving as a Member of Parliament from 1906 to 1910. In his twenties he wrote several books of light verse, which poke sly fun at late-Victorian moralizing about childrearing and the virtues of piety, discipline, and work. His hilarious collection The Bad Child's Book of Beasts *(1897) was followed by* More Beasts for Worse Children *(1898), including "The Llama," given here, and* A Moral Alphabet *(1899), in which an Indian ascetic illustrates the letter I.*

I the Poor Indian

I the Poor Indian, justly called "The Poor,"
He has to eat his Dinner off the floor.

MORAL.

The Moral these delightful lines afford
Is: "Living cheaply is its own reward."

The Llama

The Llama is a woolly sort of fleecy hairy goat,
With an indolent expression and an undulating throat
 Like an unsuccessful literary man.

And I know the place he lives in (or at least—I think I do)
It is Ecuador, Brazil or Chili—possibly Peru;
 You must find it in the Atlas if you can.

The Llama of the Pampasses[1] you never should confound
(In spite of a deceptive similarity of sound)
 With the Lhama who is Lord of Turkestan.[2]

[1]Grassy plains.

[2]A "lama" is a Tibetan priest. In the 19th c., "Turkestan" referred to the region of central Asia north of Tibet and the Shan Mountains of northern China.

For the former is a beautiful and valuable beast,
But the latter is not lovable nor useful in the least;
And the Ruminant is preferable surely to the Priest
Who battens on the woful superstitions of the East,
    The Mongol of the Monastery of Shan.

W. S. Gilbert (1836–1911)

*A master of light verse, William Schwenck Gilbert first became known
for comic poems he contributed to periodicals under the name "Bab,"
illustrating them with his own cartoons. He collected his verses in* The
Bab Ballads *(1869) and* More Bab Ballads *(1873); Kipling's* Departmental Ditties *and* Barrack-Room Ballads *carry on* The Bab Ballads'
*mode of satirical verse, ludicrously exaggerating real-life speech and
situations. In 1871, Gilbert began an immensely successful collabora-
tion with composer Arthur Sullivan and theater producer Richard
D'Oyly Carte. Gilbert and Sullivan created a brilliant series of comic
operas, including* The Pirates of Penzance, H.M.S. Pinafore *(for which
Gilbert wrote "The British Tar," included here), and* The Mikado.
*While "The British Tar" presents the sailor as a figure of heroic resolve
and strength, "The Darned Mounseer" shows a British sloop beating a
hasty retreat under cover of a blustery rhetoric of bold confidence.
"The King of Canoodle-Dum" stages a strange adventure of disguise*

and thwarted conquest, showing the limits of comic verse in dealing with the deepest tensions of empire. It makes interesting, unsettling reading next to Kipling's "The Man Who Would Be King" and Conrad's Heart of Darkness.

The British Tar[1]

A British tar is a soaring soul,
  As free as a mountain bird,
His energetic fist should be ready to resist
  A dictatorial word.
His nose should pant and his lip should curl,   5
His cheeks should flame and his brow should furl,
His bosom should heave and his heart should glow,
And his fist be ever ready for a knock-down blow.

His eyes should flash with an inborn fire,
  His brow with scorn be rung;   10
He never should bow down to a domineering frown,
  Or the tang of a tyrant tongue.
His foot should stamp and his throat should growl,
His hair should twirl and his face should scowl;
His eyes should flash and his breast protrude,   15
And this should be his customary attitude!

[1]Sailor.

The Darned Mounseer[1]

I shipped, d'ye see, in a Revenue sloop,
  And, off Cape Finisteere,[2]
    A merchantman we see,
    A Frenchman, going free,
So we made for the bold Mounseer.   5
      D'ye see?
We made for the bold Mounseer!
But she proved to be a Frigate[3]—and she up with her ports,
  And fires with a thirty-two!
    It come uncommon near,   10
    But we answered with a cheer,
Which paralysed the Parley-voo,[4]
      D'ye see?
Which paralysed the Parley-voo!

Then our Captain he up and he says, says he,   15
  "That chap we need not fear,—
    We can take her, if we like,
    She is sartin for to strike,[5]
For she's only a darned Mounseer,
      D'ye see?   20
She's only a darned Mounseer!
But to fight a French fal-lal—it's like hittin' of a gal—
  It's a lubberly thing for to do;
    For we, with all our faults,
    Why, we're sturdy British salts,   25
While she's but a Parley-voo,
      D'ye see?
A miserable Parley-voo!"

[1]Monsieur, referring to a French merchant ship. The poem is set in a time of conflict between England and France, when British "revenue sloops" (small, fast, armed ships) were allowed to plunder enemy merchant ships.

[2]Cape Finisterre ("land's end"), at the northern tip of Spain.

[3]The ship is a disguised warship carrying 32 cannon on each side, far surpassing the weapons of the small British sloop.

[4]Frenchman (a mocking corruption of the phrase "Parlez-vous français?"—"Do you speak French?").

[5]Lower her flag in surrender.

So we up with our helm, and we scuds before the breeze,
    As we gives a compassionating cheer;   30
        Froggee answers with a shout
        As he sees us go about,
    Which was grateful of the poor Mounseer,
        D'ye see?
    Which was grateful of the poor Mounseer!   35
And I'll wager in their joy they kissed each other's cheek
    (Which is what them furriners do),
        And they blessed their lucky stars
        We were hardy British tars
    Who had pity on a poor Parley-voo,   40
        D'ye see?
    Who had pity on a poor Parley-voo!

The King of Canoodle-Dum

The story of FREDERICK GOWLER,
    A mariner of the sea,
Who quitted his ship, the *Howler*,
    A-sailing in Caribbee.
For many a day he wandered   5
    Till he met, in a state of rum,
CALAMITY POP VON PEPPERMINT DROP,
    The King of Canoodle-Dum.

That monarch addressed him gaily,
    "Hum! Golly de do to-day?   10
Hum! Lily-white Buckra[1] Sailee"—
    (You notice his playful way?)—
"What dickens you doin' here, sar?
    Why debbil you want to come?
Hum! Picaninnee,[2] dere isn't no sea   15
    In City Canoodle-Dum!"

[1] British sailors wore uniforms of white buckram (heavy cotton).
[2] "Silly little one," a word of West Indian origin (from Spanish *pequeño*).

And GOWLER he answered sadly,
  "Oh, mine is a doleful tale!
They've treated me werry badly
  In Lunnon,[3] from where I hail.   20
I'm one of the Family Royal—
  No common Jack Tar you see;
I'm WILLIAM THE FOURTH,[4] far up in the North,
  A King in my own countree!"

Bang-bang! How the tom-toms thundered!   25
  Bang-bang! How they thumped the gongs!
Bang-bang! How the people wondered!
  Bang-bang! At it, hammer and tongs!
Alliance with Kings of Europe
  Is an honour Canoodlers seek;   30
Her monarchs don't stop[5] with PEPPERMINT DROP
  Every day in the week!

---

[3]London.

[4]Queen Victoria's predecessor, her uncle William IV (reigned 1830–37), had been known as "the sailor king," after serving in his youth in the British navy, where he was stationed in the West Indies to protect the interests of slave-owning plantations. In pretending to be William, the sailor trusts that the locals don't know that the king had been dead for many years.

[5]Visit.

FRED told them that he was undone,
    For his people all went insane,
And fired the Tower of London,   35
    And Grinnidge's Naval Fame.
And some of them racked St. James's,
    And vented their rage upon
The Church of St. Paul, the Fishmongers' Hall,
    And the "Angel" at Islington.[6]   40

CALAMITY POP implored him
    At Canoodle-Dum to remain
Till those people of his restored him
    To power and rank again.
CALAMITY POP he made him   45
    A Prince of Canoodle-Dum,
With a couple of caves, some beautiful slaves,
    And the run of the royal rum.

[6]They have set fire to major landmarks such as the Tower of London, Greenwich's naval cathedral, and Saint Paul's Cathedral, and also to the "Angel" pub in north-central London.

POP gave him his only daughter,
   HUM PICKETY WIMPLE TIP: 50
FRED vowed that if over the water
   He went, in an English ship,
He'd make her his Queen,—though truly,
   It is an unusual thing
For a Caribbee brat who's as black as your hat   55
   To be wife of an English King.

And all the Canoodle-Dummers
   They copied his rolling walk,
His method of draining rummers,[7]
   His emblematical talk.   60
For his dress and his graceful breeding,
   His delicate taste in rum,
And his nautical way, were the talk of the day
   In the Court of Canoodle-dum.

CALAMITY POP most wisely   65
   Determined in everything
To model his Court precisely
   On that of the English King;
And ordered that every lady
   And every lady's lord   70
Should masticate jacky[8] (a kind of tobaccy)
   And scatter its juice abroad.

They signified wonder roundly
   At any astounding yarn,
By darning their dear eyes roundly   75
   ('Twas all that they had to darn).
They "hoisted their slacks," adjusting
   Garments of plantain-leaves
With nautical twitches (as if they wore—stitches,
   Instead of a dress like EVE's!)   80

---

[7]Large glasses of rum.
[8]Should chew tobacco.

They shivered their timbers proudly,
  At a phantom fore-lock dragged,
And called for a hornpipe loudly
  Whenever amusement flagged.
"Hum! Golly! him POP resemble,   85
  Him Britisher sov'reign, hum!
CALAMITY POP VON PEPPERMINT DROP,
  De King of Canoodle-Dum!"

The mariner's lively "Hollo!"
  Enlivened Canoodle's plain   90
(For blessings unnumbered follow
  In Civilisation's train).
But Fortune, who loves a bathos,[9]
  A terrible ending planned,
For ADMIRAL D. CHICKABIDDY, C.B.,   95
  Placed foot on Canoodle land!

[9]Anticlimax.

That officer seized KING GOWLER,
   He threatened his royal brains,
And put him aboard the *Howler,*
   And fastened him down with chains.   100
The *Howler* she weighed her anchor,
   With FREDERICK nicely nailed,
And off to the North with WILLIAM THE FOURTH
   That Admiral slowly sailed.

CALAMITY said (with folly)   105
   "Hum! nebber want him again—
Him civilise all of us, golly!
   CALAMITY suck him brain!"
The people, however, were pained when
   They saw him aboard the ship,   110
But none of them wept for their FREDDY, except
   HUM PICKITY WIMPLE TIP.

Christina Rossetti (1830–1894)

Part of the circle of Pre-Raphaelite Victorian artists and poets, Christina Rossetti declined offers of marriage and pursued a life as a poet, writing passionately of love, religion, and anticipations of death. All these themes come together in Rossetti's response to the "Mutiny" of 1857, depicting the last conversation of a young British couple, Captain Alexander Skene and his wife. They were among a group of sixty-one British residents of the north Indian city of Jhansi, who took refuge in the city's fort and were then massacred after being offered safe passage out of the city.

In the Round Tower at Jhansi, June 8, 1857

A hundred, a thousand to one: even so;
   Not a hope in the world remained:
The swarming howling wretches below
   Gained and gained and gained.

Skene looked at his pale young wife.   5
   "Is the time come?"—"The time is come."

Young, strong, and so full of life,
   The agony struck them dumb.

Close his arm about her now,
   Close her cheek to his,   10
Close the pistol to her brow—
   God forgive them this!

"Will it hurt much?" "No, mine own:
   I wish I could bear the pang for both."—
"I wish I could bear the pang alone: 15
   Courage, dear, I am not loth."

Kiss and kiss: "It is not pain
   Thus to kiss and die.
One kiss more."—"And yet one again."—
   "Good-bye."—"Good-bye."   20

Ghalib (1797–1869)

One of the greatest poets of modern times, Ghalib observed his era with a compelling blend of passion and detachment. Born in Muslim northern India, the son of Turkish aristocrats in India to improve their fortunes, and named Mirza Asadullah Beg Khan, he developed a precocious talent for poetry. As a young teenager he began writing under the pen name Ghalib ("victorious"), composing brilliant lyrics both in Urdu and in Persian in the lyrical form known as the ghazal *or conversation with the beloved—either an earthly lover or God. Though he was dependent on support by powerful patrons, he was skeptical of political power and of religious orthodoxy alike. The Mughal emperor Bahadur Shah only reluctantly appointed him late in life as his court poet, following the death of the Shah's less talented poetry teacher, Zauq. Ghalib's memoir* Dastambu *recounts the revolt of 1857, which he survived, horrified by the violence on both sides. Several of his friends were killed outright, and others were executed or exiled afterwards. During the turmoil, many of Ghalib's manuscript poems were lost when the houses and libraries of two close friends were destroyed. Ghalib's memoir and his poem "Now every English soldier that bears arms" register deeply felt tensions between restrictive British rule and the horrific violence of the revolt.*

from *Dastambu: A Bouquet of Flowers*[1]

All praise to Him Who confers existence and sets a term to nothingness, Who nurtures equity and stamps out oppression, Whose justice saps the might of the mighty, and Whose kindness gives strength to the weak.

Yes, that God Who can transform nothingness into being, can in the same way annihilate all that is. If He who said "Be," and in a moment brought the whole universe into being, should in another moment say "Cease!" and annihilate all, what man would dare to murmur against Him?

In short, God is great, and God is good, and the wise man who knows this, accepts with equanimity and joy all that God sends.

* * *

Let the reader of this book understand that I, the motion of whose pen spills pearls upon the page, have from my childhood eaten the salt of the English government. So to say, since I cut my first teeth my bread has come from the table of these conquerors of the world. Some seven or eight years have passed since the king of Delhi summoned me and desired that in return for six hundred rupees a year I should write the history of the Timurid kings.[2] I accepted, and set myself to my task. After some time, when the old ustad[3] of the king passed away, the correction of his verses too fell to me. I was old and infirm, accustomed to ease and solitude. And more than all this, my deafness made me a burden to the hearts of others, as in every assembly I gazed intently at the lips of every speaker. Willy-nilly, I would go once or twice a week to the Fort. If the king came out of his apartments I would stand for some time ready to serve him; if not, I would sit there for a little while writing, and then return home. Whatever I had written I would either take to the king myself or send it to him by another's hand. Such was my occupation when the far-ranging thought of the swift-moving sky planned a fresh revolution, to destroy my insignificant and harmless ease.

[1]Translated by Ralph Russell and Khurshidul Islam (1994).
[2]14th-c. dynasty founded by Timur or Tamerlaine.
[3]Court composer.

I swear by His name, Whose unheeding sword
Strikes down impartially both friend and foe.

* * *

This year, at midday on Monday 16th Ramzan, 1273 AH,[4] which
corresponds to 11 May 1857 . . . the gates and walls of the Fort and
the battlements of Delhi were suddenly shaken. It was not an earth-
quake: on that inauspicious day a handful of ill-starred soldiers
from Meerut, frenzied with malice, invaded the city—every man of
them shameless and turbulent, and with murderous hate for his
masters, thirsting for British blood. . . .

There were humble, quiet men, who passed their days drawing
some modest sum from British bounty and eating their crust of
bread, living scattered in different areas of the city. No man among
them knew an arrow from an axe. . . . In truth, such men are made
to people the lanes and by-lanes, not to gird up their loins and go
out to battle. These men, when they saw that a dam of dust and
straw cannot stem the fast-flowing flood, took to their only remedy,
and every man of them went to his home and resigned himself to
grief. I too am one of these grief-stricken men. I was in my home.
When I heard the noise and uproar, I would have made enquiry, but
in the twinkling of an eye . . . every street and every lane was full of
galloping horsemen, and the sound of marching men, coming wave
upon wave, rose in the air. Then there was not so much as a handful
of dust which was not red with the blood of men whose bodies were
like the rose; and it seemed that every corner of every garden was
stripped of its leaves and fruits, the graveyard of a hundred spring-
times. Alas for those wise and just rulers, of good nature and good
name! And woe for those fair ladies of delicate form, with faces
radiant as the moon and bodies gleaming like new-mined silver!
And alas for those children who had barely yet seen the world,
whose smiling faces put the flowers to shame and whose dainty
steps reproached the partridge's gait! For all of these were dragged
down to drown in the vortex of blood. If Death itself, that rains
burning coals and issues flames of fire, Death at whose hands men
are compelled to lacerate their faces and blacken their clothes,

---

[4] "After the Hejirah" (flight, or departure): the Muslim starting point for modern history when the Prophet Muhammed left Mecca, where his life was in danger, to found
Islam in Medina (622 C.E.).

should stand sobbing and lamenting at these victims' graves, and don black raiment in mourning for them, it would be no more than just. And if the heavens should turn to dust and settle on the earth, and the earth in panic move like a whirlwind from its station, it would be no more than fitting.

> Spring, wallow in your own blood, like a stricken bird;
> Age, plunge in blackness, like a night without a moon;
> Sun, beat your head until your face is bruised and black;
> Moon, make yourself the scar upon the age's heart.

At last, when evening fell on that black day, and blacker darkness overspread the earth, then these black-hearted men in their head-strong pride pitched their camps throughout the city and in the Fort, where they made the royal orchards a stable for their horses and the royal abode their sleeping quarters. Little by little, from distant towns the news came in, that in every cantonment sepoys[5] had shed their officers' blood, and as the minstrel draws the melody from his strings, so had these faithless ones, with beating of drums raised the tumult of rebellion. Band upon band of soldiers and peasants had become as one, and far and near, one and all, without even speaking or conferring together, girded their loins to their single aim, and girded them so strongly that the buffetings of a torrent of blood could alone ungird them. It seemed that legions without number and warriors without count were bound in unity as a single thread binds the twigs that make the broom. . . . And now you will see a thousand armies, marshalled without marshals, and unnumbered bands, led by no commander and yet ready for war. Their guns and shells, their shot and powder are all taken from English arsenals, and are bent to war against the masters of those arsenals. All the ways of war they learned from the English, and now their faces are inflamed with hate and malice against their teachers. My heart is not stone or iron: how should it not burn in sorrow? My eyes are not sightless windows: how should they not shed tears? Yes, a man must both feel anguish at the death of its English rulers, and shed tears for the destruction of Hindustan.[6] City after city lies open, without protectors, filled with

[5]Native Indians serving in the British army.
[6]India.

men who have none to watch over them, like gardens bereft of their gardeners, studded with trees stripped bare of leaves and fruit. Robbers go freed from the fetters of the law, and merchants released from the burden of levy. House after house lies desolate, and the abodes of grieving men invite despoliation.

* * *

On Monday, 24th of the lunar month and 14th of September— when they who lay in the shade of the hill made an assault on Kashmiri gate with such majestic force that the black forces had no choice but to flee before them. . . . And if May drove justice out of Delhi, September drove out oppression and brought justice back. . . . Smiting the enemy and driving him before them, the victors overran the city in all directions. All whom they found in the streets they cut down. Those distinguished in the city by rank and wisdom one and all took to their houses and shut the doors, that their honour might be safe. Of the army of scoundrels still in the city many determined upon flight, while a few raged to resist the attackers. These few now grappled with the brave conquerors of the city to spill, as they thought, the blood of the alien enemy, but as I deem, the honour of the capital. For two to three days every road in the city, from the Kashmiri Gate to Chandni Chauk, was a battlefield. Three gates— the Ajmeri, the Turcoman and the Delhi—were still held by the rebels. My house . . . is situated, between the Kashmiri and the Delhi Gate, in the centre of the city, so that both are equidistant from my lane. When the raging lion-hearts set foot in the city, they held it lawful to slaughter the helpless and burn the houses, and indeed, in every territory taken by force of arms these are the sufferings that people must endure. At the naked spectacle of this vengeful wrath and malevolent hatred the colour fled from men's faces, and a vast concourse of men and women, past all computing, owning much or owning nothing, took to precipitate flight through these three gates. Seeking the little villages and shrines outside the city, they there drew breath to wait until such time as might favour their return. Or if even there they could not feel at ease, they journeyed on day and night to some other place. As for the writer of these words, his heart did not quake, nor did his step falter. I stayed where I was, saying "I have committed no crime and need pay no penalty. The English do not slay the innocent, nor is the air of this city uncongenial to me.

Why should I fall a prey to groundless fancies and wander stumbling from place to place? Let me sit in some deserted corner blending my voice with my lamenting pen, while the tears fall from my eyelashes to mingle with the words of blood I write."

* * *

In the same week in which the British army conquered the city, Amin ud Din Ahmad Khan Bahadur and Muhammad Ziya ud Din Khan Bahadur, men renowned for their wisdom and justice, bethought them that their honour might best be safeguarded and their hopes for the future made stronger if they left the city. They set out with their wives and children, with three elephants and about forty fine horses, and took the road to the domain of Loharu, which had always been their estate. They first halted at Mihrauli,[7] where in the radiance of that blessed burying ground they partook of the provisions for their journey and rested for two or three days. While they were there, robber soldiers surrounded them, and robbed them of everything except the clothes they wore. Only the three elephants, whom their loyal and faithful companions had led away the moment the tumult began, survived to remind them of their former state, like three burnt granaries. You may well imagine the plight of these victims of robbery and ruin, and they set out, without provisions and without equipment, for Dujana. They were welcomed by Hasan Ali Khan Bahadur, of noble name and fairest fame, who gave proof of his humanity and courage, telling them "My home is yours" and escorting them to Dujana. I will not speak at length: this laudable leader of men acted towards his peers with all the gracious generosity that Iran's emperor . . . showed to Humayun.[8]

When the Commissioner[9] Sahib Bahadur heard the news, he sent for them to come to Delhi. Accordingly they returned to the city and presented themselves before him. For some time he spoke to them with unkind taunts, but they returned soft answers to him, and he fell silent. He directed them to a place in the Fort, next to the hall of the king's steward-in-chief, and commanded them to take up residence there. Regard for the even flow of his writing did not per-

---

[7]Burial place of a Muslim saint, Qutub ud Din Baktyar.
[8]Mughal king (reigned 1530–56), who spent early years in exile in Persia.
[9]Of Delhi.

mit the writer of these words to tell the full tale of loss and ruin that befell this family. Know then that while their owners fell a prey to pillage in Mihrauli, their empty houses in Delhi were plundered and laid waste. Of all they had taken with them, they brought only their fainting lives to Dujana, while the rest in its entirety fell to the robbers. While here, of their mansions and palaces nothing remained but bricks and stones and pebbles. They were stripped bare; not a trace of their silver and gold remained, and not a thread of their carpets and their clothing. God grant His mercy to these guiltless men, and an auspicious end to this inauspicious beginning, bringing them comfort out of distress. It was Saturday, the 17 October when these two men, unrivalled in wisdom, returned to the city, and, as I have said, took up their residence in the Fort.

About the princes no more than this can be said, that some fell victims to the rifle bullet and were sent into the jaws of the dragon of death, and the souls of some froze in the noose of the hangman's rope, and some lie in prisons, and some are wanderers on the face of the earth. The old and infirm king, confined in the Fort, is under trial. The lords of Jhajjar and Ballabgarh and he who adorned the throne of Farrukhnagar, have been taken separately, on separate days, and hung on the gallows tree, that none might say that their blood has been shed.

Now every English soldier that bears arms[1]

Now every English soldier that bears arms
Is sovereign, and free to work his will.

Men dare not venture out into the street
And terror chills their hearts within them still.

Their homes enclose them as in prison walls
And in the Chauk the victors hang and kill.[2]

The city is athirst for Muslim blood
And every grain of dust must drink its fill. . . .

---

[1]Translated by Ralph Russell and Khurshidul Islam (1994). This poem comes from a letter Ghalib wrote in 1858 to a friend, in which he was more open than in his *Dastambu* about his reactions to the British tactics in suppressing the revolt.

[2]Chandni Chauk was the name of the street where the British hanged captured rebels, in front of the police station.

Bahadur Shah II (1775–1862)

The last Mughal emperor in northern India, Bahadur Shah came to the throne in 1837 and was the figurehead of the "Mutiny" of 1857. When the British regained Delhi, two of his sons were summarily beheaded and he himself was exiled to Rangoon in Burma. Ghalib was one of his court poets, and the Shah was a notable poet in his own right, composing poetry under the pen name Zafar ("victory" or "success"), taken from the full name given to him at birth, Abu Zafar Siraj-ud-Din Muhammad Bahadur Shah. He is best known and loved for the following two ghazals. Though some scholars have questioned their dating and even attribution, most read them as expressing his coming to terms with exile in the aftermath of the revolt.

I am not the light of anyone's eye[1]

I am not the light of anyone's eye
     I am no comfort to anyone's heart.
I am no more than a handful of dust
     That's of no use to anyone at all.

My splendour is all gone to pieces
     From me my beloved is separated.
I am Spring come too late
     To a garden laid waste by Fall.

I am not a darling of anyone
     I am not a rival to anyone.
I am Fate that turns against someone
     I am a blasted landscape.

Why should anyone sing a dirge
     Or at my grave should flowers place
Why light a candle for me—
     A monument to helplessness.

[1]Translated by Harish Trivedi (2005).

I cannot bring myself to like this despoiled wilderness

I cannot bring myself to like this despoiled wilderness.
But who has had it all his way in this mutable world.

O tell my longings to depart and find some far-off home
There isn't room enough for them in my now blighted heart.

I had begged God for a long life, and got all of four days.
Two went by in yearning and two in futile waiting.

My numbered days are over and now evening falls.
I hope to stretch my legs straight out in my grave at last.

How terrible is the fate of Zafar! For his burial
Two yards of land could not be had in his beloved's lane.

* * *

I wouldn't have gone to sleep in such deep dust
But nodded off worn out by sleepless misery.

* * *

O God, you should have made me an overlord[1] of kings.
Or else made me the uncrowned king of fakirs.[2]

Major R. C. W. Mitford (1839–c. 1900)

A British army officer serving in northern India, Reginald Colville William Mitford became involved in the adventure of his life in 1879. For years, Afghanistan had been a prime goal in what Kipling called "the Great Game" of Western competition for imperial influence and control. Russia and England in particular had been jockeying for influence in Afghanistan, Persia, and Turkey. While the poor and mountainous region of Afghanistan had little economic value to England, the British viewed it as a crucial buffer between India and Russian power.

[1]The Urdu term is "afsar," from the English "officer." This may be one of the earliest instances in Urdu poetry of a word derived from English.
[2]Wandering ascetic holy men.

Hence the alarm in 1878, when the Afghan leader agreed to receive a Russian mission. Future British Prime Minister Sir Neville Chamberlain was sent from India to counter the Russian initiative, but he was turned away at the Khyber Pass leading into Afghanistan. The British army then attacked the forces that had stood in his way; a treaty was negotiated allowing a British envoy, Louis Cavagnari, to settle in the capital, Kabul (also spelled "Cabul" or "Caubul"). Soon after his arrival, riots broke out—probably with the tacit support of the Afghan ruler, Yakub Khan—and Cavagnari and his men were massacred. The British organized a swift, brutally effective response under the leadership of General F. S. Roberts. Mitford's vivid narrative of this expedition compels comparisons to the account of "Kafiristan" given by the solider-narrator Peachey Carnehan in Kipling's "The Man Who Would Be King."

from *To Caubul with the Cavalry Brigade*

We had been encamped at Koorum[1] for some three months during the summer of 1879, and all, Europeans and Natives alike, had suffered more or less from the intense heat and malaria, sufferings made much more unendurable in the case of the former by the intense dulness and ennui which prevailed, and which were but little ameliorated by an occasional languid game of lawn tennis or polo. Men were talking of furlough, and looking eagerly for the time when leave to England would again be granted, when the news of the attack on the Residency at Cabul, and of the massacre of poor Cavagnari and almost all his followers, burst upon us like a thunder-clap. All were in the wildest state of excitement, not diminished when, two days later, came the order for our regiment to advance and join the leading column at Kooshi, the first halting place in the Logur Valley. A very short time sufficed for the officers' preparations, few of us having more than the authorized weight of "kit," consisting of a tiny double-roofed tent, seven feet square, weighing eighty pounds; personal baggage restricted to the same weight (this required much consideration, even to the possibility of taking an extra toothbrush!); twenty-five pounds of baggage for each camp-follower, and a like amount for each charger. Little enough when it is considered that we were starting on a campaign

---

[1]A river and town in northwest India (now Pakistan) near the border with Afghanistan.

of indefinite duration in an almost unknown country, but we were not long in finding out that our General had been quite right in thus restricting the amount of baggage. The arrangements for the men took more consideration and a longer time. They all marched out of Koorum *on foot*, carrying five days' provisions for man and horse on the latter, packed in two canvas bags and slung across the saddle. This measure was necessitated by the scarcity of supplies between Koorum and the valley of the Logur River. The men were crowded four in a tent, instead of two, as usual, and all spare tents, baggage, &c., were stored in one of the Koorum forts, and left in charge of the sick and weakly men, all of whom were ordered to be left behind, to their intense disappointment. Almost every patient in the hospital implored the Doctor to discharge him, so that he might accompany the regiment to Caubul; but our Esculapius[2] was inflexible, and most rightly so, as the sequel proved, for any man not in robust health must undoubtedly have succumbed to the cold and exposure of the campaign, which claimed many a victim even amongst those who started strong and in perfect health.

All our preparations having been thoroughly and rapidly completed, at 7 A.M. on the 23rd of September we marched from Koorum, the men shouting and in the highest spirits at the prospect of active service, and the regiment presenting a very unwonted appearance. Blue, scarlet, and gold had all been discarded, and all were dressed from top to toe in *Khâkee*, or mud colour; the lances were stripped of their gay scarlet and white pennons (we afterwards resumed these as a distinguishing mark), and the long jackboots replaced by ammunition "high-lows" and *putties*, or bandages of woollen stuff rolled round the leg from knee to ankle after the fashion of Cashmere sportsmen and Italian organ-grinders. This is a much better dress for walking in than long boots, and as we rightly expected a good deal of dismounted work in rocky ground, we adopted it with—need I say?—a total disregard to appearances.

*   *   *

Here we were joined by the General and some of his Staff, the ubiquitous "Parson Adams" amongst them, of course. I hope he will excuse my taking the liberty of introducing our Protestant Chaplain to my readers, as he was quite a foreground figure in camp. A

[2]In classical myth, the god of medicine.

strongly-built, fresh-complexioned man, very keen about his own work and almost equally devoted to sport: I do not think he shoots, but he is certainly thoroughly at home in the saddle, and used, when Chaplain of Peshawur,[3] to be a regular attendant at the meets of the "Peshawur Vale Hounds," when he frequently showed the way to the best lay riders in the station. Cheery of voice, hardy of frame, and indefatigable at work or play, he was just "the right man in the right place," and was thoroughly liked and respected by all, from highest to lowest, especially those (and they were many) whom he cheered and comforted in sickness or sorrow.

Our poor tired horses had hardly had time to swallow their meagre allowance of millet-stalks, of which we had procured a small supply in the village at an exorbitant price, when we were ordered to fall in again and return to camp. Instead of continuing our rout to Killa Kâzi, we turned off to our left (north), and followed the main road to Caubul. The distance proved greater than our leaders had expected, and we (14th) did not enter the suburbs till night had fairly fallen. We first passed through the straggling outlying village, or rather suburb, called Dêh Muzung; then, leaving some high half-ruined blank walls looming threateningly through the startlit air, on our right, we rode along a narrow rocky path hemmed in on the left by precipitous rock, and on the right by a deep and broad watercourse, which we had to cross twice by rough bridges formed of unhewn slabs of stone. Fortunately even the most timid or skittish horses were far too tired to think of shying, or we might have had some bad accidents in the dark, for these bridges were overshadowed by weeping willows and other trees, so that we lost even the small benefit of the starlight. After some distance the road turned sharply to the right, under a lofty building, and crossing a particularly uncomfortable hog-backed bridge, we entered the city of Caubul.

We soon found ourselves in total darkness, threading our way through one of the two great bazaars, which are roofed in as a protection from the weather. We now saw evidences of a friendly feeling, for every here and there a man or child—invariably Hindu, be it observed[4]—would come out holding an oil lamp to show us the way,

---

[3]City near the Khyber Pass.

[4]These immigrants from India are less hostile to the British than the natives.

or a hand, evidently a woman's, would be pushed through a peep-hole in the curtains of the upper story with a light for the same purpose, or *possibly* to gratify feminine curiosity. There were several Caubulis sitting on the platforms in front of the now closed shops, who favoured us with a diabolical scowl of hatred and defiance, of which no notice was taken, save an occasional significant inclination of a revolver-muzzle in the direction of the ill-looking ruffians.

We frequently remarked afterwards, when we began to know the city well, that though many of the children were almost beautiful, they yet contrived to develop into most villainous-looking scoundrels—Shylock, Caliban, and Sycorax his dam, all have numerous representatives,[5] though I think the first is the commonest type, on account of the decidedly Jewish cast of most Caubulis' features, and the low cunning and cruelty which supplies the only animation in their otherwise stolid countenances, true indices of the mind beneath—fatalist by creed, false, murderous, and tyrannical by education. In this description I do not include the Kizil Bâsh (Persian) or Khuttri (Hindoo) settlers, who preserve their own distinctive features, both mental and physical.

* * *

After proceeding for about five hundred yards through this street, we entered the great Bazaar, of course at the opposite end to that by which we had gained admittance on the night of the 9th. Here the sight was certainly one of the most picturesque and animated that I have ever seen. Imagine a roughly-paved street, about eighteen feet wide; on each side is a sort of wooden dresser or daïs three feet high and two wide, carried uninterruptedly along the front of the shops, the floors of which are on a level with the daïs. These shops are wooden booths, open in front during the day, and closed at night by roughly-finished but strong and sufficiently well-fitting wooden shutters. Above the shops rises a single story with a small verandah in front, forming the sleeping rooms and women's apartments of the shop keepers. Then comes an open space of from three to four feet for ventilation, and over all a flat roof of poplar beams and pine planks, protecting passengers, customers, and merchants from sun,

---

[5]All Shakespeare characters: Shylock is the vengeful Jewish merchant in *The Merchant of Venice*; Caliban is a monstrous primitive islander in *The Tempest*; his "dam" (mother) is the witch Sycorax.

rain, and above all else, snow, which would otherwise block up the street, and render the space under the daïs useless. This space, which may be called the "area," is now utilised in many ways— either as a workshop for the stall above, a cook-room for the shop keeper, a store-room, or even as a second shop altogether, hired out at a small rental to some of the numerous vendors of "Brummagem" goods,[6] sham embroidery, glass beads, thumb-glasses, embroidery-silks, and other miscellaneous rubbish.

The wall-spaces between the shop-fronts are filled with wooden frames, pegs, and projecting rods, on which are displayed gaily embroidered Persian caps, called "Koollahs," bright-coloured handkerchiefs of silk or cotton, strips of cloth, Cashmere woollen stuffs, Manchester goods, Bokhâra silks, and endless varieties and oddities of apparel affected by a mixed people just beginning to import from the outer world of civilisation and tinsel. Many of the articles exposed for sale were of native manufacture, and of the prices demanded for these we could not judge, but we found the charges for poshteens, sashes, scarves, and many other things we had been accustomed to purchase in the Punjâb, quite thirty per cent. higher than we had ever been asked before.

Certainly if rapacity and greed, combined with Jewish observances and features can be admitted as evidence, the much besneered idea that the Affghâns are descended from the "lost tribes" seems infinitely more worthy of consideration than most of our ethnologists are prepared to admit. Many of their names, too, are unmistakeably Jewish, such, for instance, as "Ibraheem" for Abraham; "Izhâq" for Isaac; "Yâkoob," Jacob; "Yoosuf," Joseph; "Ayoob," Job; "Ismael," Ishmael or Samuel; "Moosa," Moses; "Zahariâh," Zachariah; and many others.[7]

The ends of the covered bazaar were occupied by silversmiths and money-changers, who sacrificed the warmth and protection from the weather afforded by the more central positions, for the sake of the better light obtainable in these more exposed places. The silversmiths' work is very rough, and they appear to have but little originality or inventive faculty, or if they indeed are so gifted, they wrap up the talent in the very thickest of napkins. At the

[6]Cheap, fake (from "Birmingham," the British manufacturing city).

[7]Mitford is unaware that these are actually Arabic names, adopted by the Afghans from Hebrew-derived names in the Islamic scripture, the Qur'an.

money-changers (all of whom are Khuttri Hindoos, it being a trade strictly forbidden by the Korân) we found a large variety of foreign gold coins, Persian "tillas," Russian five rouble pieces, Hindustâni "mohurs," and others. The Affghâns had no gold coinage of their own until Sher Ali returned from India in 1869, when he caused a few handsome "Ashruffis" to be struck, which are valued at eighteen rupees for the metal alone, the gold being very pure and rich-coloured. I may here mention that on examining the contents of the Ameer's treasury no fewer than thirteen thousand Russian gold coins were found. What were they paid for?

* * *

Next morning (the 22nd) we marched to Dhâkâ, and thence, *viâ* Lundi Kotul and Ali Musjid, through the Khyber to Jumrood, where we found the old fort looking quite clean and in good repair.

The whole of our march down from Caubul had lain through barren, rocky, and uncultivated country, forming a marked contrast to that which we had traversed between the Peiwâr Kotul and the capital. The road also was much worse, and the only counterbalancing benefit derived from the Khyber route lay in its being considerably shorter than that by the Koorum Valley, the distances from the two bases of operations, Peshawur and Kohât to Caubul being respectively twelve and twenty-one marches.

At Ali Musjid a new stone fort had been erected by us since the commencement of the war; this had apparently already produced the good effect of over-awing or tranquillising the neighbouring robber tribes, whose principal inducement to seek their living by plundering passing caravans had been the perfect immunity from punishment which they had hitherto enjoyed. This really has also led to the petty, but most troublesome and costly, border wars in which we have been so frequently and fruitlessly engaged from our first occupation of Peshawur to the Jowâki skirmishes in 1877–78. Now that we have troops located not only in their front and rear, but even in the very heart of their hill fastnesses, our predatory neighbours may possibly be brought to see the error of their ways, especially if "Exeter Hall tactics"[8] are abandoned till a more suitable time, and we treat these murdering freebooters as the savages they really are,

---

[8]Rules of fair play, of the sort observed at the elite British school at Exeter.

instead of dealing with them as civilised people, which they are certainly *very* far from being.

We left Jumrood early on Tuesday, the 27th of January, and before we had proceeded far we met the 2nd Battalion of the 14th Foot, commanded by Colonel Dawson Warren, an old friend, and well known throughout the Service for his soldierly abilities and social qualities. Of course we drew up by the roadside to pay the usual compliments to the senior regiment, (in India, all Native regiments, of whatever branch, salute all British troops,) but our comrades of the same number, though of different race, insisted on reversing the usual order of proceeding, and paid us the very high honour of forming up and saluting while their band played us, the junior regiment, past their front. This was as gratifying to us as it was well meant, and the compliment was most fully appreciated by all in our ranks, both British and Native.

At noon we marched into the station of Peshawur, and the officers breakfasted with those of the 8th Hussars, amongst whom I had the unexpected pleasure of meeting a kinsman.

In the afternoon we enjoyed the unaccustomed luxury of a drive; and the sight of church and gardens, barracks and bungalows, carriages and shops, and—last, but most welcome of all—*ladies*, assured us that we were once more in a British cantonment.

Howard Hensman (?–1916)

When the Second Afghan War broke out, journalist Howard Hensman was the chief political correspondent for The Pioneer, *one of India's leading newspapers, located in the north Indian city of Allahabad. Having gotten permission to join General Roberts's expeditionary force, he sent a series of dispatches to* The Pioneer *and gathered them together in 1881 in a book expansively titled* The Afghan War of 1879–80: Being a Complete Narrative of the Capture of Cabul, the Seige of Sherpur, the Battle of Ahmed Khel, the Brilliant March to Candahar, and the Defeat of Ayub Khan, with the Operations of the Helmund, and the Settlement with Abdur Rahman Khan. *Kipling certainly had this account in mind when framing "The Man Who Would Be King," which he wrote in 1888 while serving his own turn at* The Pioneer *as assistant editor and correspondent.*

from *The Afghan War of 1879–80*

Preface

The interest aroused by the massacre of our ill-fated Embassy to the Amir Yakub Khan, the subsequent capture of Cabul, and the hard-won successes of our armies during the occupation of the city, can scarcely yet have passed away; and I have, therefore, ventured to republish the series of letters which, as a special correspondent, I wrote in the field. They are a simple diary of the war; and though in this form they may lack conciseness, they have at least the merit of such accuracy as an eye-witness can alone hope to attain. It was my good-fortune to be the only special correspondent with the gallant little army which moved out of Ali Kheyl in September, 1879. The Government of India had notified that "non-combatant correspondents" would not be allowed to join the force, the history of whose achievements was to be left to regimental officers, who might in their spare hours supply information carefully *visé*,[1] to such newspapers as chose to accept it. So carelessly was this strange order issued, that Sir Frederick Roberts never received official intimation of its existence, and he welcomed me at Ali Kheyl on the eve of his departure for Kushi as, I am sure, he would have welcomed any other correspondent who had chosen to cross the frontier, and push on without escort and with their own baggage animals. I make this explanation in justice to General Roberts, upon whom the responsibility of excluding correspondents has been falsely thrown. Regarding the letters now republished, Mr. Frederick Harrison in the *Fortnightly Review* has been good enough to describe them as "admirably written, with very great precision and knowledge." While not sympathizing in the least with Mr. Harrison's criticism of Sir Frederick Roberts's punishment of Cabul, in support of which criticism he mainly relied upon my letters, I am grateful for his estimate of my work. I can scarcely hope that all my critics will be equally generous.

I have carefully gone into details where military movements of importance had to be described, and the sketch maps can be relied upon as showing exact distances and positions.

HOWARD HENSMAN,

Special Correspondent of the *Pioneer,* Allahabad

Cabul, *August,* 1880.

---

[1] "Overseen," selected.

* * *

Having joined General Roberts at Ali Kheyl[2] on the evening of September 26th, I may take up the story of the advance from about that period. I will therefore give my letters as they were published at the time:—

ALI KHEYL, *28th September.*

The unexpected news of the arrival of the Amir Yakub Khan at Kushi last night has been received with general satisfaction, as affairs are much simplified as regards the military position. There has been much doubt all along as to the sincerity of Yakub's protestations, and it was not easy to determine the line of action when Cabul should be finally reached. But the Amir's authority has plainly crumbled to the dust in his capital; and, if not a fugitive, he must have come as a suppliant to us to reinstate him on the throne, at the same time that we avenge the Massacre of the Embassy. It seems far more probable, however, that he is a fugitive; for it is stated that Cabul is in a state of anarchy, which can only mean that the populace have fraternized with the mutinous troops and have driven out a sovereign who had made terms with the Kafirs.[3] If this be really so, the fate of the city, in case any opposition is shown when our army moves forward, should be sealed. The only argument an Afghan understands is direct and severe punishment for offences committed, and the punishment should now be dealt out without stint, even if Cabul has to be sacked. Not a man in the force that is now about to make the final advance would feel other than the keenest pleasure in seeing Cabul burn, for it is hopeless to expect an armed rabble, such as that which now holds the city, to show a steady front when General Roberts's army closes with them. They lack leaders to direct their movements, and though arms and ammunition may be plentiful in their midst, their organization is about equal to that of a European mob suddenly placed in power after a long period of strict government. Their capacity for mischief is as limited as that of any other rabble, for their future movements are all dependent upon outside influences. If left to their own will, they would probably split up into factions, of which the strongest would eventually sweep away all rivals; but

---

[2]About 50 miles south of Kabul.
[3]Infidels, foreigners.

when menaced by a stronger power, they must either dissolve, or by sheer doggedness attempt to dispute possession of that which they have gained. The Cabul mutineers are not of a type which "die but never surrender," and although they may risk a brush with the British forces, they will most likely seek safety in flight before any severe thrashing can be given them. It will be most aggravating if this proves to be the case, but until the Amir has explained in detail the course of events from the time of Sir Louis Cavagnari's death, an exact estimate of the position at Cabul cannot be arrived at. The conference which is sure to take place with Sir Frederick Roberts in a day or two will settle what course is to be taken, and it is to be hoped no undue tenderness will be shown in laying down the lines upon which the policy of the next few weeks is to be carried forward. By Wednesday at the latest a completely equipped force of over 6,000 men will be at Kushi, and on the following morning the march will begin. Sunday next should see the British troops encamped before Cabul, and then will begin the punishment of a city which is only connected in the saddest way with the expansion of our power in Asia.

* * *

There was no slackness in the pursuit when once it began, but the enemy had too great a start to be overtaken, and it now seems probable they dispersed to the hills and made for their homes, many doubtless taking refuge in the city. One piece of experience was certainly gained, and that was that the villagers about Cabul are hostile to us almost to a man. Five of them belonging to Aoshahr were made an example of by Colonel Ross, of the 14th Bengal Lancers. They treacherously fired into the Lancers, after having salaamed to them as they passed. The ruffians were captured with their guns still in their hands, and were shot without further parley. If is only by such severity, and by taking no prisoners in action, that any impression can be made upon the Afghan mind. Such prisoners as are brought in are tried by a military commission, and the great majority are shot. There is just a fear that too much leniency may be shown, as the work is rather distasteful to British officers; but as we are an "avenging army," scruples must be cast aside.

* * *

It must be more than thirty-five years since British infantry marched through the filthy streets of this much-vaunted citadel[4]; and our only regret was that they had now entered it so peacefully. Sir Frederick Roberts was accompanied by the Mustaufi, the Wazir, and Daoud Shah, the Commander-in-Chief.[5] After a few minutes' stay in this square, we retraced our steps and entered a narrow lane with a high wall on the right, shutting in the Amir's garden. On the left were the stables in which the horses of the Royal household were tethered in the open air, rude bins being made in the mud walls on a pattern which is common where Afghan cavalry are quartered. The lane led to the high ground on which the buildings assigned to Sir Louis Cavagnari and his companions stood. From this the city could be seen lying at our feet, to the north.

Our first view of the Residency was of the rear wall, still intact, but blackened on the top where the smoke from the burning ruins had swept across. At each angle where the side walls joined were seen the loop-holes from which the fire of the little force on the roof had been directed against the overwhelming numbers attacking them. Every square foot round these loop-holes was pitted with bullet-marks, the balls having cut deeply into the hard mud plaster. The western wall, which faced towards the Upper Bala Hissar, commanding it, was scarred with these marks, proving only too well how severe had been the fire from the higher level occupied by the mutineers in the Arsenal. At this end the Residency was of three stories, but the present wall does not indicate the height of more than two, the upper part having collapsed when the fire obtained a mastery over the building. A lane six or eight feet wide runs between this wall and the buildings on the right in which the Guides were quartered. Plans hitherto published have made the Residency and these quarters one block; but this is a mistake; they were quite distinct.

* * *

The courtyard of the Residency is about 90 feet square, and at its northern end, where formerly stood a three-storied building like that I have just described, are nothing but the bare walls, blackened

[4]The First Afghan War, 1838–42; the triumphant British occupation of Kabul in 1839 was undone when the army was massacred when it left the city in 1842, suffering the loss of almost all 4,500 troops.

[5]The principal local leaders.

and scarred by fire, and a huge heap of rubbish, the ruins of the walls and roof which fell in as the woodwork was destroyed. Portions of the partition walls still remain, jutting sullenly out from the mass of *débris*, and these only serve to make the place more desolate. The whitewashed walls on the left are here and there bespattered with blood, and on the raised basement on which the building stood are the remains of a large fire, the half-charred beams still resting among the ashes. The ruins are still smouldering. Whether, as suggested, any bodies were burned there, is still an unsettled point; but in one room into which I went there can be no doubt fire had been used for such a purpose. The ashes were in the middle of the chamber, and near them were two skulls and a heap of human bones, still fetid. It would seem as if a desperate struggle had taken place in this room, the bloodstains on the floor and walls being clearly discernible. The skulls are to be examined by surgeons, as it is possible they may be those of Europeans. The Residency was looted so thoroughly, that not even a peg has been left in the walls. In Sir Louis Cavagnari's quarters the windows overlooking the Bala Hissar wall have been torn out even to the sashes, and a few bits of glass on the floor alone remain of them. The chintz hangings and purdahs[6] have been stripped away, a fluttering bit of coloured rag on a stray nail being the only sign of such cheerfulness as these once gave. Bare cross-poles and rafters, floors rough with dirt and defiled with filth, staring white walls with here and there a bullet-mark— such are the once comfortable quarters of our Envoy. The view over the Cabul plain is still as peaceful as when poor Jenkyns described it so enthusiastically; but all else is changed. The one consolation is that a British army is encamped within gunshot of the walls.

It is still difficult to make out the point at which the mutineers obtained entry into the Residency buildings, unless it was by a hole in the eastern wall, a little to the right of a small doorway leading to a lower range of houses adjoining. Round this hole are scores of bullet-holes, and their direction seems to show that the defenders on the roof fired down as the men streamed in, in the vain hope of checking them before they could rush forward and set fire to the woodwork. Once the lower part of the three-storied building was in flames, nothing could save the brave men on the roof, as all retreat

[6]Curtains.

was cut off. We viewed the scene of desolation for some time from the roof of Sir Louis Cavagnari's quarters; and General Roberts gave orders that nothing should be disturbed until careful sketches had been made of the interior of the Residency and its surroundings. Careful excavations for bodies will also be made among the ruins. It is absurd to talk of the Residency being a safe place for a garrison; it is commanded completely from the walls of the Arsenal in the Upper Bala Hissar, and also from the roofs of some high houses to the southwest. In addition, houses closely adjoin it on the eastern side; and an attacking party sapping[7] the walls would have perfect cover in this direction the whole time: this may account for the breach in the walls through which I have suggested the mutineers made their rush. Riding into the quarters occupied by the Guides' escort, on the western side of the lane, I found but few bullet-marks on the walls. Facing was a high door firmly closed and seemingly uninjured; but on going into the Sikh quarters on my right, and following a broad passage which turned at right angles towards the wall, a huge breach was visible. This was where the Afghans had blown in the gate after Lieutenant Hamilton's noble, but ineffectual, efforts to check them. Three times he charged out, killing many men with his sword and pistol, but what could one hero do against a mob of fanatics? No doubt when it was seen that a breach was made the Guides withdrew to the Residency proper, and there made the last stand, first in the courtyard guarding the doors and afterwards on the roof.

On returning we stayed for a short time in the Amir's garden, where fruit and tea were served to us. Afterwards we visited Shere Ali's palace on the wall near the gate. Two or three dark passages had to be traversed before a staircase was gained which led to his State rooms. Persian carpets of value were spread in two rooms, in the second of which hung gaudy glass chandeliers, while on the ground (as if purposely placed out of harm's way) was a collection of glassware of sorts showing all the colours of the rainbow. A few cheap prints, including one of the Czar Alexander, hung on the walls, and on a chair near was a *Graphic* folded so as to show a portrait of Cavagnari. On taking this up I came across a diary of Sir Louis Cavagnari's, which seemed to have been used chiefly for

[7]Undermining.

recording lists of visits and visitors. The book was handed over to Major Hastings. Two or three maps of Central Asia were also among the papers; but it is doubtful to whom they belonged.

* * *

There is a probability that the taking of Cabul may not be so barren as we first thought in the matter of loot. The city itself having been respected, there was not much to get out of the Bala Hissar beyond warlike stores and ammunition. But to-day the news has been made known that a vast store of treasure is hidden in houses belonging to Yakub Khan, or his near relatives living within the walls. Our treasure-chest has sunk very low of late by reason of the enormous purchases made by the Commissariat, which has to provide five months' stores for the army. Carriage was so scarce when we marched up from Ali Kheyl, that only a few lakhs[8] were brought up, and poverty is staring us in the face. Such expedients as giving bills upon India to Hindu and Kizilbash merchants in Cabul, or in receiving from Wali Mahomed and his sirdars many thousands of Bokhara gold *tillahs* (worth Rs. 9 or Rs. 10 each), or Russian five-rouble pieces said to be worth Rs. 11-8, though nobody really knows their legitimate market value—such expedients could not last long; and as nothing has been done to exact the fine imposed upon the Cabulis, it was clear that specie[9] would have to be raised from some source yet untouched. It is said that Yakub Khan, on assuming the Amirship, appropriated many lakhs of rupees which his father had given to the mother of Abdullah Jan, Shere Ali's favourite son, and these he had cleared out of the Bala Hissar, and, with other property of value, had hidden in the city. A little party of British soldiers filed off to the house indicated by our informers this morning, and the officer in charge of our treasure-chest (Major Moriarty) and Lieutenant Neville Chamberlain, Assistant Political Officer, had soon their eyes gladdened by bags and boxes of gold coins, besides finding on all sides rich silks, brocades, and other portable property of enormous value. About eight lakhs in gold were secured, and native rumour affirms that before the examination comes to an end, a million sterling may be unearthed. Boxes innumerable have still to be opened, and our spies are firm in their

[8]Bunches of rupees.
[9]Hard cash.

assurance that the value in coin and precious stones alone is eighty lakhs of rupees. To-morrow the examination of the place will be continued, and it is hoped another good day's find will be the result. This prize-money, for no doubt it will be considered as such, if it is confiscated, will be a just reward for the energy and dash our commander and his troops have shown in the capture of Cabul; and even if it is found necessary to use the money now for our immediate wants, the debtor and creditor account should be carefully kept in view of future distribution.

Joseph Conrad

Heart of Darkness

Joseph Conrad

Heart of Darkness

In 1889, Conrad settled in England and began to write, yet he was unsure of his prospects and still thought of returning to the merchant marine. In the summer of 1890, he decided to take a break from writing; using an aunt's influence, he went to Brussels and gained appointment to pilot an aging steamboat upriver—the basis for his most famous novella, *Heart of Darkness* (serialized in *Blackwood's Magazine* in 1899, published in book form in 1902). The Congo was controlled by a private corporation set up by King Leopold II of Belgium for personal profit. The Company was being promoted as a perfect marriage of the noble work of civilization and the profits of free enterprise, and so the colony was named the Congo Free State, a deeply ironic name in view of the conditions of virtual slavery that prevailed there. While the explorer-journalist Henry Morton Stanley extolled the benefits of King Leopold's enterprise, Conrad encountered a much grimmer reality on his journey. His work included transporting a sick agent of the Belgian Company downriver; his passenger, Georges Klein, died en route. The meeting with Klein ("Little," in German) provided the germ of Conrad's novella, in which Marlow journeys upriver to encounter the mysterious, threatening, eloquent Company agent Mr. Kurtz.

Conrad's great, enigmatic novella draws us into the heart of darkness. Yet what do we really see, and what does the story's unnamed narrator see as he listens to the tale told by his sailor friend Charlie Marlow? As dusk grows around the yacht where the tale is told, fog and obscurity seem to gather around the tale as well as the teller. Do we see Africa through Marlow's words, or do we see only

Marlow's hallucination of a dark night of the soul, projected outward? In a preface to his early novella *The Nigger of the "Narcissus"* (1897), Conrad issued a personal manifesto for the critical responsibility of the artist, who must seek the truth of life by descending "within himself, and in that lonely region of stress and strife, if he be deserving and fortunate, he finds the terms of his appeal. . . . to snatch in a moment of courage, from the remorseless rush of time, a passing phase of life." Conrad insisted that this lonely descent into self isn't a matter of aesthetic withdrawal but the basis for "the solidarity . . . which binds men to each other and all mankind to the visible world."

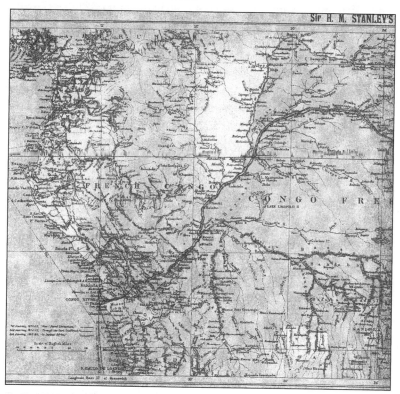

Sir H. M. Stanley's Three African Journeys, c. 1895; detail. When Conrad's Marlow dreamed of voyaging "into the yellow" of the empty spaces on African maps, he would have been looking at a map like this one. The Congo Free State is shown in yellow on the map, with red, green, and blue lines tracing Stanley's travels in the 1870s and 1880s across east and central Africa and up and down the Congo River, as he explored the borders of King Leopold's African domain.

Not only this solidarity but also the visibility of the world itself are severely tested in *Heart of Darkness*. Like many of Conrad's works, it presents shifting uncertainties of vision, understanding, and moral choice. From its multiple framing of stories inside stories to its portrayal of the uncanny African landscape, the Congolese, and the displaced Europeans, Conrad's narrative has provoked wide controversy. Many critics, including the postcolonial critic Edward Said, have seen the novella as a pivotal exposure of hollow imperial rhetoric and vicious imperial practice. Others, though, have argued that, whatever his intentions, Conrad created a picture of timeless primitivism that only reinforces a racist imperialism. In a now famous article, the Nigerian novelist Chinua Achebe sharply criticized Conrad for portraying Africa as

> a metaphysical battlefield devoid of all recognizable humanity, into which the wandering European enters at his peril. Can nobody see the preposterous and perverse arrogance in thus reducing Africa to the role of props for the breakup of one petty European mind? . . . And the question is whether a novel which celebrates this dehumanization, which depersonalizes a portion of the human race, can be called a great work of art. My answer is: No, it cannot. ("An Image of Africa: Racism in Conrad's *Heart of Darkness*," 1977)

Other readers have contested Achebe's answer by pointing to the complexity of Conrad's storytelling: Why *does* he wrap Marlow's story inside the frame-tale of an anonymous narrator aboard the *Nellie*? How closely are we to identify Conrad and Marlow? Just what horrors are evoked in the voyage upriver in search of the mysterious ivory trader Mr. Kurtz?

Marlow tries to see imperialism as redeemed either by "the idea" behind it or, more modestly, by the concrete practicalities of manly work, but Conrad asks his readers to decide how far these rationales can hold up in practice, as work is interrupted, speeches trail off, and texts disintegrate. Showing us an image of Africa through Marlow's troubled eyes, Conrad challenges us to hone our own vision and to deepen our reflections, as we encounter a world in which civilization and barbarism are inextricably intertwined.

Heart of Darkness

1

The *Nellie,* a cruising yawl,[1] swung to her anchor without a flutter of the sails, and was at rest. The flood had made, the wind was nearly calm, and being bound down the river, the only thing for it was to come to and wait for the turn of the tide.

The sea-reach of the Thames stretched before us like the beginning of an interminable waterway. In the offing the sea and the sky were welded together without a joint, and in the luminous space the tanned sails of the barges drifting up with the tide seemed to stand still in red clusters of canvas sharply peaked, with gleams of varnished sprits. A haze rested on the low shores that ran out to sea in vanishing flatness. The air was dark above Gravesend, and farther back still seemed condensed into a mournful gloom, brooding motionless over the biggest, and the greatest, town on earth.[2]

The Director of Companies was our captain and our host. We four affectionately watched his back as he stood in the bows looking to seaward. On the whole river there was nothing that looked half so nautical. He resembled a pilot, which to a seaman is trustworthiness personified. It was difficult to realise his work was not out there in the luminous estuary, but behind him, within the brooding gloom.

Between us there was, as I have already said somewhere, the bond of the sea. Besides holding our hearts together through long periods of separation, it had the effect of making us tolerant of each other's yarns—and even convictions. The Lawyer—the best of old fellows—had, because of his many years and many virtues, the only cushion on deck, and was lying on the only rug. The Accountant had brought out already a box of dominoes, and was toying architecturally with the bones. Marlow sat cross-legged right aft, leaning against the mizzen-mast.[3] He had sunken cheeks, a yellow complexion, a straight back, an ascetic aspect, and, with his arms dropped, the palms of hands outwards, resembled an idol. The

[1]A two-masted ship.

[2]London. Gravesend is the last major town on the Thames estuary, from which the river joins the North Sea.

[3]A secondary mast at the stern of the ship.

Director, satisfied the anchor had good hold, made his way aft and sat down amongst us. We exchanged a few words lazily. Afterwards there was silence on board the yacht. For some reason or other we did not begin that game of dominoes. We felt meditative, and fit for nothing but placid staring. The day was ending in a serenity of still and exquisite brilliance. The water shone pacifically; the sky, without a speck, was a benign immensity of unstained light; the very mist on the Essex marshes was like a gauzy and radiant fabric, hung from the wooded rises inland, and draping the low shores in diaphanous folds. Only the gloom to the west, brooding over the upper reaches, became more sombre every minute, as if angered by the approach of the sun.

And at last, in its curved and imperceptible fall, the sun sank low, and from glowing white changed to a dull red without rays and without heat, as if about to go out suddenly, stricken to death by the touch of that gloom brooding over a crowd of men.

Forthwith a change came over the waters, and the serenity became less brilliant but more profound. The old river in its broad reach rested unruffled at the decline of day, after ages of good service done to the race that peopled its banks, spread out in the tranquil dignity of a waterway leading to the uttermost ends of the earth. We looked at the venerable stream not in the vivid flush of a short day that comes and departs for ever, but in the august light of abiding memories. And indeed nothing is easier for a man who has, as the phrase goes, "followed the sea" with reverence and affection, than to evoke the great spirit of the past upon the lower reaches of the Thames. The tidal current runs to and fro in its unceasing service, crowded with memories of men and ships it has borne to the rest of home or to the battles of the sea. It had known and served all the men of whom the nation is proud, from Sir Francis Drake to Sir John Franklin, knights all, titled and untitled—the great knights-errant of the sea.[4] It had borne all the ships whose names are like jewels flashing in the night of time, from the *Golden Hind* returning with her round flanks full of treasure, to be visited

[4]Sir Francis Drake (1540–96) was captain of *The Golden Hind* in the service of Queen Elizabeth I; his reputation came from the successful raids he mounted against Spanish ships returning laden with gold from the New World (South America). In 1845 Sir John Franklin led an expedition in the *Erebus* and *Terror* in search of the Northwest Passage (to the Pacific); all perished.

by the Queen's Highness and thus pass out of the gigantic tale, to the *Erebus* and *Terror*, bound on other conquests—and that never returned. It had known the ships and the men. They had sailed from Deptford, from Greenwich, from Erith—the adventurers and the settlers; kings' ships and the ships of men on 'Change; captains, admirals, the dark "interlopers" of the Eastern trade, and the commissioned "generals" of East India fleets.[5] Hunters for gold or pursuers of fame, they all had gone out on that stream, bearing the sword, and often the torch, messengers of the might within the land, bearers of a spark from the sacred fire. What greatness had not floated on the ebb of that river into the mystery of an unknown earth! . . . The dreams of men, the seed of commonwealths, the germs of empires.

The sun set; the dusk fell on the stream, and lights began to appear along the shore. The Chapman lighthouse, a three-legged thing erect on a mudflat, shone strongly. Lights of ships moved in the fairway—a great stir of lights going up and going down. And farther west on the upper reaches the place of the monstrous town was still marked ominously on the sky, a brooding gloom in sunshine, a lurid glare under the stars.

"And this also," said Marlow suddenly, "has been one of the dark places of the earth."

He was the only man of us who still "followed the sea." The worst that could be said of him was that he did not represent his class. He was a seaman, but he was a wanderer too, while most seamen lead, if one may so express it, a sedentary life. Their minds are of the stay-at-home order, and their home is always with them—the ship; and so is their country—the sea. One ship is very much like another, and the sea is always the same. In the immutability of their surroundings the foreign shores, the foreign faces, the changing immensity of life, glide past, veiled not by a sense of mystery but by a slightly disdainful ignorance; for there is nothing mysterious to a seaman unless it be the sea itself, which is the mistress of his existence and as inscrutable as Destiny. For the rest, after his hours of work, a casual stroll or a casual spree on

[5]Deptford, Greenwich, and Erith lie on the Thames between London and Gravesend; "men on 'Change" are brokers on the Stock Exchange; the East India Company, a commercial and trading concern, became *de facto* ruler of large tracts of India in the 18th and 19th c.

shore suffices to unfold for him the secret of a whole continent, and generally he finds the secret not worth knowing. The yarns of seamen have a direct simplicity, the whole meaning of which lies within the shell of a cracked nut. But Marlow was not typical (if his propensity to spin yarns be excepted), and to him the meaning of an episode was not inside like a kernel but outside, enveloping the tale which brought it out only as a glow brings out a haze, in the likeness of one of these misty halos that sometimes are made visible by the spectral illumination of moonshine.

His remark did not seem at all surprising. It was just like Marlow. It was accepted in silence. No one took the trouble to grunt even; and presently he said, very slow,—

"I was thinking of very old times, when the Romans first came here, nineteen hundred years ago[6]—the other day. . . . Light came out of this river since—you say Knights? Yes; but it is like a running blaze on a plain, like a flash of lightning in the clouds. We live in the flicker—may it last as long as the old earth keeps rolling! But darkness was here yesterday. Imagine the feelings of a commander of a fine—what d'ye call 'em?—trireme in the Mediterranean, ordered suddenly to the north; run overland across the Gauls in a hurry[7]; put in charge of one of these craft the legionaries,—a wonderful lot of handy men they must have been too—used to build, apparently by the hundred, in a month or two, if we may believe what we read. Imagine him here—the very end of the world, a sea the colour of lead, a sky the colour of smoke, a kind of ship about as rigid as a concertina—and going up this river with stores, or orders, or what you like. Sandbanks, marshes, forests, savages,— precious little to eat fit for a civilised man, nothing but Thames water to drink. No Falernian wine here, no going ashore. Here and there a military camp lost in a wilderness, like a needle in a bundle of hay—cold, fog, tempests, disease, exile, and death,—death skulking in the air, in the water, in the bush. They must have been dying like flies here. Oh yes—he did it. Did it very well, too, no doubt, and without thinking much about it either, except after-

---

[6]A Roman force under Julius Caesar landed in Britain in 55 B.C.E., but it was not until 43 C.E. that the Emperor Claudius decided to conquer the island.

[7]A *trireme* is an ancient warship, propelled by oarsmen; the Gauls were the pre-Roman tribes who occupied present-day France; they were subdued by Julius Caesar between 58 and 50 B.C.E.

wards to brag of what he had gone through in his time, perhaps. They were men enough to face the darkness. And perhaps he was cheered by keeping his eye on a chance of promotion to the fleet at Ravenna by-and-by, if he had good friends in Rome and survived the awful climate. Or think of a decent young citizen in a toga—perhaps too much dice, you know—coming out here in the train of some prefect, or tax-gatherer, or trader even, to mend his fortunes. Land in a swamp, march through the woods, and in some inland post feel the savagery, the utter savagery, had closed round him,—all that mysterious life of the wilderness that stirs in the forest, in the jungles, in the hearts of wild men. There's no initiation either into such mysteries. He has to live in the midst of the incomprehensible, which is also detestable. And it has a fascination, too, that goes to work upon him. The fascination of the abomination—you know. Imagine the growing regrets, the longing to escape, the powerless disgust, the surrender, the hate."

He paused.

"Mind," he began again, lifting one arm from the elbow, the palm of the hand outwards, so that, with his legs folded before him, he had the pose of a Buddha preaching in European clothes and without a lotus-flower—"Mind, none of us would feel exactly like this. What saves us is efficiency—the devotion to efficiency. But these chaps were not much account, really. They were no colonists; their administration was merely a squeeze, and nothing more, I suspect. They were conquerors, and for that you want only brute force—nothing to boast of, when you have it, since your strength is just an accident arising from the weakness of others. They grabbed what they could get for the sake of what was to be got. It was just robbery with violence, aggravated murder on a great scale, and men going at it blind—as is very proper for those who tackle a darkness. The conquest of the earth, which mostly means the taking it away from those who have a different complexion or slightly flatter noses than ourselves, is not a pretty thing when you look into it too much. What redeems it is the idea only. An idea at the back of it; not a sentimental pretence but an idea; and an unselfish belief in the idea—something you can set up, and bow down before, and offer a sacrifice to. . . ."

He broke off. Flames glided in the river, small green flames, red flames, white flames, pursuing, overtaking, joining, crossing each other—then separating slowly or hastily. The traffic of the great city went on in the deepening night upon the sleepless river. We looked on, waiting patiently—there was nothing else to do till the end of the flood; but it was only after a long silence, when he said, in a hesitating voice, "I suppose you fellows remember I did once turn fresh-water sailor for a bit," that we knew we were fated, before the ebb began to run, to hear about one of Marlow's inconclusive experiences.

"I don't want to bother you much with what happened to me personally," he began, showing in this remark the weakness of many tellers of tales who seem so often unaware of what their audience would best like to hear; "yet to understand the effect of it on me you ought to know how I got out there, what I saw, how I went up that river to the place where I first met the poor chap. It was the farthest point of navigation and the culminating point of my experience. It seemed somehow to throw a kind of light on everything about me—and into my thoughts. It was sombre enough too—and pitiful—not extraordinary in any way—not very clear either. No, not very clear. And yet it seemed to throw a kind of light.

"I had then, as you remember, just returned to London after a lot of Indian Ocean, Pacific, China Seas—a regular dose of the East—six years or so, and I was loafing about, hindering you fellows in your work and invading your homes, just as though I had got a heavenly mission to civilise you. It was very fine for a time, but after a bit I did get tired of resting. Then I began to look for a ship—I should think the hardest work on earth. But the ships wouldn't even look at me. And I got tired of that game too.

"Now when I was a little chap I had a passion for maps. I would look for hours at South America, or Africa, or Australia, and lose myself in all the glories of exploration. At that time there were many blank spaces on the earth, and when I saw one that looked particularly inviting on a map (but they all look that) I would put my finger on it and say, When I grow up I will go there. The North Pole was one of these places, I remember. Well, I haven't been there yet, and shall not try now. The glamour's off. Other places were scattered about the Equator, and in every sort of latitude all over the two hemispheres. I have been in some of them, and . . . well, we won't talk about that. But there was one yet—the biggest, the most blank, so to speak—that I had a hankering after.

"True, by this time it was not a blank space any more. It had got filled since my boyhood with rivers and lakes and names. It had ceased to be a blank space of delightful mystery—a white patch for a boy to dream gloriously over. It had become a place of darkness. But there was in it one river especially, a mighty big river, that you could see on the map, resembling an immense snake uncoiled, with its head in the sea, its body at rest curving afar over a vast country, and its tail lost in the depths of the land. And as I looked at the map of it in a shop-window, it fascinated me as a snake would a bird—a silly little bird. Then I remembered there was a big concern, a Company for trade on that river. Dash it all! I thought to myself, they can't trade without using some kind of craft on that lot of fresh water—steamboats! Why shouldn't I try to get charge of one. I went on along Fleet Street, but could not shake off the idea. The snake had charmed me.

"You understand it was a Continental concern, that Trading Society; but I have a lot of relations living on the Continent, because it's cheap and not so nasty as it looks, they say.

"I am sorry to own I began to worry them. This was already a fresh departure for me. I was not used to get things that way, you know. I always went my own road and on my own legs where I had a mind to go. I wouldn't have believed it of myself; but, then—you see—I felt somehow I must get there by hook or by crook. So I worried them. The men said 'My dear fellow,' and did nothing. Then—would you believe it?—I tried the women. I, Charlie Marlow, set the women to work—to get a job. Heavens! Well, you see, the notion drove me. I had an aunt, a dear enthusiastic soul. She wrote: 'It will be delightful. I am ready to do anything, anything for you. It is a glorious idea. I know the wife of a very high personage in the Administration, and also a man who has lots of influence with,' &c., &c. She was determined to make no end of fuss to get me appointed skipper of a river steamboat, if such was my fancy.

"I got my appointment—of course; and I got it very quick. It appears the Company had received news that one of their captains had been killed in a scuffle with the natives. This was my chance, and it made me the more anxious to go. It was only months and months afterwards, when I made the attempt to recover what was left of the body, that I heard the original quarrel arose from a misunderstanding about some hens. Yes, two black hens. Fresleven—

that was the fellow's name, a Dane—thought himself wronged somehow in the bargain, so he went ashore and started to hammer the chief of the village with a stick. Oh, it didn't surprise me in the least to hear this, and at the same time to be told that Fresleven was the gentlest, quietest creature that ever walked on two legs. No doubt he was; but he had been a couple of years already out there engaged in the noble cause, you know, and he probably felt the need at last of asserting his self-respect in some way. Therefore he whacked the old nigger mercilessly, while a big crowd of his people watched him, thunderstruck, till some man,—I was told the chief's son,—in desperation at hearing the old chap yell, made a tentative jab with a spear at the white man—and of course it went quite easy between the shoulder-blades. Then the whole population cleared into the forest, expecting all kinds of calamities to happen, while, on the other hand, the steamer Fresleven commanded left also in a bad panic, in charge of the engineer, I believe. Afterwards nobody seemed to trouble much about Fresleven's remains, till I got out and stepped into his shoes. I couldn't let it rest, though; but when an opportunity offered at last to meet my predecessor, the grass growing through his ribs was tall enough to hide his bones. They were all there. The supernatural being had not been touched after he fell. And the village was deserted, the huts gaped black, rotting, all askew within the fallen enclosures. A calamity had come to it, sure enough. The people had vanished. Mad terror had scattered them, men, women, and children, through the bush, and they had never returned. What became of the hens I don't know either. I should think the cause of progress got them, anyhow. However, through this glorious affair I got my appointment, before I had fairly begun to hope for it.

"I flew around like mad to get ready, and before forty-eight hours I was crossing the Channel to show myself to my employers, and sign the contract. In a very few hours I arrived in a city that always makes me think of a whited sepulchre.[8] Prejudice no doubt. I had no difficulty in finding the Company's offices. It was the biggest thing in the town, and everybody I met was full of it. They were going to run an over-sea empire, and make no end of coin by trade.

[8]Brussels was the headquarters of the Société Anonyme Belge pour le Commerce du Haut-Congo (Belgian Corporation for Trade in the Upper Congo), with which Conrad obtained his post through the influence of his aunt, Marguerite Poradowska.

"A narrow and deserted street in deep shadow, high houses, innumerable windows with venetian blinds, a dead silence, grass sprouting between the stones, imposing carriage archways right and left, immense double doors standing ponderously ajar. I slipped through one of these cracks, went up a swept and ungarnished staircase, as arid as a desert, and opened the first door I came to. Two women, one fat and the other slim, sat on straw-bottomed chairs, knitting black wool. The slim one got up and walked straight at me—still knitting with downcast eyes—and only just as I began to think of getting out of her way, as you would for a somnambulist, stood still, and looked up. Her dress was as plain as an umbrella-cover, and she turned round without a word and preceded me into a waiting-room. I gave my name, and looked about. Deal table in the middle, plain chairs all round the walls, on one end a large shining map, marked with all the colours of a rainbow. There was a vast amount of red—good to see at any time, because one knows that some real work is done in there, a deuce of a lot of blue, a little green, smears of orange, and, on the East Coast, a purple patch, to show where the jolly pioneers of progress drink the jolly lager-beer.[9] However, I wasn't going into any of these. I was going into the yellow. Dead in the centre. And the river was there—fascinating—deadly—like a snake. Ough! A door opened, a white-haired secretarial head, but wearing a compassionate expression, appeared, and a skinny forefinger beckoned me into the sanctuary. Its light was dim, and a heavy writing-desk squatted in the middle. From behind that structure came out an impression of pale plumpness in a frock-coat. The great man himself. He was five feet six, I should judge, and had his grip on the handle-end of ever so many millions. He shook hands, I fancy, murmured vaguely, was satisfied with my French. *Bon voyage.*

"In about forty-five seconds I found myself again in the waiting-room with the compassionate secretary, who, full of desolation and sympathy, made me sign some document. I believe I undertook amongst other things not to disclose any trade secrets. Well, I am not going to.

"I began to feel slightly uneasy. You know I am not used to such ceremonies, and there was something ominous in the atmos-

[9]British territories were traditionally marked in red on colonial maps; lager was originally a Continental beer, not much drunk in England.

phere. It was just as though I had been let into some conspiracy—I don't know—something not quite right; and I was glad to get out. In the outer room the two women knitted black wool feverishly. People were arriving, and the younger one was walking back and forth introducing them. The old one sat on her chair. Her flat cloth slippers were propped up on a foot-warmer, and a cat reposed on her lap. She wore a starched white affair on her head, had a wart on one cheek, and silver-rimmed spectacles hung on the tip of her nose. She glanced at me above the glasses. The swift and indifferent placidity of that look troubled me. Two youths with foolish and cheery countenances were being piloted over, and she threw at them the same quick glance of unconcerned wisdom. She seemed to know all about them and about me too. An eerie feeling came over me. She seemed uncanny and fateful. Often far away there I thought of these two, guarding the door of Darkness, knitting black wool as for a warm pall, one introducing, introducing continuously to the unknown, the other scrutinising the cheery and foolish faces with unconcerned old eyes. *Ave!* Old knitter of black wool. *Morituri te salutant.*[10] Not many of those she looked at ever saw her again—not half, by a long way.

"There was yet a visit to the doctor. 'A simple formality,' assured me the secretary, with an air of taking an immense part in all my sorrows. Accordingly a young chap wearing his hat over the left eyebrow, some clerk I suppose,—there must have been clerks in the business, though the house was as still as a house in a city of the dead,—came from somewhere upstairs, and led me forth. He was shabby and careless, with ink-stains on the sleeves of his jacket, and his cravat was large and billowy, under a chin shaped like the toe of an old boot. It was a little too early for the doctor, so I proposed a drink, and thereupon he developed a vein of joviality. As we sat over our vermouths he glorified the Company's business, and by-and-by I expressed casually my surprise at him not going out there. He became very cool and collected all at once. 'I am not such a fool as I look, quoth Plato to his disciples,' he said sententiously, emptied his glass with great resolution, and we rose.

"The old doctor felt my pulse, evidently thinking of something else the while. 'Good, good for there,' he mumbled, and then with

[10]Hail! . . . Those who are about to die salute you!—traditional cry of Roman gladiators.

a certain eagerness asked me whether I would let him measure my head. Rather surprised, I said Yes, when he produced a thing like calipers and got the dimensions back and front and every way, taking notes carefully. He was an unshaven little man in a threadbare coat like a gaberdine, with his feet in slippers, and I thought him a harmless fool. 'I always ask leave, in the interests of science, to measure the crania of those going out there,' he said. 'And when they come back too?' I asked. 'Oh, I never see them,' he remarked; 'and moreover, the changes take place inside, you know.' He smiled, as if at some quiet joke. 'So you are going out there. Famous. Interesting too.' He gave me a searching glance, and made another note. 'Ever any madness in your family?' he asked, in a matter-of-fact tone. I felt very annoyed. 'Is that question in the interests of science too?' 'It would be,' he said, without taking notice of my irritation, 'interesting for science to watch the mental changes of individuals, on the spot, but . . .' 'Are you an alienist?'[11] I interrupted. 'Every doctor should be—a little,' answered that original, imperturbably. 'I have a little theory which you Messieurs who go out there must help me to prove. This is my share in the advantages my country shall reap from the possession of such a magnificent dependency. The mere wealth I leave to others. Pardon my questions, but you are the first Englishman coming under my observation . . .' I hastened to assure him I was not in the least typical. 'If I were,' said I, 'I wouldn't be talking like this with you.' 'What you say is rather profound, and probably erroneous,' he said, with a laugh. 'Avoid irritation more than exposure to the sun. Adieu. How do you English say, eh? Good-bye. Ah! Good-bye. Adieu. In the tropics one must before everything keep calm.' . . . He lifted a warning forefinger. . . . '*Du calme, du calme. Adieu.*'

"One thing more remained to do—say good-bye to my excellent aunt. I found her triumphant. I had a cup of tea—the last decent cup of tea for many days—and in a room that most soothingly looked just as you would expect a lady's drawing-room to look, we had a long quiet chat by the fireside. In the course of these confidences it became quite plain to me I had been represented to the wife of the high dignitary, and goodness knows to how many more people besides, as an exceptional and gifted creature—

[11]A psychologist.

a piece of good fortune for the Company—a man you don't get hold of every day. Good heavens! and I was going to take charge of a twopenny-half-penny river-steamboat with a penny whistle attached! It appeared, however, I was also one of the Workers, with a capital—you know. Something like an emissary of light, something like a lower sort of apostle. There had been a lot of such rot let loose in print and talk just about that time, and the excellent woman, living right in the rush of all that humbug, got carried off her feet. She talked about 'weaning those ignorant millions from their horrid ways,' till, upon my word, she made me quite uncomfortable. I ventured to hint that the Company was run for profit.

"'You forget, dear Charlie, that the labourer is worthy of his hire,' she said, brightly.[12] It's queer how out of touch with truth women are. They live in a world of their own, and there had never been anything like it, and never can be. It is too beautiful altogether, and if they were to set it up it would go to pieces before the first sunset. Some confounded fact we men have been living contentedly with ever since the day of creation would start up and knock the whole thing over.

"After this I got embraced, told to wear flannel, be sure to write often, and so on—and I left. In the street—I don't know why—a queer feeling came to me that I was an impostor. Odd thing that I, who used to clear out for any part of the world at twenty-four hours' notice, with less thought than most men give to the crossing of a street, had a moment—I won't say of hesitation, but of startled pause, before this commonplace affair. The best way I can explain it to you is by saying that, for a second or two, I felt as though, instead of going to the centre of a continent, I were about to set off for the centre of the earth.

"I left in a French steamer, and she called in every blamed port they have out there, for, as far as I could see, the sole purpose of landing soldiers and custom-house officers. I watched the coast. Watching a coast as it slips by the ship is like thinking about an enigma. There it is before you—smiling, frowning, inviting, grand, mean, insipid, or savage, and always mute with an air of whispering, Come and find out. This one was almost featureless, as if still

---

[12] 1 Timothy 5:18.

in the making, with an aspect of monotonous grimness. The edge of a colossal jungle, so dark-green as to be almost black, fringed with white surf, ran straight, like a ruled line, far, far away along a blue sea whose glitter was blurred by a creeping mist. The sun was fierce, the land seemed to glisten and drip with steam. Here and there greyish-whitish specks showed up, clustered inside the white surf, with a flag flying above them perhaps—settlements some centuries old, and still no bigger than pin-heads on the untouched expanse of their background. We pounded along, stopped, landed soldiers; went on, landed custom-house clerks to levy toll in what looked like a Godforsaken wilderness, with a tin shed and a flagpole lost in it; landed more soldiers—to take care of the custom-house clerks, presumably. Some, I heard, got drowned in the surf; but whether they did or not, nobody seemed particularly to care. They were just flung out there, and on we went. Every day the coast looked the same, as though we had not moved; but we passed various places—trading places—with names like Gran' Bassam, Little Popo,[13] names that seemed to belong to some sordid farce acted in front of a sinister backcloth. The idleness of a passenger, my isolation amongst all these men with whom I had no point of contact, the oily and languid sea, the uniform sombreness of the coast, seemed to keep me away from the truth of things, within the toil of a mournful and senseless delusion. The voice of the surf heard now and then was a positive pleasure, like the speech of a brother. It was something natural, that had its reason, that had a meaning. Now and then a boat from the shore gave one a momentary contact with reality. It was paddled by black fellows. You could see from afar the white of their eyeballs glistening. They shouted, sang; their bodies streamed with perspiration; they had faces like grotesque masks—these chaps; but they had bone, muscle, a wild vitality, an intense energy of movement, that was as natural and true as the surf along their coast. They wanted no excuse for being there. They were a great comfort to look at. For a time I would feel I belonged still to a world of straightforward facts; but the feeling would not last long. Something would turn up to scare it away. Once, I remember, we came upon a man-of-war anchored off the coast. There wasn't even a shed there, and she was shelling

[13]Grand Bassam and Grand Popo are the names of ports where Conrad's ship called on its way to the Congo.

the bush. It appears the French had one of their wars going on thereabouts. Her ensign dropped limp like a rag; the muzzles of the long eight-inch guns stuck out all over the low hull; the greasy, slimy swell swung her up lazily and let her down, swaying her thin masts. In the empty immensity of earth, sky, and water, there she was, incomprehensible, firing into a continent. Pop, would go one of the eight-inch guns; a small flame would dart and vanish, a little white smoke would disappear, a tiny projectile would give a feeble screech—and nothing happened. Nothing could happen. There was a touch of insanity in the proceeding, a sense of lugubrious drollery in the sight; and it was not dissipated by somebody on board assuring me earnestly there was a camp of natives—he called them enemies!—hidden out of sight somewhere.

"We gave her letters (I heard the men in that lonely ship were dying of fever at the rate of three a day) and went on. We called at some more places with farcical names, where the merry dance of death and trade goes on in a still and earthy atmosphere as of an overheated catacomb[14]; all along the formless coast bordered by dangerous surf, as if Nature herself had tried to ward off intruders; in and out of rivers, streams of death in life, whose banks were rotting into mud, whose waters, thickened into slime, invaded the contorted mangroves, that seemed to writhe at us in the extremity of an impotent despair. Nowhere did we stop long enough to get a particularised impression, but the general sense of vague and oppressive wonder grew upon me. It was like a weary pilgrimage amongst hints for nightmares.

"It was upward of thirty days before I saw the mouth of the big river. We anchored off the seat of the government. But my work would not begin till some two hundred miles farther on. So as soon as I could I made a start for a place thirty miles higher up.

"I had my passage on a little sea-going steamer. Her captain was a Swede, and knowing me for a seaman, invited me on the bridge. He was a young man, lean, fair, and morose, with lanky

---

[14]In a letter in May 1890 Conrad wrote: "What makes me rather uneasy is the information that 60 per cent. of our Company's employés return to Europe before they have completed even six months' service. Fever and dysentery! There are others who are sent home in a hurry at the end of a year, so that they shouldn't die in the Congo." According to a 1907 report, 150 out of every 2,000 native Congolese laborers died each month while in company employ; "All along the [railroad] track one would see corpses."

hair and a shuffling gait. As we left the miserable little wharf, he tossed his head contemptuously at the shore. 'Been living there?' he asked. I said, 'Yes.' 'Fine lot these government chaps—are they not?' he went on, speaking English with great precision and considerable bitterness. 'It is funny what some people will do for a few francs a month. I wonder what becomes of that kind when it goes up country?' I said to him I expected to see that soon. 'So-o-o!' he exclaimed. He shuffled athwart, keeping one eye ahead vigilantly. 'Don't be too sure,' he continued. 'The other day I took up a man who hanged himself on the road. He was a Swede, too.' 'Hanged himself! Why, in God's name?' I cried. He kept on looking out watchfully. 'Who knows? The sun too much for him, or the country perhaps.'

"At last we opened a reach. A rocky cliff appeared, mounds of turned-up earth by the shore, houses on a hill, others, with iron roofs, amongst a waste of excavations, or hanging to the declivity. A continuous noise of the rapids above hovered over this scene of inhabited devastation. A lot of people, mostly black and naked, moved about like ants. A jetty projected into the river. A blinding sunlight drowned all this at times in a sudden recrudescence of glare. 'There's your Company's station,' said the Swede, pointing to three wooden barrack-like structures on the rocky slope. 'I will send your things up. Four boxes did you say? So. Farewell.'

"I came upon a boiler wallowing in the grass, then found a path leading up the hill. It turned aside for the boulders, and also for an undersized railway-truck lying there on its back with its wheels in the air. One was off. The thing looked as dead as the carcass of some animal. I came upon more pieces of decaying machinery, a stack of rusty rails. To the left a clump of trees made a shady spot, where dark things seemed to stir feebly. I blinked, the path was steep. A horn tooted to the right, and I saw the black people run. A heavy and dull detonation shook the ground, a puff of smoke came out of the cliff, and that was all. No change appeared on the face of the rock. They were building a railway. The cliff was not in the way or anything; but this objectless blasting was all the work going on.

"A slight clinking behind me made me turn my head. Six black men advanced in a file, toiling up the path. They walked erect and slow, balancing small baskets full of earth on their heads, and the clink kept time with their footsteps. Black rags were wound round their loins, and the short ends behind wagged to and fro like tails. I could see every rib, the joints of their limbs were like knots in a rope; each had an iron collar on his neck, and all were connected together with a chain whose bights swung between them, rhythmically clinking. Another report from the cliff made me think suddenly of that ship of war I had seen firing into a continent. It was the same kind of ominous voice; but these men could by no stretch of imagination be called enemies. They were called criminals, and the outraged law, like the bursting shells, had come to them, an insoluble mystery from over the sea. All their meagre breasts panted together, the violently dilated nostrils quivered, the eyes stared stonily up-hill. They passed me within six inches, without a glance, with that complete, deathlike indifference of unhappy savages. Behind this raw matter one of the reclaimed, the product of the new forces at work, strolled despondently, carrying a rifle by its middle. He had a uniform jacket with one button off, and seeing a white man on the path, hoisted his weapon to his shoulder with alacrity. This was simple prudence, white men being so much alike at a distance that he could not tell who I might be. He was speedily reassured, and with a large, white, rascally grin, and a glance at his charge, seemed to take me into partnership in his exalted trust. After all, I also was a part of the great cause of these high and just proceedings.

"Instead of going up, I turned and descended to the left. My idea was to let that chain-gang get out of sight before I climbed the hill. You know I am not particularly tender; I've had to strike and to fend off. I've had to resist and to attack sometimes—that's only one way of resisting—without counting the exact cost, according to the demands of such sort of life as I had blundered into. I've seen the devil of violence, and the devil of greed, and the devil of hot desire; but, by all the stars! these were strong, lusty, red-eyed devils, that swayed and drove men—men, I tell you. But as I stood on this hillside, I foresaw that in the blinding sunshine of that land I would become acquainted with a flabby, pretending, weak-eyed devil of a rapacious and pitiless folly. How insidious he could be, too, I was only to find out several months later and a thousand miles farther. For a moment I stood appalled, as though by a warning. Finally I descended the hill, obliquely, towards the trees I had seen.

"I avoided a vast artificial hole somebody had been digging on the slope, the purpose of which I found it impossible to divine. It wasn't a quarry or a sandpit, anyhow. It was just a hole. It might have been connected with the philanthropic desire of giving the criminals something to do. I don't know. Then I nearly fell into a very narrow ravine, almost no more than a scar in the hillside. I discovered that a lot of imported drainage-pipes for the settlement had been tumbled in there. There wasn't one that was not broken. It was a wanton smash-up. At last I got under the trees. My purpose was to stroll into the shade for a moment; but no sooner within than it seemed to me I had stepped into the gloomy circle of some Inferno. The rapids were near, and an uninterrupted, uniform, headlong, rushing noise filled the mournful stillness of the grove, where not a breath stirred, not a leaf moved, with a mysterious sound—as though the tearing pace of the launched earth had suddenly become audible.

"Black shapes crouched, lay, sat between the trees, leaning against the trunks, clinging to the earth, half coming out, half effaced within the dim light, in all the attitudes of pain, abandonment, and despair. Another mine on the cliff went off, followed by a slight shudder of the soil under my feet. The work was going on. The work! And this was the place where some of the helpers had withdrawn to die.

"They were dying slowly—it was very clear. They were not enemies, they were not criminals, they were nothing earthly now,—nothing but black shadows of disease and starvation, lying confusedly in the greenish gloom. Brought from all the recesses of the coast in all the legality of time contracts, lost in uncongenial surroundings, fed on unfamiliar food, they sickened, became inefficient, and were then allowed to crawl away and rest. These moribund shapes were free as air—and nearly as thin. I began to distinguish the gleam of eyes under the trees. Then, glancing down, I saw a face near my hand. The black bones reclined at full length with one shoulder against the tree, and slowly the eyelids rose and the sunken eyes looked up at me, enormous and vacant, a kind of blind, white flicker in the depths of the orbs, which died out slowly. The man seemed young—almost a boy—but you know with them it's hard to tell. I found nothing else to do but to offer him one of my good Swede's ship's biscuits I had in my pocket. The fingers closed slowly on it and held—there was no other movement and no other glance. He had tied a bit of white worsted round his neck—Why? Where did he get it? Was it a badge—an ornament—a charm—a propitiatory act? Was there any idea at all connected with it? It looked startling round his black neck, this bit of white thread from beyond the seas.

"Near the same tree two more bundles of acute angles sat with their legs drawn up. One, with his chin propped on his knees, stared at nothing, in an intolerable and appalling manner: his brother phantom rested its forehead, as if overcome with a great weariness; and all about others were scattered in every pose of contorted collapse, as in some picture of a massacre or a pestilence. While I stood horror-struck, one of these creatures rose to his hands and knees, and went off on all-fours towards the river to drink. He lapped out of his hand, then sat up in the sunlight, crossing his shins in front of him, and after a time let his woolly head fall on his breastbone.

"I didn't want any more loitering in the shade, and I made haste towards the station. When near the buildings I met a white man, in such an unexpected elegance of get-up that in the first moment I took him for a sort of vision. I saw a high starched collar, white cuffs, a light alpaca jacket, snowy trousers, a clear silk necktie, and varnished boots. No hat. Hair parted, brushed, oiled, under a green-lined parasol held in a big white hand. He was amazing, and had a penholder behind his ear.

"I shook hands with this miracle, and I learned he was the Company's chief accountant, and that all the book-keeping was done at this station. He had come out for a moment, he said, 'to get a breath of fresh air.' The expression sounded wonderfully odd, with its suggestion of sedentary desk-life. I wouldn't have mentioned the fellow to you at all, only it was from his lips that I first heard the name of the man who is so indissolubly connected with the memories of that time. Moreover, I respected the fellow. Yes; I respected his collars, his vast cuffs, his brushed hair. His appearance was certainly that of a hairdresser's dummy; but in the great demoralisation of the land he kept up his appearance. That's backbone. His starched collars and got-up shirt-fronts were achievements of character. He had been out nearly three years; and, later on, I could not help asking him how he managed to sport such linen. He had just the faintest blush, and said modestly, 'I've been teaching one of the native women about the station. It was difficult. She had a distaste for the work.' Thus this man had verily accomplished something. And he was devoted to his books, which were in apple-pie order.

"Everything else in the station was in a muddle,—heads, things, buildings. Strings of dusty niggers with splay feet arrived and departed; a stream of manufactured goods, rubbishy cottons, beads, and brass-wire set into the depths of darkness, and in return came a precious trickle of ivory.

"I had to wait in the station for ten days—an eternity. I lived in a hut in the yard, but to be out of the chaos I would sometimes get into the accountant's office. It was built of horizontal planks, and so badly put together that, as he bent over his high desk, he was barred from neck to heels with narrow strips of sunlight. There was no need to open the big shutter to see. It was hot there too; big flies buzzed fiendishly, and did not sting, but stabbed. I sat generally on the floor, while, of faultless appearance (and even slightly scented), perching on a high stool, he wrote, he wrote. Sometimes he stood up for exercise. When a truckle-bed with a sick man (some invalided agent from up-country) was put in there, he exhibited a gentle annoyance. 'The groans of this sick person,' he said, 'distract my attention. And without that it is extremely difficult to guard against clerical errors in this climate.'

"One day he remarked, without lifting his head, 'In the interior you will no doubt meet Mr Kurtz.' On my asking who Mr Kurtz was, he said he was a first-class agent; and seeing my disappointment at this information, he added slowly, laying down his pen, 'He is a very remarkable person.' Further questions elicited from him that Mr Kurtz was at present in charge of a trading-post, a very important one, in the true ivory-country, at 'the very bottom of there. Sends in as much ivory as all the others put together . . .' He began to write again. The sick man was too ill to groan. The flies buzzed in a great peace.

"Suddenly there was a growing murmur of voices and a great tramping of feet. A caravan had come in. A violent babble of uncouth sounds burst out on the other side of the planks. All the carriers were speaking together, and in the midst of the uproar the lamentable voice of the chief agent was heard 'giving it up' tearfully for the twentieth time that day. . . . He rose slowly. 'What a frightful row,' he said. He crossed the room gently to look at the sick man, and returning, said to me, 'He does not hear.' 'What! Dead?' I asked, startled. 'No, not yet,' he answered, with great composure. Then, alluding with a toss of the head to the tumult in the station-yard, 'When one has got to make correct entries, one comes to hate those savages—hate them to the death.' He remained thoughtful for a moment. 'When you see Mr Kurtz,' he went on, 'tell him from me that everything here'—he glanced at the desk—'is very satisfactory. I don't like to write to him—with those messengers of ours you never know who may get hold of your letter—at that Central Station.' He stared at me for a moment with his mild, bulging eyes. 'Oh, he will go far, very far,' he began again. 'He will be a somebody in the Administration before long. They, above—the Council in Europe, you know—mean him to be.'

"He turned to his work. The noise outside had ceased, and presently in going out I stopped at the door. In the steady buzz of flies the homeward-bound agent was lying flushed and insensible; the other, bent over his books, was making correct entries of perfectly correct transactions; and fifty feet below the doorstep I could see the still tree-tops of the grove of death.

"Next day I left that station at last, with a caravan of sixty men, for a two-hundred-mile tramp.

"No use telling you much about that. Paths, paths, everywhere; a stamped-in network of paths spreading over the empty land, through long grass, through burnt grass, through thickets, down and up chilly ravines, up and down stony hills ablaze with heat; and a solitude, a solitude, nobody, not a hut. The population had cleared out a long time ago. Well, if a lot of mysterious niggers armed with all kinds of fearful weapons suddenly took to travelling on the road between Deal[15] and Gravesend, catching the yokels right and left to carry heavy loads for them, I fancy every farm and cottage thereabouts would get empty very soon. Only here the dwellings were gone too. Still, I passed through several abandoned villages. There's something pathetically childish in the ruins of grass walls. Day after day, with the stamp and shuffle of

[15]An English port.

sixty pair of bare feet behind me, each pair under a 60-lb. load. Camp, cook, sleep, strike camp, march. Now and then a carrier dead in harness, at rest in the long grass near the path, with an empty water-gourd and his long staff lying by his side. A great silence around and above. Perhaps on some quiet night the tremor of far-off drums, sinking, swelling, a tremor vast, faint; a sound weird, appealing, suggestive, and wild—and perhaps with as profound a meaning as the sound of bells in a Christian country. Once a white man in an unbuttoned uniform, camping on the path with an armed escort of lank Zanzibaris,[16] very hospitable and festive— not to say drunk. Was looking after the upkeep of the road, he declared. Can't say I saw any road or any upkeep, unless the body of a middle-aged negro, with a bullet-hole in the forehead, upon which I absolutely stumbled three miles farther on, may be considered as a permanent improvement. I had a white companion too, not a bad chap, but rather too fleshy and with the exasperating habit of fainting on the hot hillsides, miles away from the least bit of shade and water. Annoying, you know, to hold your own coat like a parasol over a man's head while he is coming-to. I couldn't help asking him once what he meant by coming there at all. 'To make money, of course. What do you think?' he said, scornfully. Then he got fever, and had to be carried in a hammock slung under a pole. As he weighed sixteen stone I had no end of rows with the carriers. They jibbed, ran away, sneaked off with their loads in the night—quite a mutiny. So, one evening, I made a speech in English with gestures, not one of which was lost to the sixty pairs of eyes before me, and the next morning I started the hammock off in front all right. An hour afterwards I came upon the whole concern wrecked in a bush—man, hammock, groans, blankets, horrors. The heavy pole had skinned his poor nose. He was very anxious for me to kill somebody, but there wasn't the shadow of a carrier near. I remembered the old doctor,—'It would be interesting for science to watch the mental changes of individuals, on the spot.' I felt I was becoming scientifically interesting. However, all that is to no purpose. On the fifteenth day I came in sight of the big river again, and hobbled into the Central Station. It was on a back water surrounded by scrub and forest, with a pretty border of smelly

---

[16]Africans from Zanzibar, in East Africa; they were widely used as mercenaries.

mud on one side, and on the three others enclosed by a crazy fence of rushes. A neglected gap was all the gate it had, and the first glance at the place was enough to let you see the flabby devil was running that show. White men with long staves in their hands appeared languidly from amongst the buildings, strolling up to take a look at me, and then retired out of sight somewhere. One of them, a stout, excitable chap with black moustaches, informed me with great volubility and many digressions, as soon as I told him who I was, that my steamer was at the bottom of the river. I was thunderstruck. What, how, why? Oh, it was 'all right.' The 'manager himself' was there. All quite correct. 'Everybody had behaved splendidly! splendidly!'—'You must,' he said in agitation, 'go and see the general manager at once. He is waiting!'

"I did not see the real significance of that wreck at once. I fancy I see it now, but I am not sure—not at all. Certainly the affair was too stupid—when I think of it—to be altogether natural. Still. . . . But at the moment it presented itself simply as a confounded nuisance. The steamer was sunk. They had started two days before in a sudden hurry up the river with the manager on board, in charge of some volunteer skipper, and before they had been out three hours they tore the bottom out of her on stones, and she sank near the south bank. I asked myself what I was to do there, now my boat was lost. As a matter of fact, I had plenty to do in fishing my command out of the river. I had to set about it the very next day. That, and the repairs when I brought the pieces to the station, took some months.

"My first interview with the manager was curious. He did not ask me to sit down after my twenty-mile walk that morning. He was commonplace in complexion, in feature, in manners, and in voice. He was of middle size and of ordinary build. His eyes, of the usual blue, were perhaps remarkably cold, and he certainly could make his glance fall on one as trenchant and heavy as an axe. But even at these times the rest of his person seemed to disclaim the intention. Otherwise there was only an indefinable, faint expression of his lips, something stealthy—a smile—not a smile—I remember it, but I can't explain. It was unconscious, this smile was, though just after he had said something it got intensified for an instant. It came at the end of his speeches like a seal applied on the words to make the meaning of the commonest phrase appear absolutely inscrutable. He was a common trader, from his youth up employed in these parts—nothing more. He was obeyed, yet he inspired neither love nor fear, nor even respect. He inspired uneasiness. That was it! Uneasiness. Not a definite mistrust—just uneasiness—nothing more. You have no idea how effective such a ... a ... faculty can be. He had no genius for organising, for initiative, or for order even. That was evident in such things as the deplorable state of the station. He had no learning, and no intelligence. His position had come to him—why? Perhaps because he was never ill ... He had served three terms of three years out there ... Because triumphant health in the general rout of constitutions is a kind of power in itself. When he went home on leave he rioted on a large scale—pompously. Jack ashore—with a difference—in externals only. This one could gather from his casual talk. He originated nothing, he could keep the routine going—that's all. But he was great. He was great by this little thing that it was impossible to tell what could control such a man. He never gave that secret away. Perhaps there was nothing within him. Such a suspicion made one pause—for out there there were no external checks. Once when various tropical diseases had laid low almost every 'agent' in the station, he was heard to say, 'Men who come out here should have no entrails.' He sealed the utterance with that smile of his, as though it had been a door opening into a darkness he had in his keeping. You fancied you had seen things—but the seal was on. When annoyed at meal-times by the constant quarrels of the white men about precedence, he ordered an immense round table to be made, for which a special house had to be built. This was the station's mess-room. Where he sat was the first place—the rest were nowhere. One felt this to be his unalterable conviction. He was neither civil nor uncivil. He was quiet. He allowed his 'boy'—an overfed young negro from the coast—to treat the white men, under his very eyes, with provoking insolence.

"He began to speak as soon as he saw me. I had been very long on the road. He could not wait. Had to start without me. The up-river stations had to be relieved. There had been so many delays already that he did not know who was dead and who was alive, and how they got on—and so on, and so on. He paid no attention to my explanations, and, playing with a stick of sealing-wax, repeated several times that the situation was 'very grave, very grave.' There were rumours that a very important station was in jeopardy, and its chief, Mr Kurtz, was ill. Hoped it was not true. Mr Kurtz was . . . I felt weary and irritable. Hang Kurtz, I thought. I interrupted him by saying I had heard of Mr Kurtz on the coast. 'Ah! So they talk of him down there,' he murmured to himself. Then he began again, assuring me Mr Kurtz was the best agent he had, an exceptional man, of the greatest importance to the Company; therefore I could understand his anxiety. He was, he said, 'very, very uneasy.' Certainly he fidgeted on his chair a good deal, exclaimed, 'Ah, Mr Kurtz!' broke the stick of sealing-wax and seemed dumbfounded by the accident. Next thing he wanted to know 'how long it would take to' . . . I interrupted him again. Being hungry, you know, and kept on my feet too, I was getting savage. 'How can I tell?' I said. 'I haven't even seen the wreck yet—some months, no doubt.' All this talk seemed to me so futile. 'Some months,' he said. 'Well, let us say three months before we can make a start. Yes. That ought to do the affair.' I flung out of his hut (he lived all alone in a clay hut with a sort of verandah) muttering to myself my opinion of him. He was a chattering idiot. Afterwards I took it back when it was borne in upon me startlingly with what extreme nicety he had estimated the time requisite for the 'affair.'

"I went to work the next day, turning, so to speak, my back on that station. In that way only it seemed to me I could keep my hold on the redeeming facts of life. Still, one must look about sometimes; and then I saw this station, these men strolling aimlessly about in the sunshine of the yard. I asked myself sometimes what it all meant. They wandered here and there with their absurd long staves in their hands, like a lot of faithless pilgrims bewitched inside a rotten fence. The word 'ivory' rang in the air, was whispered, was sighed. You would think they were praying to it. A taint of imbecile rapacity blew through it all, like a whiff from some corpse. By Jove! I've never seen anything so unreal in my life. And outside, the silent wilderness surrounding this cleared speck on the earth struck me as something great and invincible, like evil or truth, waiting patiently for the passing away of this fantastic invasion.

"Oh, those months! Well, never mind. Various things happened. One evening a grass shed full of calico, cotton prints, beads, and I don't know what else, burst into a blaze so suddenly that you would have thought the earth had opened to let an avenging fire consume all that trash. I was smoking my pipe quietly by my dismantled steamer, and saw them all cutting capers in the light, with their arms lifted high, when the stout man with moustaches came tearing down to the river, a tin pail in his hand, assured me that everybody was 'behaving splendidly, splendidly,' dipped about a quart of water and tore back again. I noticed there was a hole in the bottom of his pail.

"I strolled up. There was no hurry. You see the thing had gone off like a box of matches. It had been hopeless from the very first. The flame had leaped high, driven everybody back, lighted up everything—and collapsed. The shed was already a heap of embers glowing fiercely. A nigger was being beaten near by. They said he had caused the fire in some way; be that as it may, he was screeching most horribly. I saw him, later on, for several days, sitting in a bit of shade looking very sick and trying to recover himself: afterwards he arose and went out—and the wilderness without a sound took him into its bosom again. As I approached the glow from the dark I found myself at the back of two men, talking. I heard the name of Kurtz pronounced, then the words, 'take advantage of this unfortunate accident.' One of the men was the manager. I wished him a good evening. 'Did you ever see anything like it—eh? it is incredible,' he said, and walked off. The other man remained. He was a first-class agent, young, gentlemanly, a bit reserved, with a forked little beard and a hooked nose. He was stand-offish with the other agents, and they on their side said he was the manager's spy upon them. As to me, I had hardly ever spoken to him before. We got into talk, and by-and-by we strolled away from the hissing ruins. Then he asked me to his room, which was in the main building of the station. He struck a match, and I perceived that this young aristocrat had not only a silver-mounted dressing-case but also a whole candle all to himself. Just at that time the manager was the only man supposed to have any right to candles. Native mats covered the clay walls; a collection of spears, assegais,[17] shields, knives was hung up in trophies. The business intrusted to this fellow was the making of bricks—so I had been informed; but there wasn't a fragment of a brick anywhere in the station, and he

[17]Slender African spears.

had been there more than a year—waiting. It seems he could not make bricks without something, I don't know what—straw maybe. Anyway, it could not be found there, and as it was not likely to be sent from Europe, it did not appear clear to me what he was waiting for. An act of special creation perhaps. However, they were all waiting—all the sixteen or twenty pilgrims of them—for something; and upon my word it did not seem an uncongenial occupation, from the way they took it, though the only thing that ever came to them was disease—as far as I could see. They beguiled the time by backbiting and intriguing against each other in a foolish kind of way. There was an air of plotting about that station, but nothing came of it, of course. It was as unreal as everything else—as the philanthropic pretence of the whole concern, as their talk, as their government, as their show of work. The only real feeling was a desire to get appointed to a trading-post where ivory was to be had, so that they could earn percentages. They intrigued and slandered and hated each other only on that account,—but as to effectually lifting a little finger—oh, no. By heavens! there is something after all in the world allowing one man to steal a horse while another must not look at a halter. Steal a horse straight out. Very well. He has done it. Perhaps he can ride. But there is a way of looking at a halter that would provoke the most charitable of saints into a kick.

"I had no idea why he wanted to be sociable, but as we chatted in there it suddenly occurred to me the fellow was trying to get at something—in fact, pumping me. He alluded constantly to Europe, to the people I was supposed to know there—putting leading questions as to my acquaintances in the sepulchral city, and so on. His little eyes glittered like mica discs—with curiosity,—though he tried to keep up a bit of superciliousness. At first I was astonished, but very soon I became awfully curious to see what he would find out from me. I couldn't possibly imagine what I had in me to make it worth his while. It was very pretty to see how he baffled himself, for in truth my body was full of chills, and my head had nothing in it but that wretched steamboat business. It was evident he took me for a perfectly shameless prevaricator. At last he got angry, and, to conceal a movement of furious annoyance, he yawned. I rose. Then I noticed a small sketch in oils, on a panel, representing a woman, draped and blind-folded, carrying a lighted torch. The background was sombre—almost black. The movement of the woman was stately, and the effect of the torchlight on the face was sinister.

"It arrested me, and he stood by civilly, holding a half-pint champagne bottle (medical comforts) with the candle stuck in it. To my question he said Mr Kurtz had painted this—in this very station more than a year ago—while waiting for means to go to his trading-post. 'Tell me, pray,' said I, 'who is this Mr Kurtz?'

"'The chief of the Inner Station,' he answered in a short tone, looking away. 'Much obliged,' I said, laughing. 'And you are the brickmaker of the Central Station. Every one knows that.' He was silent for a while. 'He is a prodigy,' he said at last. 'He is an emissary of pity, and science, and progress, and devil knows what else. We want,' he began to declaim suddenly, 'for the guidance of the cause intrusted to us by Europe, so to speak, higher intelligence, wide sympathies, a singleness of purpose.' 'Who says that?' I asked. 'Lots of them,' he replied. 'Some even write that; and so *he* comes here, a special being, as you ought to know.' 'Why ought I to know?' I interrupted, really surprised. He paid no attention. 'Yes. To-day he is chief of the best station, next year he will be assistant-manager, two years more and . . . but I daresay you know what he will be in two years' time. You are of the new gang—the gang of virtue. The same people who sent him specially also recommended you. Oh, don't say no. I've my own eyes to trust.' Light dawned upon me. My dear aunt's influential acquaintances were producing an unexpected effect upon that young man. I nearly burst into a laugh. 'Do you read the Company's confidential correspondence?' I asked. He hadn't a word to say. It was great fun. 'When Mr Kurtz,' I continued severely, 'is General Manager, you won't have the opportunity.'

"He blew the candle out suddenly, and we went outside. The moon had risen. Black figures strolled about listlessly, pouring water on the glow, whence proceeded a sound of hissing; steam ascended in the moonlight; the beaten nigger groaned somewhere. 'What a row the brute makes!' said the indefatigable man with the moustaches, appearing near us. 'Serve him right. Transgression—punishment—bang! Pitiless, pitiless. That's the only way. This will prevent all conflagrations for the future. I was just telling the manager . . .' He noticed my companion, and became crestfallen all at once. 'Not in bed yet,' he said, with a kind of servile heartiness; 'it's so natural.

Ha! Danger—agitation.' He vanished. I went on to the river-side, and the other followed me. I heard a scathing murmur at my ear, 'Heap of muffs—go to.' The pilgrims could be seen in knots gesticulating, discussing. Several had still their staves in their hands. I verily believe they took these sticks to bed with them. Beyond the fence the forest stood up spectrally in the moonlight, and through the dim stir, through the faint sounds of that lamentable courtyard, the silence of the land went home to one's very heart,—its mystery, its greatness, the amazing reality of its concealed life. The hurt nigger moaned feebly somewhere near by, and then fetched a deep sigh that made me mend my pace away from there. I felt a hand introducing itself under my arm. 'My dear sir,' said the fellow, 'I don't want to be misunderstood, and especially by you, who will see Mr Kurtz long before I can have that pleasure. I wouldn't like him to get a false idea of my disposition. . . .'

"I let him run on, this papier-mâché Mephistopheles,[18] and it seemed to me that if I tried I could poke my forefinger through him, and would find nothing inside but a little loose dirt, maybe. He, don't you see, had been planning to be assistant-manager by-and-by under the present man, and I could see that the coming of that Kurtz had upset them both not a little. He talked precipitately, and I did not try to stop him. I had my shoulders against the wreck of my steamer, hauled up on the slope like a carcass of some big river animal. The smell of mud, of primeval mud, by Jove! was in my nostrils, the high stillness of primeval forest was before my eyes; there were shiny patches on the black creek. The moon had spread over everything a thin layer of silver—over the rank grass, over the mud, upon the wall of matted vegetation standing higher than the wall of a temple, over the great river I could see through a sombre gap glittering, glittering, as it flowed broadly by without a murmur. All this was great, expectant, mute, while the man jabbered about himself. I wondered whether the stillness on the face of the immensity looking at us two were meant as an appeal or as a menace. What were we who had strayed in here? Could we handle that dumb thing, or would it handle us? I felt how big, how confoundedly big, was that thing that couldn't talk, and perhaps was deaf as well. What was in there? I could see a little ivory coming

[18]One of the devils who tempts Faust.

out from there, and I had heard Mr Kurtz was in there. I had heard enough about it too—God knows! Yet somehow it didn't bring any image with it—no more than if I had been told an angel or a fiend was in there. I believed it in the same way one of you might believe there are inhabitants in the planet Mars. I knew once a Scotch sail-maker who was certain, dead sure, there were people in Mars. If you asked him for some idea how they looked and behaved, he would get shy and mutter something about 'walking on all-fours.' If you as much as smiled, he would—though a man of sixty—offer to fight you. I would not have gone so far as to fight for Kurtz, but I went for him near enough to a lie. You know I hate, detest, and can't bear a lie, not because I am straighter than the rest of us, but simply because it appals me. There is a taint of death, a flavour of mortality in lies,—which is exactly what I hate and detest in the world—what I want to forget. It makes me miserable and sick, like biting something rotten would do. Temperament, I suppose. Well, I went near enough to it by letting the young fool there believe any-thing he liked to imagine as to my influence in Europe. I became in an instant as much of a pretence as the rest of the bewitched pil-grims. This simply because I had a notion it somehow would be of help to that Kurtz whom at the time I did not see—you under-stand. He was just a word for me. I did not see the man in the name any more than you do. Do you see him? Do you see the sto-ry? Do you see anything? It seems to me I am trying to tell you a dream—making a vain attempt, because no relation of a dream can convey the dream-sensation, that commingling of absurdity, sur-prise, and bewilderment in a tremor of struggling revolt, that notion of being captured by the incredible which is of the very essence of dreams. . . ."

He was silent for a while.

". . . No, it is impossible; it is impossible to convey the life-sensation of any given epoch of one's existence,—that which makes its truth, its meaning—its subtle and penetrating essence. It is im-possible. We live, as we dream—alone. . . ."

He paused again as if reflecting, then added—

"Of course in this you fellows see more than I could then. You see me, whom you know. . . ."

It had become so pitch dark that we listeners could hardly see one another. For a long time already he, sitting apart, had been no more to us than a voice. There was not a word from anybody. The others might have been asleep, but I was awake. I listened, I listened on the watch for the sentence, for the word, that would give me the clue to the faint uneasiness inspired by this narrative that seemed to shape itself without human lips in the heavy night-air of the river.

". . . Yes—I let him run on," Marlow began again, "and think what he pleased about the powers that were behind me. I did! And there was nothing behind me! There was nothing but that wretched, old, mangled steamboat I was leaning against, while he talked fluently about 'the necessity for every man to get on.' 'And when one comes out here, you conceive, it is not to gaze at the moon.' Mr Kurtz was a 'universal genius,' but even a genius would find it easier to work with 'adequate tools—intelligent men.' He did not make bricks—why, there was a physical impossibility in the way—as I was well aware; and if he did secretarial work for the manager, it was because 'no sensible man rejects wantonly the confidence of his superiors.' Did I see it? I saw it. What more did I want? What I really wanted was rivets, by heaven! Rivets. To get on with the work—to stop the hole. Rivets I wanted. There were cases of them down at the coast—cases—piled up—burst—split! You kicked a loose rivet at every second step in that station yard on the hillside. Rivets had rolled into the grove of death. You could fill your pockets with rivets for the trouble of stooping down—and there wasn't one rivet to be found where it was wanted. We had plates that would do, but nothing to fasten them with. And every week the messenger, a lone negro, letter-bag on shoulder and staff in hand, left our station for the coast. And several times a week a coast caravan came in with trade goods,—ghastly glazed calico that made you shudder only to look at it, glass beads value about a penny a quart, confounded spotted cotton handkerchiefs. And no rivets. Three carriers could have brought all that was wanted to set that steamboat afloat.

"He was becoming confidential now, but I fancy my unresponsive attitude must have exasperated him at last, for he judged it necessary to inform me he feared neither God nor devil, let alone any mere man. I said I could see that very well, but what I wanted was a certain quantity of rivets—and rivets were what really Mr

Kurtz wanted, if he had only known it. Now letters went to the coast every week. . . . 'My dear sir,' he cried, 'I write from dictation.' I demanded rivets. There was a way—for an intelligent man. He changed his manner; became very cold, and suddenly began to talk about a hippopotamus; wondered whether sleeping on board the steamer (I stuck to my salvage night and day) I wasn't disturbed. There was an old hippo that had the bad habit of getting out on the bank and roaming at night over the station grounds. The pilgrims used to turn out in a body and empty every rifle they could lay hands on at him. Some even had sat up o' nights for him. All this energy was wasted, though. 'That animal has a charmed life,' he said; 'but you can say this only of brutes in this country. No man—you apprehend me?—no man here bears a charmed life.' He stood there for a moment in the moonlight with his delicate hooked nose set a little askew, and his mica eyes glittering without a wink, then, with a curt Good night, he strode off. I could see he was disturbed and considerably puzzled, which made me feel more hopeful than I had been for days. It was a great comfort to turn from that chap to my influential friend, the battered, twisted, ruined, tin-pot steamboat. I clambered on board. She rang under my feet like an empty Huntley & Palmer[19] biscuit-tin kicked along a gutter; she was nothing so solid in make, and rather less pretty in shape, but I had expended enough hard work on her to make me love her. No influential friend would have served me better. She had given me a chance to come out a bit—to find out what I could do. No, I don't like work. I had rather laze about and think of all the fine things that can be done. I don't like work—no man does— but I like what is in the work,—the chance to find yourself. Your own reality—for yourself, not for others—what no other man can ever know. They can only see the mere show, and never can tell what it really means.

"I was not surprised to see somebody sitting aft, on the deck, with his legs dangling over the mud. You see I rather chummed with the few mechanics there were in that station, whom the other pilgrims naturally despised—on account of their imperfect manners, I suppose. This was the foreman—a boiler-maker by trade—a good worker. He was a lank, bony, yellow-faced man, with big

---

[19]A brand of English cookies.

intense eyes. His aspect was worried, and his head was as bald as the palm of my hand; but his hair in falling seemed to have stuck to his chin, and had prospered in the new locality, for his beard hung down to his waist. He was a widower with six young children (he had left them in charge of a sister of his to come out there), and the passion of his life was pigeon-flying. He was an enthusiast and a connoisseur. He would rave about pigeons. After work hours he used sometimes to come over from his hut for a talk about his children and his pigeons; at work, when he had to crawl in the mud under the bottom of the steamboat, he would tie up that beard of his in a kind of white serviette[20] he brought for the purpose. It had loops to go over his ears. In the evening he could be seen squatted on the bank rinsing that wrapper in the creek with great care, then spreading it solemnly on a bush to dry.

"I slapped him on the back and shouted 'We shall have rivets!' He scrambled to his feet exclaiming 'No! Rivets!' as though he couldn't believe his ears. Then in a low voice, 'You . . . eh?' I don't know why we behaved like lunatics. I put my finger to the side of my nose and nodded mysteriously. 'Good for you!' he cried, snapped his fingers above his head, lifting one foot. I tried a jig. We capered on the iron deck. A frightful clatter came out of that hulk, and the virgin forest on the other bank of the creek sent it back in a thundering roll upon the sleeping station. It must have made some of the pilgrims sit up in their hovels. A dark figure obscured the lighted doorway of the manager's hut, vanished, then, a second or so after, the doorway itself vanished too. We stopped, and the silence driven away by the stamping of our feet flowed back again from the recesses of the land. The great wall of vegetation, an exuberant and entangled mass of trunks, branches, leaves, boughs, festoons, motionless in the moonlight, was like a rioting invasion of soundless life, a rolling wave of plants, piled up, crested, ready to topple over the creek, to sweep every little man of us out of his little existence. And it moved not. A deadened burst of mighty splashes and snorts reached us from afar, as though an ichthyosaurus had been taking a bath of glitter in the great river. 'After all,' said the boiler-maker in a reasonable tone, 'why shouldn't we get the rivets?' Why not, indeed! I did not know

---

[20]Napkin.

of any reason why we shouldn't. 'They'll come in three weeks,' I said, confidently.

"But they didn't. Instead of rivets there came an invasion, an infliction, a visitation. It came in sections during the next three weeks, each section headed by a donkey carrying a white man in new clothes and tan shoes, bowing from that elevation right and left to the impressed pilgrims. A quarrelsome band of footsore sulky niggers trod on the heels of the donkey; a lot of tents, camp-stools, tin boxes, white cases, brown bales would be shot down in the courtyard, and the air of mystery would deepen a little over the muddle of the station. Five such instalments came, with their absurd air of disorderly flight with the loot of innumerable outfit shops and provision stores, that, one would think, they were lugging, after a raid, into the wilderness for equitable division. It was an inextricable mess of things decent in themselves but that human folly made look like the spoils of thieving.

"This devoted band called itself the Eldorado Exploring Expedition,[21] and I believe they were sworn to secrecy. Their talk, however, was the talk of sordid buccaneers: it was reckless without hardihood, greedy without audacity, and cruel without courage; there was not an atom of foresight or of serious intention in the whole batch of them, and they did not seem aware these things are wanted for the work of the world. To tear treasure out of the bowels of the land was their desire, with no more moral purpose at the back of it than there is in burglars breaking into a safe. Who paid the expenses of the noble enterprise I don't know; but the uncle of our manager was leader of that lot.

"In exterior he resembled a butcher in a poor neighbourhood, and his eyes had a look of sleepy cunning. He carried his fat paunch with ostentation on his short legs, and during the time his gang infested the station spoke to no one but his nephew. You could see these two roaming about all day long with their heads close together in an everlasting confab.

"I had given up worrying myself about the rivets. One's capacity for that kind of folly is more limited than you would suppose. I said Hang!—and let things slide. I had plenty of time for meditation, and now and then I would give some thought to Kurtz. I wasn't

[21]Eldorado, legendary land of gold in South America and the object of many fruit-less 16th-c. Spanish expeditions.

very interested in him. No. Still, I was curious to see whether this man, who had come out equipped with moral ideas of some sort, would climb to the top after all, and how he would set about his work when there."

2

"One evening as I was lying flat on the deck of my steamboat, I heard voices approaching—and there were the nephew and the uncle strolling along the bank. I laid my head on my arm again, and had nearly lost myself in a doze, when somebody said in my ear, as it were: 'I am as harmless as a little child, but I don't like to be dictated to. Am I the manager—or am I not? I was ordered to send him there. It's incredible.' . . . I became aware that the two were standing on the shore alongside the forepart of the steamboat, just below my head. I did not move; it did not occur to me to move: I was sleepy. 'It is unpleasant,' grunted the uncle. 'He has asked the Administration to be sent there,' said the other, 'with the idea of showing what he could do; and I was instructed accordingly. Look at the influence that man must have. Is it not frightful?' They both agreed it was frightful, then made several bizarre remarks: 'Make rain and fine weather—one man—the Council—by the nose'—bits of absurd sentences that got the better of my drowsiness, so that I had pretty near the whole of my wits about me when the uncle said, 'The climate may do away with this difficulty for you. Is he alone there?' 'Yes,' answered the manager; 'he sent his assistant down the river with a note to me in these terms: "Clear this poor devil out of the country, and don't bother sending more of that sort. I had rather be alone than have the kind of men you can dispose of with me." It was more than a year ago. Can you imagine such impudence?' 'Anything since then?' asked the other, hoarsely. 'Ivory,' jerked the nephew; 'lots of it—prime sort—lots—most annoying, from him.' 'And with that?' questioned the heavy rumble. 'Invoice,' was the reply fired out, so to speak. Then silence. They had been talking about Kurtz.

"I was broad awake by this time, but, lying perfectly at ease, remained still, having no inducement to change my position. 'How did that ivory come all this way?' growled the elder man, who seemed very vexed. The other explained that it had come with a fleet of canoes in charge of an English half-caste clerk Kurtz had with him; that Kurtz had apparently intended to return himself, the station being by that time bare of goods and stores, but after coming three hundred miles, had suddenly decided to go back, which he started to do alone in a small dug-out with four paddlers, leaving the half-caste to continue down the river with the ivory. The two fellows there seemed astounded at anybody attempting such a thing. They were at a loss for an adequate motive. As to me, I seemed to see Kurtz for the first time. It was a distinct glimpse: the dug-out, four paddling savages, and the lone white man turning his back suddenly on the headquarters, on relief, on thoughts of home—perhaps; setting his face towards the depths of the wilderness, towards his empty and desolate station. I did not know the motive. Perhaps he was just simply a fine fellow who stuck to his work for its own sake. His name, you understand, had not been pronounced once. He was 'that man.' The half-caste, who, as far as I could see, had conducted a difficult trip with great prudence and pluck, was invariably alluded to as 'that scoundrel.' The 'scoundrel' had reported that the 'man' had been very ill—had recovered imperfectly. . . . The two below me moved away then a few paces, and strolled back and forth at some little distance. I heard: 'Military post—doctor—two hundred miles—quite alone now—unavoidable delays—nine months—no news—strange rumours.' They approached again, just as the manager was saying, 'No one, as far as I know, unless a species of wandering trader—a pestilential fellow, snapping ivory from the natives.' Who was it they were talking about now? I gathered in snatches that this was some man supposed to be in Kurtz's district, and of whom the manager did not approve. 'We will not be free from unfair competition till one of these fellows is hanged for an example,' he said. 'Certainly,' grunted the other; 'get him hanged! Why not? Anything—anything can be done in this country. That's what I say; nobody here, you understand, *here*, can endanger your position. And why? You stand the climate—you outlast them all. The danger is in Europe; but there before I left I took care to—' They moved off and whispered, then their voices rose again. 'The extraordinary series of delays is not my fault. I did my possible.' The fat man sighed, 'Very sad.' 'And the pestiferous absurdity of his talk,' continued the other; 'he bothered me enough when he was here. "Each station should be like a beacon on the road towards better things, a centre for trade of course, but also for humanising, improving, instructing." Conceive you—that ass! And he wants to be manager! No, it's—' Here he got choked by excessive indignation, and I lifted my head the least bit. I was surprised to see how near they were—right under me. I could have spat upon their hats. They were looking on the ground, absorbed in thought. The manager was switching his leg with a slender twig: his sagacious relative lifted his head. 'You have been well since you came out this time?' he asked. The other gave a start. 'Who? I? Oh! Like a charm—like a charm. But the rest—oh, my goodness! All sick. They die so quick, too, that I haven't the time to send them out of the country—it's incredible!' 'H'm. Just so,' grunted the uncle. 'Ah! my boy, trust to this—I say, trust to this.' I saw him extend his short flipper of an arm for a gesture that took in the forest, the creek, the mud, the river,—seemed to beckon with a dishonouring flourish before the sunlit face of the land a treacherous appeal to the lurking death, to the hidden evil, to the profound darkness of its heart. It was so startling that I leaped to my feet and looked back at the edge of the forest, as though I had expected an answer of some sort to that black display of confidence. You know the foolish notions that come to one sometimes. The high stillness confronted these two figures with its ominous patience, waiting for the passing away of a fantastic invasion.

"They swore aloud together—out of sheer fright, I believe—then, pretending not to know anything of my existence, turned back to the station. The sun was low; and leaning forward side by side, they seemed to be tugging painfully uphill their two ridiculous shadows of unequal length, that trailed behind them slowly over the tall grass without bending a single blade.

"In a few days the Eldorado Expedition went into the patient wilderness, that closed upon it as the sea closes over a diver. Long afterwards the news came that all the donkeys were dead. I know nothing as to the fate of the less valuable animals. They, no doubt, like the rest of us, found what they deserved. I did not inquire. I was then rather excited at the prospect of meeting Kurtz very soon. When I say very soon I mean it comparatively. It was just two months from the day we left the creek when we came to the bank below Kurtz's station.

"Going up that river was like travelling back to the earliest beginnings of the world, when vegetation rioted on the earth and the big trees were kings. An empty stream, a great silence, an impenetrable forest. The air was warm, thick, heavy, sluggish. There was no joy in the brilliance of sunshine. The long stretches of the waterway ran on, deserted, into the gloom of overshadowed distances. On silvery sandbanks hippos and alligators sunned themselves side by side. The broadening waters flowed through a mob of wooded islands; you lost your way on that river as you would in a desert, and butted all day long against shoals, trying to find the channel, till you thought yourself bewitched and cut off for ever from everything you had known once—somewhere—far away—in another existence perhaps. There were moments when one's past came back to one, as it will sometimes when you have not a moment to spare to yourself; but it came in the shape of an unrestful and noisy dream, remembered with wonder amongst the overwhelming realities of this strange world of plants, and water, and silence. And this stillness of life did not in the least resemble a peace. It was the stillness of an implacable force brooding over an inscrutable intention. It looked at you with a vengeful aspect. I got used to it afterwards; I did not see it any more; I had no time. I had to keep guessing at the channel; I had to discern, mostly by inspiration, the signs of hidden banks; I watched for sunken stones; I was learning to clap my teeth smartly before my heart flew out, when I shaved by a fluke some infernal sly old snag that would have ripped the life out of the tin-pot steamboat and drowned all the pilgrims; I had to keep a look-out for the signs of dead wood we could cut up in the night for next day's steaming. When you have to attend to things of that sort, to the mere incidents of the surface, the reality—the reality, I tell you—fades. The inner truth is hidden—luckily, luckily. But I felt it all the same; I felt often its mysterious stillness watching me at my monkey tricks, just as it watches you fellows performing on your respective tight-ropes for—what is it? half-a-crown a tumble—"

"Try to be civil, Marlow," growled a voice, and I knew there was at least one listener awake besides myself.

"I beg your pardon. I forgot the heartache which makes up the rest of the price. And indeed what does the price matter, if the trick be well done? You do your tricks very well. And I didn't do badly either, since I managed not to sink that steamboat on my first trip. It's a wonder to me yet. Imagine a blindfolded man set to drive a van over a bad road. I sweated and shivered over that business considerably, I can tell you. After all, for a seaman, to scrape the bottom of the thing that's supposed to float all the time under his care is the unpardonable sin. No one may know of it, but you never forget the thump—eh? A blow on the very heart. You remember it, you dream of it, you wake up at night and think of it—years after—and go hot and cold all over. I don't pretend to say that steamboat floated all the time. More than once she had to wade for a bit, with twenty cannibals splashing around and pushing. We had enlisted some of these chaps on the way for a crew. Fine fellows—cannibals—in their place. They were men one could work with, and I am grateful to them. And, after all, they did not eat each other before my face: they had brought along a provision of hippo-meat which went rotten, and made the mystery of the wilderness stink in my nostrils. Phoo! I can sniff it now. I had the manager on board and three or four pilgrims with their staves—all complete. Sometimes we came upon a station close by the bank, clinging to the skirts of the unknown, and the white men rushing out of a tumble-down hovel, with great gestures of joy and surprise and welcome, seemed very strange,—had the appearance of being held there captive by a spell. The word 'ivory' would ring in the air for a while—and on we went again into the silence, along empty reaches, round the still bends, between the high walls of our winding way, reverberating in hollow claps the ponderous beat of the stern-wheel. Trees, trees, millions of trees, massive, immense, running up high; and at their foot, hugging the bank against the stream, crept the little begrimed steamboat, like a sluggish beetle crawling on the floor of a lofty portico. It made you feel very small, very lost, and yet it was not altogether depressing that feeling. After all, if you were small, the grimy beetle crawled on—which was just what you wanted it to do. Where the pilgrims imagined it crawled to I don't know. To some place where they expected to get something, I bet! For me it crawled towards Kurtz—exclusively; but when the steam-pipes started leaking we crawled very slow. The reaches opened before us and closed behind, as if the forest had stepped leisurely across the water to bar the way for our return. We penetrated deeper and deeper into the heart of darkness. It was very quiet there. At night sometimes the roll of drums behind the curtain of trees would run up the river and remain sustained faintly, as if hovering in the air high over our heads, till the first break of day. Whether it meant war, peace, or prayer we could not tell. The dawns were heralded by the descent of a chill stillness; the woodcutters slept, their fires burned low; the snapping of a twig would make you start. We were wanderers on a prehistoric earth, on an earth that wore the aspect of an unknown planet. We could have fancied ourselves the first of men taking possession of an accursed inheritance, to be subdued at the cost of profound anguish and of excessive toil. But suddenly, as we struggled round a bend, there would be a glimpse of rush walls, of peaked grass-roofs, a burst of yells, a whirl of black limbs, a mass of hands clapping, of feet stamping, of bodies swaying, of eyes rolling, under the droop of heavy and motionless foliage. The steamer toiled along slowly on the edge of a black and incomprehensible frenzy. The prehistoric man was cursing us, praying to us, welcoming us—who could tell? We were cut off from the comprehension of our surroundings; we glided past like phantoms, wondering and secretly appalled, as sane men would be before an enthusiastic outbreak in a madhouse. We could not understand, because we were too far and could not remember, because we were travelling in the night of first ages, of those ages that are gone, leaving hardly a sign—and no memories.

"The earth seemed unearthly. We are accustomed to look upon the shackled form of a conquered monster, but there—there you could look at a thing monstrous and free. It was unearthly, and the men were—No, they were not inhuman. Well, you know, that was the worst of it—this suspicion of their not being inhuman. It would come slowly to one. They howled, and leaped, and spun, and made horrid faces; but what thrilled you was just the thought of their humanity—like yours—the thought of your remote kinship with this wild and passionate uproar. Ugly. Yes, it was ugly enough; but if you were man enough you would admit to yourself that there was in you just the faintest trace of a response to the terrible frankness of that noise, a dim suspicion of there being a meaning in it which you—you so remote from the night of first ages—could comprehend. And why not? The mind of man is capable of anything—because everything is in it, all the past as well as all the future. What was there after all? Joy, fear, sorrow, devotion, valour, rage—who can tell?—but truth—truth stripped of its cloak of time. Let the fool gape and shudder—the man knows, and can look on without a wink. But he must at least be as much of a man as these on the shore. He must meet that truth with his own true stuff—with his own inborn strength. Principles? Principles won't do. Acquisitions, clothes, pretty rags—rags that would fly off at the first good shake. No; you want a deliberate belief. An appeal to me in this fiendish row—is there? Very well; I hear; I admit, but I have a voice too, and for good or evil mine is the speech that cannot be silenced. Of course, a fool, what with sheer fright and fine sentiments, is always safe. Who's that grunting? You wonder I didn't go ashore for a howl and a dance? Well, no—I didn't. Fine sentiments, you say? Fine sentiments be hanged! I had no time. I had to mess about with white-lead and strips of woollen blanket helping to put bandages on those leaky steam-pipes—I tell you. I had to watch the steering, and circumvent those snags, and get the tin-pot along by hook or by crook. There was surface-truth enough in these things to save a wiser man. And between whiles I had to look after the savage who was fireman. He was an improved specimen; he could fire up a vertical boiler. He was there below me, and, upon my word, to look at him was as edifying as seeing a dog in a parody of breeches and a feather hat, walking on his hind-legs. A few months of training had done for that really fine chap. He squinted at the steam-gauge and at the water-gauge with an evident effort of intrepidity—and he had filed teeth too, the poor devil, and the wool of his pate shaved into queer patterns, and three ornamental scars on each of his cheeks. He ought to have been clapping his hands and stamping his feet on the bank, instead of which he was hard at work, a thrall to strange witchcraft, full of improving knowledge. He was useful because he had been instructed; and what he knew was this—that should the water in that transparent thing disappear, the evil spirit inside the boiler would get angry through the greatness of his thirst, and take a terrible vengeance. So he sweated and fired up and watched the glass fearfully (with an impromptu charm, made of rags, tied to his arm, and a piece of polished bone, as big as a watch, stuck flatways through his lower lip), while the wooded banks slipped past us slowly, the short noise was left behind, the interminable miles of silence—and we crept on, towards Kurtz. But the snags were thick, the water was treacherous and shallow, the boiler seemed indeed to have a sulky devil in it, and thus neither that fireman nor I had any time to peer into our creepy thoughts.

"Some fifty miles below the Inner Station we came upon a hut of reeds, an inclined and melancholy pole, with the unrecognisable tatters of what had been a flag of some sort flying from it, and a neatly stacked wood-pile. This was unexpected. We came to the bank, and on the stack of firewood found a flat piece of board with some faded pencil-writing on it. When deciphered it said: 'Wood for you. Hurry up. Approach cautiously.' There was a signature, but it was illegible—not Kurtz—a much longer word. Hurry up. Where? Up the river? 'Approach cautiously.' We had not done so. But the warning could not have been meant for the place where it could be only found after approach. Something was wrong above. But what—and how much? That was the question. We commented adversely upon the imbecility of that telegraphic style. The bush around said nothing, and would not let us look very far, either. A torn curtain of red twill hung in the doorway of the hut, and flapped sadly in our faces. The dwelling was dismantled; but we could see a white man had lived there not very long ago. There remained a rude table—a plank on two posts; a heap of rubbish reposed in a dark corner, and by the door I picked up a book. It had lost its covers, and the pages had been thumbed into a state of extremely dirty softness; but the back had been lovingly stitched afresh with white cotton thread, which looked clean yet. It was an extraordinary find. Its title was, 'An Inquiry into some Points of Seamanship,' by a man Tower, Towson—some such name—Master in his Majesty's Navy. The matter looked dreary reading enough, with illustrative diagrams and repulsive tables of figures, and the copy was sixty years old. I handled this amazing antiquity with the greatest possible tenderness, lest it should dissolve in my hands. Within, Towson or Towser was inquiring earnestly into the break-ing strain of ships' chains and tackle, and other such matters. Not a very enthralling book; but at the first glance you could see there a singleness of intention, an honest concern for the right way of going to work, which made these humble pages, thought out so many years ago, luminous with another than a professional light. The simple old sailor, with his talk of chains and purchases, made me forget the jungle and the pilgrims in a delicious sensation of having come upon something unmistakably real. Such a book being there was wonderful enough; but still more astounding were the notes pencilled in the margin, and plainly referring to the text. I couldn't believe my eyes! They were in cipher! Yes, it looked like cipher. Fancy a man lugging with him a book of that description into this nowhere and studying it—and making notes—in cipher at that! It was an extravagant mystery.

"I had been dimly aware for some time of a worrying noise, and when I lifted my eyes I saw the wood-pile was gone, and the manager, aided by all the pilgrims, was shouting at me from the river-side. I slipped the book into my pocket. I assure you to leave off reading was like tearing myself away from the shelter of an old and solid friendship.

"I started the lame engine ahead. 'It must be this miserable trader—this intruder,' exclaimed the manager, looking back malevolently at the place we had left. 'He must be English,' I said. 'It will not save him from getting into trouble if he is not careful,' muttered the manager darkly. I observed with assumed innocence that no man was safe from trouble in this world.

"The current was more rapid now, the steamer seemed at her last gasp, the stern-wheel flopped languidly, and I caught myself listening on tiptoe for the next beat of the float, for in sober truth I expected the wretched thing to give up every moment. It was like watching the last flickers of a life. But still we crawled. Sometimes I would pick out a tree a little way ahead to measure our progress towards Kurtz by, but I lost it invariably before we got abreast. To keep the eyes so long on one thing was too much for human patience. The manager displayed a beautiful resignation. I fretted and fumed and took to arguing with myself whether or no I would talk openly with Kurtz; but before I could come to any conclusion it occurred to me that my speech or my silence, indeed any action of mine, would be a mere futility. What did it matter what any one knew or ignored? What did it matter who was manager? One gets sometimes such a flash of insight. The essentials of this affair lay deep under the surface, beyond my reach, and beyond my power of meddling.

"Towards the evening of the second day we judged ourselves about eight miles from Kurtz's station. I wanted to push on; but the manager looked grave, and told me the navigation up there was so dangerous that it would be advisable, the sun being very low already, to wait where we were till next morning. Moreover, he pointed out that if the warning to approach cautiously were to be followed, we must approach in daylight—not at dusk, or in the dark. This was sensible enough. Eight miles meant nearly three hours' steaming for us, and I could also see suspicious ripples at the upper end of the reach. Nevertheless, I was annoyed beyond expression at the delay, and most unreasonably too, since one night more could not matter much after so many months. As we had plenty of wood, and caution was the word, I brought up in the middle of the stream. The reach was narrow, straight, with high sides like a railway cutting. The dusk came gliding into it long before the sun had set. The current ran smooth and swift, but a dumb immobility sat on the banks. The living trees, lashed together by the creepers and every living bush of the undergrowth, might have been changed into stone, even to the slenderest twig, to the lightest leaf. It was not sleep—it seemed unnatural, like a state of trance. Not the faintest sound of any kind could be heard. You looked on amazed, and began to suspect yourself of being deaf— then the night came suddenly, and struck you blind as well. About three in the morning some large fish leaped, and the loud splash made me jump as though a gun had been fired. When the sun rose there was a white fog, very warm and clammy, and more blinding than the night. It did not shift or drive; it was just there, standing all round you like something solid. At eight or nine, perhaps, it lifted as a shutter lifts. We had a glimpse of the towering multitude of trees, of the immense matted jungle, with the blazing little ball of the sun hanging over it—all perfectly still—and then the white shutter came down again, smoothly, as if sliding in greased grooves. I ordered the chain, which we had begun to heave in, to be paid out again. Before it stopped running with a muffled rattle, a cry, a very loud cry, as of infinite desolation, soared slowly in the opaque air. It ceased. A complaining clamour, modulated in savage discords, filled our ears. The sheer unexpectedness of it made my hair stir under my cap. I don't know how it struck the others: to me it seemed as though the mist itself had screamed, so suddenly, and apparently from all sides at once, did this tumultuous and mournful uproar arise. It culminated in a hurried outbreak of almost intolerably excessive shrieking, which stopped short, leaving us stiffened in a variety of silly attitudes, and obstinately listening to the nearly as appalling and excessive silence. 'Good God! What is the meaning—?' stammered at my elbow one of the pilgrims,—a little fat man, with sandy hair and red whiskers, who wore side-spring boots, and pink pyjamas tucked into his socks. Two others remained open-mouthed a whole minute, then dashed into the little cabin, to rush out incontinently and stand darting scared glances, with Winchesters at 'ready' in their hands. What we could see was just the steamer we were on, her outlines blurred as though she had been on the point of dissolving, and a misty strip of water, perhaps two feet broad, around her—and that was all. The rest of the world was nowhere, as far as our eyes and ears were concerned. Just nowhere. Gone, disappeared; swept off without leaving a whisper or a shadow behind.

"I went forward, and ordered the chain to be hauled in short, so as to be ready to trip the anchor and move the steamboat at once if necessary. 'Will they attack?' whispered an awed voice. 'We will all be butchered in this fog,' murmured another. The faces twitched with the strain, the hands trembled slightly, the eyes forgot to wink. It was very curious to see the contrast of expressions of the white men and of the black fellows of our crew, who were as much strangers to that part of the river as we, though their homes were only eight hundred miles away. The whites, of course greatly discomposed, had besides a curious look of being painfully shocked by such an outrageous row. The others had an alert, naturally interested expression; but their faces were essentially quiet, even those of the one or two who grinned as they hauled at the chain. Several exchanged short, grunting phrases, which seemed to settle the matter to their satisfaction. Their headman, a young, broad-chested black, severely draped in dark-blue fringed cloths, with fierce nostrils and his hair all done up artfully in oily ringlets, stood near me. 'Aha!' I said, just for good fellowship's sake. 'Catch 'im,' he snapped, with a bloodshot widening of his eyes and a flash of sharp teeth—'catch 'im. Give 'im to us.' 'To you, eh?' I asked; 'what would you do with them?' 'Eat 'im!' he said, curtly, and, leaning his elbow on the rail, looked out into the fog in a dignified and profoundly pensive attitude. I would no doubt have been properly horrified, had it not occurred to me that he and his chaps must be very hungry: that they must have been growing increasingly hungry for at least this month past. They had been engaged for six months (I don't think a single one of them had any clear idea of time, as we at the end of countless ages have. They still belonged to the beginnings of time—had no inherited experience to teach them, as it were), and of course, as long as there was a piece of paper written over in accordance with some farcical law or other made down the river, it didn't enter anybody's head to trouble how they would live. Certainly they had brought with them some rotten hippo-meat, which couldn't have lasted very long, anyway, even if the pilgrims hadn't, in the midst of a shocking hullabaloo, thrown a considerable quantity of it overboard. It looked like a high-handed proceeding; but it was really a case of legitimate self-defence. You can't breathe dead hippo waking, sleeping, and eating, and at the same time keep your precarious grip on existence. Besides that, they had given them every week three pieces of brass wire, each about nine inches long; and the theory was they were to buy their provisions with that currency in river-side villages. You can see how *that* worked. There were either no villages, or the people were hostile, or the director, who like the rest of us fed out of tins, with an occasional old he-goat thrown in, didn't want to stop the steamer for some more or less recondite reason. So, unless they swallowed the wire itself, or made loops of it to snare the fishes with, I don't see what good their extravagant salary could be to them. I must say it was paid with a regularity worthy of a large and honourable trading company. For the rest, the only thing to eat—though it didn't look eatable in the least—I saw in their possession was a few lumps of some stuff like half-cooked dough, of a dirty lavender colour, they kept wrapped in leaves, and now and then swallowed a piece of, but so small that it seemed done more for the looks of the thing than for any serious purpose of sustenance. Why in the name of all the gnawing devils of hunger they didn't go for us—they were thirty to five—and have a good tuck-in for once, amazes me now when I think of it. They were big powerful men, with not much capacity to weigh the consequences, with courage, with strength, even yet, though their skins were no longer glossy and their muscles no longer hard. And I saw that something restraining, one of those human secrets that baffle probability, had come into play there. I looked at them with a swift quickening of interest—not because it occurred to me I might be eaten by them before very long, though I own to you that just then I perceived—

in a new light, as it were—how unwholesome the pilgrims looked, and I hoped, yes, I positively hoped, that my aspect was not so—what shall I say?—so—unappetising: a touch of fantastic vanity which fitted well with the dream-sensation that pervaded all my days at that time. Perhaps I had a little fever too. One can't live with one's finger everlastingly on one's pulse. I had often 'a little fever,' or a little touch of other things—the playful paw-strokes of the wilderness, the preliminary trifling before the more serious onslaught which came in due course. Yes; I looked at them as you would on any human being, with a curiosity of their impulses, motives, capacities, weaknesses, when brought to the test of an inexorable physical necessity. Restraint! What possible restraint? Was it superstition, disgust, patience, fear—or some kind of primitive honour? No fear can stand up to hunger, no patience can wear it out, disgust simply does not exist where hunger is; and as to superstition, beliefs, and what you may call principles, they are less than chaff in a breeze. Don't you know the devilry of lingering starvation, its exasperating torment, its black thoughts, its sombre and brooding ferocity? Well, I do. It takes a man all his inborn strength to fight hunger properly. It's really easier to face bereavement, dishonour, and the perdition of one's soul—than this kind of prolonged hunger. Sad, but true. And these chaps too had no earthly reason for any kind of scruple. Restraint! I would just as soon have expected restraint from a hyena prowling amongst the corpses of a battlefield. But there was the fact facing me—the fact dazzling, to be seen, like the foam on the depths of the sea, like a ripple on an unfathomable enigma, a mystery greater—when I thought of it—than the curious, inexplicable note of desperate grief in this savage clamour that had swept by us on the river-bank, behind the blind whiteness of the fog.

"Two pilgrims were quarrelling in hurried whispers as to which bank. 'Left.' 'No, no; how can you? Right, right, of course.' 'It is very serious,' said the manager's voice behind me; 'I would be desolated if anything should happen to Mr Kurtz before we came up.' I looked at him, and had not the slightest doubt he was sincere. He was just the kind of man who would wish to preserve appearances. That was his restraint. But when he muttered something about going on at once, I did not even take the trouble to answer him. I knew, and he knew, that it was impossible. Were we to let go our hold of the bottom, we would be absolutely in the air—in space. We wouldn't be able to tell where we were going to—whether up or down stream, or across—till we fetched against one bank or the other,—and then we wouldn't know at first which it was. Of course I made no move. I had no mind for a smash-up. You couldn't imagine a more deadly place for a shipwreck. Whether drowned at once or not, we were sure to perish speedily in one way or another. 'I authorise you to take all the risks,' he said, after a short silence. 'I refuse to take any,' I said shortly; which was just the answer he expected, though its tone might have surprised him. 'Well, I must defer to your judgment. You are captain,' he said, with marked civility. I turned my shoulder to him in sign of my appreciation, and looked into the fog. How long would it last? It was the most hopeless look-out. The approach to this Kurtz grubbing for ivory in the wretched bush was beset by as many dangers as though he had been an enchanted princess sleeping in a fabulous castle. 'Will they attack, do you think?' asked the manager, in a confidential tone.

"I did not think they would attack, for several obvious reasons. The thick fog was one. If they left the bank in their canoes they would get lost in it, as we would be if we attempted to move. Still, I had also judged the jungle of both banks quite impenetrable and yet eyes were in it, eyes that had seen us. The river-side bushes were certainly very thick; but the undergrowth behind was evidently penetrable. However, during the short lift I had seen no canoes anywhere in the reach—certainly not abreast of the steamer. But what made the idea of attack inconceivable to me was the nature of the noise—of the cries we had heard. They had not the fierce character boding of immediate hostile intention. Unexpected, wild, and violent as they had been, they had given me an irresistible impression of sorrow. The glimpse of the steamboat had for some reason filled those savages with unrestrained grief. The danger, if any, I expounded, was from our proximity to a great human passion let loose. Even extreme grief may ultimately vent itself in violence—but more generally takes the form of apathy. . . .

"You should have seen the pilgrims stare! They had no heart to grin, or even to revile me; but I believe they thought me gone mad—with fright, maybe. I delivered a regular lecture. My dear boys, it was no good bothering. Keep a look-out? Well, you may guess I watched the fog for the signs of lifting as a cat watches a mouse; but for anything else our eyes were of no more use to us than if we had been buried miles deep in a heap of cotton-wool. It felt like it too—choking, warm, stifling. Besides, all I said, though it sounded extravagant, was absolutely true to fact. What we afterwards alluded to as an attack was really an attempt at repulse. The action was very far from being aggressive—it was not even defensive, in the usual sense: it was undertaken under the stress of desperation, and in its essence was purely protective.

"It developed itself, I should say, two hours after the fog lifted, and its commencement was at a spot, roughly speaking, about a mile and a half below Kurtz's station. We had just floundered and flopped round a bend, when I saw an islet, a mere grassy hummock of bright green, in the middle of the stream. It was the only thing of the kind; but as we opened the reach more, I perceived it was the head of a long sandbank, or rather of a chain of shallow patches stretching down the middle of the river. They were discoloured, just awash, and the whole lot was seen just under the water, exactly as a man's backbone is seen running down the middle of his back under the skin. Now, as far as I did see, I could go to the right or to the left of this. I didn't know either channel, of course. The banks looked pretty well alike, the depth appeared the same; but as I had been informed the station was on the west side, I naturally headed for the western passage.

"No sooner had we fairly entered it than I became aware it was much narrower than I had supposed. To the left of us there was the long uninterrupted shoal, and to the right a high, steep bank heavily overgrown with bushes. Above the bush the trees stood in serried ranks. The twigs overhung the current thickly, and from distance to distance a large limb of some tree projected rigidly over the stream. It was then well on in the afternoon, the face of the forest was gloomy, and a broad strip of shadow had already fallen on the water. In this shadow we steamed up—very slowly, as you may imagine. I sheered her well inshore—the water being deepest near the bank, as the sounding-pole informed me.

"One of my hungry and forbearing friends was sounding in the bows just below me. This steamboat was exactly like a decked scow.[22] On the deck there were two little teak-wood houses, with

[22] A flat-bottomed boat.

doors and windows. The boiler was in the fore-end, and the machinery right astern. Over the whole there was a light roof, supported on stanchions. The funnel projected through that roof, and in front of the funnel a small cabin built of light planks served for a pilot-house. It contained a couch, two camp-stools, a loaded Martini-Henry[23] leaning in one corner, a tiny table, and the steering-wheel. It had a wide door in front and a broad shutter at each side. All these were always thrown open, of course. I spent my days perched up there on the extreme fore-end of that roof, before the door. At night I slept, or tried to, on the couch. An athletic black belonging to some coast tribe, and educated by my poor predecessor, was the helmsman. He sported a pair of brass earrings, wore a blue cloth wrapper from the waist to the ankles, and thought all the world of himself. He was the most unstable kind of fool I had ever seen. He steered with no end of a swagger while you were by; but if he lost sight of you, he became instantly the prey of an abject funk, and would let that cripple of a steamboat get the upper hand of him in a minute.

"I was looking down at the sounding-pole, and feeling much annoyed to see at each try a little more of it stick out of that river, when I saw my poleman give up the business suddenly, and stretch himself flat on the deck, without even taking the trouble to haul his pole in. He kept hold on it though, and it trailed in the water. At the same time the fireman, whom I could also see below me, sat down abruptly before his furnace and ducked his head. I was amazed. Then I had to look at the river mighty quick, because there was a snag in the fairway. Sticks, little sticks, were flying about— thick: they were whizzing before my nose, dropping below me, striking behind me against my pilot-house. All this time the river, the shore, the woods, were very quiet—perfectly quiet. I could only hear the heavy splashing thump of the stern-wheel and the patter of these things. We cleared the snag clumsily. Arrows, by Jove! We were being shot at! I stepped in quickly to close the shutter on the landside. That fool-helmsman, his hands on the spokes, was lifting his knees high, stamping his feet, champing his mouth, like a reined-in horse. Confound him! And we were staggering within ten feet of the bank. I had to lean right out to swing the heavy shutter,

[23]A rifle.

and I saw a face amongst the leaves on the level with my own, looking at me very fierce and steady; and then suddenly, as though a veil had been removed from my eyes, I made out, deep in the tangled gloom, naked breasts, arms, legs, glaring eyes,—the bush was swarming with human limbs in movement, glistening, of bronze colour. The twigs shook, swayed, and rustled, the arrows flew out of them, and then the shutter came to. 'Steer her straight,' I said to the helmsman. He held his head rigid, face forward; but his eyes rolled, he kept on lifting and setting down his feet gently, his mouth foamed a little. 'Keep quiet!' I said in a fury. I might just as well have ordered a tree not to sway in the wind. I darted out. Below me there was a great scuffle of feet on the iron deck; confused exclamations; a voice screamed, 'Can you turn back?' I caught sight of a V-shaped ripple on the water ahead. What? Another snag! A fusillade burst out under my feet. The pilgrims had opened with their Winchesters, and were simply squirting lead into that bush. A deuce of a lot of smoke came up and drove slowly forward. I swore at it. Now I couldn't see the ripple or the snag either. I stood in the doorway, peering, and the arrows came in swarms. They might have been poisoned, but they looked as though they wouldn't kill a cat. The bush began to howl. Our wood-cutters raised a warlike whoop; the report of a rifle just at my back deafened me. I glanced over my shoulder, and the pilot-house was yet full of noise and smoke when I made a dash at the wheel. The fool-nigger had dropped everything, to throw the shutter open and let off that Martini-Henry. He stood before the wide opening, glaring, and I yelled at him to come back, while I straightened the sudden twist out of that steamboat. There was no room to turn even if I had wanted to, the snag was somewhere very near ahead in that confounded smoke, there was no time to lose, so I just crowded her into the bank—right into the bank, where I knew the water was deep.

"We tore slowly along the overhanging bushes in a whirl of broken twigs and flying leaves. The fusillade below stopped short, as I had foreseen it would when the squirts got empty. I threw my head back to a glinting whizz that traversed the pilot-house, in at one shutter-hole and out at the other. Looking past that mad helmsman, who was shaking the empty rifle and yelling at the shore, I saw vague forms of men running bent double, leaping, gliding, distinct, incomplete, evanescent. Something big appeared in the air before the shutter, the rifle went overboard, and the man stepped back swiftly, looked at me over his shoulder in an extraordinary, profound, familiar manner, and fell upon my feet. The side of his head hit the wheel twice, and the end of what appeared a long cane clattered round and knocked over a little camp-stool. It looked as though after wrenching that thing from somebody ashore he had lost his balance in the effort. The thin smoke had blown away, we were clear of the snag, and looking ahead I could see that in another hundred yards or so I would be free to sheer off, away from the bank; but my feet felt so very warm and wet that I had to look down. The man had rolled on his back and stared straight up at me; both his hands clutched that cane. It was the shaft of a spear that, either thrown or lunged through the opening, had caught him in the side just below the ribs; the blade had gone in out of sight, after making a frightful gash; my shoes were full; a pool of blood lay very still, gleaming dark-red under the wheel; his eyes shone with an amazing lustre. The fusillade burst out again. He looked at me anxiously, gripping the spear like something precious, with an air of being afraid I would try to take it away from him. I had to make an effort to free my eyes from his gaze and attend to the steering. With one hand I felt above my head for the line of the steam-whistle, and jerked out screech after screech hurriedly. The tumult of angry and warlike yells was checked instantly, and then from the depths of the woods went out such a tremulous and prolonged wail of mournful fear and utter despair as may be imagined to follow the flight of the last hope from the earth. There was a great commotion in the bush; the shower of arrows stopped, a few dropping shots rang out sharply—then silence, in which the languid beat of the stern-wheel came plainly to my ears. I put the helm hard astarboard at the moment when the pilgrim in pink pyjamas, very hot and agitated, appeared in the doorway. 'The manager sends me—' he began in an official tone, and stopped short. 'Good God!' he said, glaring at the wounded man.

"We two whites stood over him, and his lustrous and inquiring glance enveloped us both. I declare it looked as though he would presently put to us some question in an understandable language; but he died without uttering a sound, without moving a limb, without twitching a muscle. Only in the very last moment, as though in response to some sign we could not see, to some whisper we could not hear, he frowned heavily, and that frown gave to his black death-mask an inconceivably sombre, brooding, and menacing expression. The lustre of inquiring glance faded swiftly into vacant glassiness. 'Can you steer?' I asked the agent eagerly. He looked very dubious; but I made a grab at his arm, and he understood at once I meant him to steer whether or no. To tell you the truth, I was morbidly anxious to change my shoes and socks. 'He is dead,' murmured the fellow, immensely impressed. 'No doubt about it,' said I, tugging like mad at the shoelaces. 'And, by the way, I suppose Mr Kurtz is dead as well by this time.'

"For the moment that was the dominant thought. There was a sense of extreme disappointment, as though I had found out I had been striving after something altogether without a substance. I couldn't have been more disgusted if I had travelled all this way for the sole purpose of talking with Mr Kurtz. Talking with . . . I flung one shoe overboard, and became aware that that was exactly what I had been looking forward to—a talk with Kurtz. I made the strange discovery that I had never imagined him as doing, you know, but as discoursing. I didn't say to myself, 'Now I will never see him,' or 'Now I will never shake him by the hand,' but, 'Now I will never hear him.' The man presented himself as a voice. Not of course that I did not connect him with some sort of action. Hadn't I been told in all the tones of jealousy and admiration that he had collected, bartered, swindled, or stolen more ivory than all the other agents together. That was not the point. The point was in his being a gifted creature, and that of all his gifts the one that stood out pre-eminently, that carried with it a sense of real presence, was his ability to talk, his words—the gift of expression, the bewildering, the illuminating, the most exalted and the most contemptible, the pulsating stream of light, or the deceitful flow from the heart of an impenetrable darkness.

"The other shoe went flying unto the devil-god of that river. I thought, By Jove! it's all over. We are too late; he has vanished—the gift has vanished, by means of some spear, arrow, or club. I will never hear that chap speak after all,—and my sorrow had a startling extravagance of emotion, even such as I had noticed in the howling sorrow of these savages in the bush. I couldn't have felt more of lonely desolation somehow, had I been robbed of a belief or had missed my destiny in life. . . . Why do you sigh in this beastly way, somebody? Absurd? Well, absurd. Good Lord! mustn't a man ever—Here, give me some tobacco." . . .

There was a pause of profound stillness, then a match flared, and Marlow's lean face appeared, worn, hollow, with downward folds and dropped eyelids, with an aspect of concentrated attention; and as he took vigorous draws at his pipe, it seemed to retreat and advance out of the night in the regular flicker of the tiny flame. The match went out.

"Absurd!" he cried. "This is the worst of trying to tell . . . Here you all are, each moored with two good addresses, like a hulk with two anchors, a butcher round one corner, a policeman round another, excellent appetites, and temperature normal—you hear— normal from year's end to year's end. And you say, Absurd! Absurd be—exploded! Absurd! My dear boys, what can you expect from a man who out of sheer nervousness had just flung overboard a pair of new shoes? Now I think of it, it is amazing I did not shed tears. I am, upon the whole, proud of my fortitude. I was cut to the quick at the idea of having lost the inestimable privilege of listening to the gifted Kurtz. Of course I was wrong. The privilege was waiting for me. Oh yes, I heard more than enough. And I was right, too. A voice. He was very little more than a voice. And I heard—him— it—this voice—other voices—all of them were so little more than voices—and the memory of that time itself lingers around me, impalpable, like a dying vibration of one immense jabber, silly, atrocious, sordid, savage, or simply mean, without any kind of sense. Voices, voices—even the girl herself—now—"

He was silent for a long time.

"I laid the ghost of his gifts at last with a lie," he began suddenly. "Girl! What? Did I mention a girl? Oh, she is out of it— completely. They—the women I mean—are out of it—should be out of it. We must help them to stay in that beautiful world of their own, lest ours gets worse. Oh, she had to be out of it. You should have heard the disinterred body of Mr Kurtz saying, "My Intended." You would have perceived directly then how completely she was out of it. And the lofty frontal bone of Mr Kurtz! They say the hair goes on growing sometimes, but this—ah—specimen was impressively bald. The wilderness had patted him on the head, and, behold, it was like a ball—an ivory ball; it had caressed him, and—lo!—he had withered; it had taken him, loved him, embraced him, got into his veins, consumed his flesh, and sealed his soul to its own by the inconceivable ceremonies of some devilish initiation. He was its spoiled and pampered favourite. Ivory? I should think so. Heaps of it, stacks of it. The old mud shanty was bursting with it. You would think there was not a single tusk left either above or below the ground in the whole country. 'Mostly fossil,' the manager had remarked disparagingly. It was no more fossil than I am; but they call it fossil when it is dug up. It appears these niggers do bury the tusks sometimes—but evidently they couldn't bury this parcel deep enough to save the gifted Mr Kurtz from his fate. We filled the steamboat with it, and had to pile a lot on the deck. Thus he could see and enjoy as long as he could see, because the appreciation of this favour had remained with him to the last. You should have heard him say, 'My ivory.' Oh yes, I heard him. 'My Intended, my ivory, my station, my river, my—' everything belonged to him. It made me hold my breath in expectation of hearing the wilderness burst into a prodigious peal of laughter that would shake the fixed stars in their places. Everything belonged to him—but that was a trifle. The thing was to know what he belonged to, how many powers of darkness claimed him for their own. That was the reflection that made you creepy all over. It was impossible—it was not good for one either—trying to imagine. He had taken a high seat amongst the devils of the land—I mean literally. You can't understand. How could you?—with solid pavement under your feet, surrounded by kind neighbours ready to cheer you or to fall on you, stepping delicately between the butcher and the policeman, in the holy terror of scandal and gallows and lunatic asylums—how can you imagine what particular region of the first ages a man's untrammelled feet may take him into by the way of solitude—utter solitude without a policeman—by the way of silence—utter silence, where no warning voice of a kind neighbour can be heard whispering of public opinion? These little things make all the great difference. When they are gone you must fall back upon your own innate strength, upon your own capacity for faithfulness. Of course you may be too much of a fool to go wrong—too dull even to know you are being assaulted by the powers of darkness. I take it, no fool ever made a bargain for his soul with the devil: the fool is too much of a fool, or the devil too much of a devil—I don't know which. Or you may be such a thunderingly exalted creature as to be altogether deaf and blind to anything but heavenly sights and sounds. Then the earth for you is only a standing place—and whether to be like this is your loss or your gain I won't pretend to say. But most of us are neither one nor the other. The earth for us is a place to live in, where we must put up with sights, with sounds, with smells too, by Jove!—breathe dead hippo, so to speak, and not be contaminated. And there, don't you see? your strength comes in, the faith in your ability for the digging of unostentatious holes to bury the stuff in—your power of devotion, not to yourself, but to an obscure, back-breaking business. And that's difficult enough. Mind, I am not trying to excuse or even explain—I am trying to account to myself for—for—Mr Kurtz— for the shade of Mr Kurtz. This initiated wraith from the back of Nowhere honoured me with its amazing confidence before it vanished altogether. This was because it could speak English to me. The original Kurtz had been educated partly in England, and—as he was good enough to say himself—his sympathies were in the right place. His mother was half-English, his father was half-French. All Europe contributed to the making of Kurtz; and by-and-by I learned that, most appropriately, the International Society for the Suppression of Savage Customs had intrusted him with the making of a report, for its future guidance. And he had written it too. I've seen it. I've read it. It was eloquent, vibrating with eloquence, but too high-strung, I think. Seventeen pages of close writing he had found time for! But this must have been before his—let us say—nerves went wrong, and caused him to preside at certain midnight dances ending with unspeakable rites, which—as far as I reluctantly gathered from what I heard at various times— were offered up to him—do you understand?—to Mr Kurtz himself. But it was a beautiful piece of writing. The opening paragraph, however, in the light of later information, strikes me now as ominous. He began with the argument that we whites, from the point of development we had arrived at, 'must necessarily appear to them [savages] in the nature of supernatural beings—we approach them with the might as of a deity,' and so on, and so on. 'By the simple exercise of our will we can exert a power for good practically unbounded,' &c., &c. From that point he soared and took me with him. The peroration was magnificent, though difficult to remember, you know. It gave me the notion of an exotic Immensity ruled by an august Benevolence. It made me tingle with enthusiasm. This was the unbounded power of eloquence—of words—of burning noble words. There were no practical hints to interrupt the magic current of phrases, unless a kind of note at the foot of the last page, scrawled evidently much later, in an unsteady hand, may be regarded as the exposition of a method. It was very simple, and at the end of that moving appeal to every altruistic sentiment it blazed at you, luminous and terrifying, like a flash of lightning in a serene sky: 'Exterminate all the brutes!' The curious part was that he had apparently forgotten all about that valuable postscriptum, because, later on, when he in a sense came to himself, he repeatedly entreated me to take good care of 'my pamphlet' (he called it), as it was sure to have in the future a good influence upon his career. I had full information about all these things, and, besides, as it turned out, I was to have the care of his memory. I've done enough for it to give me the indisputable right to lay it, if I choose, for an everlasting rest in the dust-bin of progress, amongst all the sweepings and, figuratively speaking, all the dead cats of civilisation. But then, you see, I can't choose. He won't be forgotten. Whatever he was, he was not common. He had the power to charm or frighten rudimentary souls into an aggravated witch-dance in his honour; he could also fill the small souls of the pilgrims with bitter misgivings: he had one devoted friend at least, and he had conquered one soul in the world that was neither rudimentary nor tainted with self-seeking. No; I can't forget him, though I am not prepared to affirm the fellow was exactly worth the life we lost in getting to him. I missed my late helmsman awfully,—I missed him even while his body was still lying in the pilot-house. Perhaps you will think it passing strange this regret for a savage who was no more account than a grain of sand in a black Sahara. Well, don't you see, he had done something, he had steered; for months I had him at my back—a help—an instrument. It was a kind of partnership. He steered for me—I had to look after him, I worried about his deficiencies, and thus a subtle bond had been created, of which I only became aware when it was suddenly broken. And the intimate profundity of that look he gave me when he received his hurt remains to this day in my memory—like a claim of distant kinship affirmed in a supreme moment.

"Poor fool! If he had only left that shutter alone. He had no restraint, no restraint—just like Kurtz—a tree swayed by the wind. As soon as I had put on a dry pair of slippers, I dragged him out, after first jerking the spear out of his side, which operation I confess I performed with my eyes shut tight. His heels leaped together over the little doorstep; his shoulders were pressed to my breast; I hugged him from behind desperately. Oh! he was heavy, heavy; heavier than any man on earth, I should imagine. Then without more ado I tipped him overboard. The current snatched him as though he had been a wisp of grass, and I saw the body roll over twice before I lost sight of it for ever. All the pilgrims and the manager were then congregated on the awning-deck about the pilothouse, chattering at each other like a flock of excited magpies, and there was a scandalised murmur at my heartless promptitude. What they wanted to keep that body hanging about for I can't guess. Embalm it, maybe. But I had also heard another, and a very ominous, murmur on the deck below. My friends the woodcutters were likewise scandalised, and with a better show of reason—though I admit that the reason itself was quite inadmissible. Oh, quite! I had made up my mind that if my late helmsman was to be eaten, the fishes alone should have him. He had been a very second-rate helmsman while alive, but now he was dead he might have become a first-class temptation, and possibly cause some startling trouble. Besides, I was anxious to take the wheel, the man in pink pyjamas showing himself a hopeless duffer at the business.

"This I did directly the simple funeral was over. We were going half-speed, keeping right in the middle of the stream, and I listened to the talk about me. They had given up Kurtz, they had given up the station; Kurtz was dead, and the station had been burnt—and so on—and so on. The red-haired pilgrim was beside himself with the thought that at least this poor Kurtz had been properly revenged. 'Say! We must have made a glorious slaughter of them in the bush. Eh? What do you think? Say?' He positively danced, the bloodthirsty little gingery beggar. And he had nearly fainted when he saw the wounded man! I could not help saying, 'You made a glorious lot of smoke, anyhow.' I had seen, from the way the tops of the bushes rustled and flew, that almost all the shots had gone too high. You can't hit anything unless you take aim and fire from the shoulder; but these chaps fired from the hip with their eyes shut. The retreat, I maintained—and I was right—was caused by the screeching of the steam-whistle. Upon this they forgot Kurtz, and began to howl at me with indignant protests.

"The manager stood by the wheel murmuring confidentially about the necessity of getting well away down the river before dark at all events, when I saw in the distance a clearing on the river-side and the outlines of some sort of building. 'What's this?' I asked. He clapped his hands in wonder. 'The station!' he cried. I edged in at once, still going half-speed.

"Through my glasses I saw the slope of a hill interspersed with rare trees and perfectly free from undergrowth. A long decaying building on the summit was half buried in the high grass; the large holes in the peaked roof gaped black from afar; the jungle and the woods made a background. There was no enclosure or fence of any kind; but there had been one apparently, for near the house half-a-dozen slim posts remained in a row, roughly trimmed, and with their upper ends ornamented with round carved balls. The rails, or whatever there had been between, had disappeared. Of course the forest surrounded all that. The river-bank was clear, and on the waterside I saw a white man under a hat like a cart-wheel beckoning persistently with his whole arm. Examining the edge of the forest above and below, I was almost certain I could see movements—human forms gliding here and there. I steamed past prudently, then stopped the engines and let her drift down. The man on the shore began to shout, urging us to land. 'We have been attacked,' screamed the manager. 'I know—I know. It's all right,' yelled back the other, as cheerful as you please. 'Come along. It's all right. I am glad.'

"His aspect reminded me of something I had seen—something funny I had seen somewhere. As I manoeuvred to get alongside, I was asking myself, 'What does this fellow look like?' Suddenly I got it. He looked like a harlequin. His clothes had been made of some stuff that was brown holland[24] probably, but it was covered with patches all over, with bright patches, blue, red, and yellow,—patches on the back, patches on front, patches on elbows, on knees; coloured binding round his jacket, scarlet edging at the bottom of his trousers; and the sunshine made him look extremely gay and wonderfully neat withal, because you could see how beautiful-

[24]A smooth linen fabric.

ly all this patching had been done. A beardless, boyish face, very fair, no features to speak of, nose peeling, little blue eyes, smiles and frowns chasing each other over that open countenance like sunshine and shadow on a wind-swept plain. 'Look out, captain!' he cried; 'there's a snag lodged in here last night.' What! Another snag? I confess I swore shamefully. I had nearly holed my cripple, to finish off that charming trip. The harlequin on the bank turned his little pug nose up to me. 'You English?' he asked, all smiles. 'Are you?' I shouted from the wheel. The smiles vanished, and he shook his head as if sorry for my disappointment. Then he brightened up. 'Never mind!' he cried encouragingly. 'Are we in time?' I asked. 'He is up there,' he replied, with a toss of the head up the hill, and becoming gloomy all of a sudden. His face was like the autumn sky, overcast one moment and bright the next.

"When the manager, escorted by the pilgrims, all of them armed to the teeth, had gone to the house, this chap came on board. 'I say, I don't like this. These natives are in the bush,' I said. He assured me earnestly it was all right. 'They are simple people,' he added; 'well, I am glad you came. It took me all my time to keep them off.' 'But you said it was all right,' I cried. 'Oh, they meant no harm,' he said; and as I stared he corrected himself, 'Not exactly.' Then vivaciously, 'My faith, your pilot-house wants a clean-up!' In the next breath he advised me to keep enough steam on the boiler to blow the whistle in case of any trouble. 'One good screech will do more for you than all your rifles. They are simple people,' he repeated. He rattled away at such a rate he quite overwhelmed me. He seemed to be trying to make up for lots of silence, and actually hinted, laughing, that such was the case. 'Don't you talk with Mr Kurtz?' I said. 'You don't talk with that man—you listen to him,' he exclaimed with severe exaltation. 'But now—' He waved his arm, and in the twinkling of an eye was in the uttermost depths of despondency. In a moment he came up again with a jump, possessed himself of both my hands, shook them continuously, while he gabbled: 'Brother sailor . . . honour . . . pleasure . . . delight . . . introduce myself . . . Russian . . . son of an arch-priest . . . Government of Tambov[25] . . . What? Tobacco! English tobacco; the excellent

[25] A province of Western Russia.

English tobacco! Now, that's brotherly. Smoke? Where's a sailor that does not smoke?'

"The pipe soothed him, and gradually I made out he had run away from school, had gone to sea in a Russian ship; ran away again; served some time in English ships; was now reconciled with the arch-priest. He made a point of that. 'But when one is young one must see things, gather experience, ideas; enlarge the mind.' 'Here!' I interrupted. 'You can never tell! Here I have met Mr Kurtz,' he said, youthfully solemn and reproachful. I held my tongue after that. It appears he had persuaded a Dutch trading-house on the coast to fit him out with stores and goods, and had started for the interior with a light heart, and no more idea of what would happen to him than a baby. He had been wandering about that river for nearly two years alone, cut off from everybody and everything. 'I am not so young as I look. I am twenty-five,' he said. 'At first old Van Shuyten would tell me to go to the devil,' he narrated with keen enjoyment; 'but I stuck to him, and talked and talked, till at last he got afraid I would talk the hind-leg off his favorite dog, so he gave me some cheap things and a few guns, and told me he hoped he would never see my face again. Good old Dutchman, Van Shuyten. I sent him one small lot of ivory a year ago, so that he can't call me a little thief when I get back. I hope he got it. And for the rest, I don't care. I had some wood stacked for you. That was my old house. Did you see?'

"I gave him Towson's book. He made as though he would kiss me, but restrained himself. 'The only book I had left, and I thought I had lost it,' he said, looking at it ecstatically. 'So many accidents happen to a man going about alone, you know. Canoes get upset sometimes—and sometimes you've got to clear out so quick when the people get angry.' He thumbed the pages. 'You made notes in Russian?' I asked. He nodded. 'I thought they were written in cipher,' I said. He laughed, then became serious. 'I had lots of trouble to keep these people off,' he said. 'Did they want to kill you?' I asked. 'Oh no!' he cried, and checked himself. 'Why did they attack us?' I pursued. He hesitated, then said shamefacedly, 'They don't want him to go.' 'Don't they?' I said, curiously. He nodded a nod full of mystery and wisdom. 'I tell you,' he cried, 'this man has enlarged my mind.' He opened his arms wide, staring at me with his little blue eyes that were perfectly round."

3

"I looked at him, lost in astonishment. There he was before me, in motley, as though he had absconded from a troupe of mimes, enthusiastic, fabulous. His very existence was improbable, inexplicable, and altogether bewildering. He was an insoluble problem. It was inconceivable how he had existed, how he had succeeded in getting so far, how he had managed to remain—why he did not instantly disappear. 'I went a little farther,' he said, 'then still a little farther—till I had gone so far that I don't know how I'll ever get back. Never mind. Plenty time. I can manage. You take Kurtz away quick—quick—I tell you.' The glamour of youth enveloped his particoloured rags, his destitution, his loneliness, the essential desolation of his futile wanderings. For months—for years—his life hadn't been worth a day's purchase; and there he was gallantly, thoughtlessly alive, to all appearance indestructible solely by the virtue of his few years and of his unreflecting audacity. I was seduced into something like admiration—like envy. Glamour urged him on, glamour kept him unscathed. He surely wanted nothing from the wilderness but space to breathe in and to push on through. His need was to exist, and to move onwards at the greatest possible risk, and with a maximum of privation. If the absolutely pure, uncalculating, unpractical spirit of adventure had ever ruled a human being, it ruled this be-patched youth. I almost envied him the possession of this modest and clear flame. It seemed to have consumed all thought of self so completely, that, even while he was talking to you, you forgot that it was he—the man before your eyes—who had gone through these things. I did not envy him his devotion to Kurtz, though. He had not meditated over it. It came to him, and he accepted it with a sort of eager fatalism. I must say that to me it appeared about the most dangerous thing in every way he had come upon so far.

"They had come together unavoidably, like two ships becalmed near each other, and lay rubbing sides at last. I suppose Kurtz wanted an audience, because on a certain occasion, when encamped in the forest, they had talked all night, or more probably Kurtz had talked. 'We talked of everything,' he said, quite transported at the recollection. 'I forgot there was such a thing as sleep. The night did not seem to last an hour. Everything! Everything! . . . Of love too.' 'Ah, he talked to you of love!' I said, much amused.

'It isn't what you think,' he cried, almost passionately. 'It was in general. He made me see things—things.'

"He threw his arms up. We were on deck at the time, and the headman of my wood-cutters, lounging near by, turned upon him his heavy and glittering eyes. I looked around, and I don't know why, but I assure you that never, never before, did this land, this river, this jungle, the very arch of this blazing sky, appear to me so hopeless and so dark, so impenetrable to human thought, so pitiless to human weakness. 'And, ever since, you have been with him, of course?' I said.

"On the contrary. It appears their intercourse had been very much broken by various causes. He had, as he informed me proudly, managed to nurse Kurtz through two illnesses (he alluded to it as you would to some risky feat), but as a rule Kurtz wandered alone, far in the depths of the forest. 'Very often coming to this station, I had to wait days and days before he would turn up,' he said. 'Ah, it was worth waiting for!—sometimes.' 'What was he doing? exploring or what?' I asked. 'Oh yes, of course'; he had discovered lots of villages, a lake too—he did not know exactly in what direction; it was dangerous to inquire too much—but mostly his expeditions had been for ivory. 'But he had no goods to trade with by that time,' I objected. 'There's a good lot of cartridges left even yet,' he answered, looking away. 'To speak plainly, he raided the country,' I said. He nodded. 'Not alone, surely!' He muttered something about the villages round that lake. 'Kurtz got the tribe to follow him, did he?' I suggested. He fidgeted a little. 'They adored him,' he said. The tone of these words was so extraordinary that I looked at him searchingly. It was curious to see his mingled eagerness and reluctance to speak of Kurtz. The man filled his life, occupied his thoughts, swayed his emotions. 'What can you expect?' he burst out; 'he came to them with thunder and lightning, you know—and they had never seen anything like it—and very terrible. He could be very terrible. You can't judge Mr Kurtz as you would an ordinary man. No, no, no! Now—just to give you an idea—I don't mind telling you, he wanted to shoot me too one day—but I don't judge him.' 'Shoot you!' I cried. 'What for?' 'Well, I had a small lot of ivory the chief of that village near my house gave me. You see I used to shoot game for them. Well, he wanted it, and wouldn't hear reason. He declared he would shoot me unless I gave him the ivory and then cleared out of the country, because he could do so, and had a fancy for it, and there was nothing on earth to prevent him killing whom he jolly well pleased. And it was true too. I gave him the ivory. What did I care! But I didn't clear out. No, no. I couldn't leave him. I had to be careful, of course, till we got friendly again for a time. He had his second illness then. Afterwards I had to keep out of the way; but I didn't mind. He was living for the most part in those villages on the lake. When he came down to the river, sometimes he would take to me, and sometimes it was better for me to be careful. This man suffered too much. He hated all this, and somehow he couldn't get away. When I had a chance I begged him to try and leave while there was time; I offered to go back with him. And he would say yes, and then he would remain; go off on another ivory hunt; disappear for weeks; forget himself amongst these people—forget himself—you know.' 'Why! he's mad,' I said. He protested indignantly. Mr Kurtz couldn't be mad. If I had heard him talk, only two days ago, I wouldn't dare hint at such a thing. . . . I had taken up my binoculars while we talked, and was looking at the shore, sweeping the limit of the forest at each side and at the back of the house. The consciousness of there being people in that bush, so silent, so quiet—as silent and quiet as the ruined house on the hill—made me uneasy. There was no sign on the face of nature of this amazing tale that was not so much told as suggested to me in desolate exclamations, completed by shrugs, in interrupted phrases, in hints ending in deep sighs. The woods were unmoved, like a mask—heavy, like the closed door of a prison—they looked with their air of hidden knowledge, of patient expectation, of unapproachable silence. The Russian was explaining to me that it was only lately that Mr Kurtz had come down to the river, bringing along with him all the fighting men of that lake tribe. He had been absent for several months—getting himself adored, I suppose—and had come down unexpectedly, with the intention to all appearance of making a raid either across the river or down stream. Evidently the appetite for more ivory had got the better of the—what shall I say?—less material aspirations. However, he had got much worse suddenly. 'I heard he was lying helpless, and so I came up—took my chance,' said the Russian. 'Oh, he is bad, very bad.' I directed my glass to the house. There were no signs of life, but there was the ruined roof, the long mud wall peeping above the grass, with three little square window-holes, no two of the same size; all this brought within reach of my hand, as it were. And then I made a brusque movement, and one of the remaining posts of that vanished fence leaped up in the field of my glass. You remember I told you I had been struck at the distance by certain attempts at ornamentation, rather remarkable in the ruinous aspect of the place. Now I had suddenly a nearer view, and its first result was to make me throw my head back as if before a blow. Then I went carefully from post to post with my glass, and I saw my mistake. These round knobs were not ornamental but symbolic; they were expressive and puzzling, striking and disturbing—food for thought and also for the vultures if there had been any looking down from the sky; but at all events for such ants as were industrious enough to ascend the pole. They would have been even more impressive, those heads on the stakes, if their faces had not been turned to the house. Only one, the first I had made out, was facing my way. I was not so shocked as you may think. The start back I had given was really nothing but a movement of surprise. I had expected to see a knob of wood there, you know. I returned deliberately to the first I had seen—and there it was, black, dried, sunken, with closed eyelids,—a head that seemed to sleep at the top of that pole, and, with the shrunken dry lips showing a narrow white line of the teeth, was smiling too, smiling continuously at some endless and jocose dream of that eternal slumber.

"I am not disclosing any trade secrets. In fact the manager said afterwards that Mr Kurtz's methods had ruined the district. I have no opinion on that point, but I want you clearly to understand that there was nothing exactly profitable in these heads being there. They only showed that Mr Kurtz lacked restraint in the gratification of his various lusts, that there was something wanting in him—some small matter which, when the pressing need arose, could not be found under his magnificent eloquence. Whether he knew of this deficiency himself I can't say. I think the knowledge came to him at last—only at the very last. But the wilderness had found him out early, and had taken on him a terrible vengeance for the fantastic invasion. I think it had whispered to him things about himself which he did not know, things of which he had no conception till he took counsel with this great solitude—and the whisper had proved irresistibly fascinating. It echoed loudly within him because he was hollow at the core. . . . I put down the glass, and the head that had appeared near enough to be spoken to seemed at once to have leaped away from me into inaccessible distance.

"The admirer of Mr Kurtz was a bit crestfallen. In a hurried, indistinct voice he began to assure me he had not dared to take these—say, symbols—down. He was not afraid of the natives; they would not stir till Mr Kurtz gave the word. His ascendancy was extraordinary. The camps of these people surrounded the place, and the chiefs came every day to see him. They would crawl . . . 'I don't want to know anything of the ceremonies used when approaching Mr Kurtz,' I shouted. Curious, this feeling that came over me that such details would be more intolerable than those heads drying on the stakes under Mr Kurtz's windows. After all, that was only a savage sight, while I seemed at one bound to have been transported into some lightless region of subtle horrors, where pure, uncomplicated savagery was a positive relief, being something that had a right to exist—obviously—in the sunshine. The young man looked at me with surprise. I suppose it did not occur to him Mr Kurtz was no idol of mine. He forgot I hadn't heard any of these splendid monologues on, what was it? on love, justice, conduct of life—or what not. If it had come to crawling before Mr Kurtz, he crawled as much as the veriest savage of them all. I had no idea of the conditions, he said: these heads were the heads of rebels. I shocked him excessively by laughing. Rebels! What would be the next definition I was to hear? There had been enemies, criminals, workers—and these were rebels. Those rebellious heads looked very subdued to me on their sticks. 'You don't know how such a life tries a man like Kurtz,' cried Kurtz's last disciple. 'Well, and you?' I said. 'I! I! I am a simple man. I have no great thoughts. I want nothing from anybody. How can you compare me to . . . ?' His feelings were too much for speech, and suddenly he broke down. 'I don't understand,' he groaned. 'I've been doing my best to keep him alive, and that's enough. I had no hand in all this. I have no abilities. There hasn't been a drop of medicine or a mouthful of invalid food for months here. He was shamefully abandoned. A man like this, with such ideas. Shamefully! Shamefully! I—I—haven't slept for the last ten nights. . . .'

"His voice lost itself in the calm of the evening. The long shadows of the forest had slipped down-hill while we talked, had gone far beyond the ruined hovel, beyond the symbolic row of stakes. All this was in the gloom, while we down there were yet in the sunshine, and the stretch of the river abreast of the clearing glittered in a still and dazzling splendour, with a murky and overshadowed bend above and below. Not a living soul was seen on the shore. The bushes did not rustle.

"Suddenly round the corner of the house a group of men appeared, as though they had come up from the ground. They waded waist-deep in the grass, in a compact body, bearing an improvised stretcher in their midst. Instantly, in the emptiness of the landscape, a cry arose whose shrillness pierced the still air like a sharp arrow flying straight to the very heart of the land; and, as if by enchantment, streams of human beings—of naked human beings—with spears in their hands, with bows, with shields, with wild glances and savage movements, were poured into the clearing by the dark-faced and pensive forest. The bushes shook, the grass swayed for a time, and then everything stood still in attentive immobility.

"'Now, if he does not say the right thing to them we are all done for,' said the Russian at my elbow. The knot of men with the stretcher had stopped too, half-way to the steamer, as if petrified. I saw the man on the stretcher sit up, lank and with an uplifted arm, above the shoulders of the bearers. 'Let us hope that the man who can talk so well of love in general will find some particular reason to spare us this time,' I said. I resented bitterly the absurd danger of our situation, as if to be at the mercy of that atrocious phantom had been a dishonouring necessity. I could not hear a sound, but through my glasses I saw the thin arm extended commandingly, the lower jaw moving, the eyes of that apparition shining darkly far in its bony head that nodded with grotesque jerks. Kurtz—Kurtz—that means 'short' in German—don't it? Well, the name was as true as everything else in his life—and death. He looked at least seven feet long. His covering had fallen off, and his body emerged from it pitiful and appalling as from a winding-sheet. I could see the cage of his ribs all astir, the bones of his arm waving. It was as though an animated image of death carved out of old ivory had been shaking its hand with menaces at a motionless crowd of men made of dark and glittering bronze. I saw him open his mouth wide—it gave him a weirdly voracious aspect, as though he had wanted to swallow all the air, all the earth, all the men before him. A deep voice reached me faintly. He must have been shouting. He fell back suddenly. The stretcher shook as the bearers staggered forward again, and almost at the same time I noticed that the crowd of savages was vanishing without any perceptible movement of retreat, as if the forest that had ejected these beings so suddenly had drawn them in again as the breath is drawn in a long aspiration.

"Some of the pilgrims behind the stretcher carried his arms—two shot-guns, a heavy rifle, and a light revolver-carbine—the thunderbolts of that pitiful Jupiter. The manager bent over him murmuring as he walked beside his head. They laid him down in one of the little cabins—just a room for a bed-place and a camp-stool or two, you know. We had brought his belated correspondence, and a lot of torn envelopes and open letters littered his bed. His hand roamed feebly amongst these papers. I was struck by the fire of his eyes and the composed languor of his expression. It was not so much the exhaustion of disease. He did not seem in pain. This shadow looked satiated and calm, as though for the moment it had had its fill of all the emotions.

"He rustled one of the letters, and looking straight in my face said, 'I am glad.' Somebody had been writing to him about me. These special recommendations were turning up again. The volume of tone he emitted without effort, almost without the trouble of moving his lips, amazed me. A voice! a voice! It was grave, profound, vibrating, while the man did not seem capable of a whisper. However, he had enough strength in him—factitious no doubt—to very nearly make an end of us, as you shall hear directly.

"The manager appeared silently in the doorway; I stepped out at once and he drew the curtain after me. The Russian, eyed curiously by the pilgrims, was staring at the shore. I followed the direction of his glance.

"Dark human shapes could be made out in the distance, flitting indistinctly against the gloomy border of the forest, and near the river two bronze figures, leaning on tall spears, stood in the sunlight under fantastic head-dresses of spotted skins, warlike and still in statuesque repose. And from right to left along the lighted shore moved a wild and gorgeous apparition of a woman.

"She walked with measured steps, draped in striped and fringed cloths, treading the earth proudly, with a slight jingle and flash of barbarous ornaments. She carried her head high; her hair was done in the shape of a helmet; she had brass leggings to the knee, brass wire gauntlets to the elbow, a crimson spot on her tawny cheek, innumerable necklaces of glass beads on her neck; bizarre things, charms, gifts of witchmen, that hung about her, glittered and trembled at every step. She must have had the value of several elephant tusks upon her. She was savage and superb, wild-eyed and magnificent; there was something ominous and stately in her deliberate progress. And in the hush that had fallen suddenly upon the whole sorrowful land, the immense wilderness, the colossal body of the fecund and mysterious life seemed to look at her, pensive, as though it had been looking at the image of its own tenebrous and passionate soul.

"She came abreast of the steamer, stood still, and faced us. Her long shadow fell to the water's edge. Her face had a tragic and fierce aspect of wild sorrow and of dumb pain mingled with the fear of some struggling, half-shaped resolve. She stood looking at us without a stir, and like the wilderness itself, with an air of brooding over an inscrutable purpose. A whole minute passed, and then she made a step forward. There was a low jingle, a glint of yellow metal, a sway of fringed draperies, and she stopped as if her heart had failed her. The young fellow by my side growled. The pilgrims murmured at my back. She looked at us all as if her life had depended upon the unswerving steadiness of her glance. Suddenly she opened her bared arms and threw them up rigid above her head, as though in an uncontrollable desire to touch the sky, and at the same time the swift shadows darted out on the earth, swept around on the river, gathering the steamer in a shadowy embrace. A formidable silence hung over the scene.

"She turned away slowly, walked on, following the bank, and passed into the bushes to the left. Once only her eyes gleamed back at us in the dusk of the thickets before she disappeared.

"'If she had offered to come aboard I really think I would have tried to shoot her,' said the man of patches, nervously. 'I had been risking my life every day for the last fortnight to keep her out of the house. She got in one day and kicked up a row about those miserable rags I picked up in the storeroom to mend my clothes with. I wasn't decent. At least it must have been that, for she talked like a fury to Kurtz for an hour, pointing at me now and then. I don't understand the dialect of this tribe. Luckily for me, I fancy Kurtz felt too ill that day to care, or there would have been mischief. I don't understand. . . . No—it's too much for me. Ah, well, it's all over now.'

"At this moment I heard Kurtz's deep voice behind the curtain, 'Save me!—save the ivory, you mean. Don't tell me. Save *me!* Why, I've had to save you. You are interrupting my plans now. Sick! Sick! Not so sick as you would like to believe. Never mind. I'll carry my ideas out yet—I will return. I'll show you what can be done. You with your little peddling notions—you are interfering with me. I will return. I . . .'

"The manager came out. He did me the honour to take me under the arm and lead me aside. 'He is very low, very low,' he said. He considered it necessary to sigh, but neglected to be consistently sorrowful. 'We have done all we could for him—haven't we? But there is no disguising the fact, Mr Kurtz has done more harm than good to the Company. He did not see the time was not ripe for vigorous action. Cautiously, cautiously—that's my principle. We must be cautious yet. The district is closed to us for a time. Deplorable! Upon the whole, the trade will suffer. I don't deny there is a remarkable quantity of ivory—mostly fossil. We must save it, at all events— but look how precarious the position is—and why? Because the method is unsound.' 'Do you,' said I, looking at the shore, 'call it "unsound method"?' 'Without doubt,' he exclaimed, hotly. 'Don't you?' . . . 'No method at all,' I murmured after a while. 'Exactly,' he exulted. 'I anticipated this. Shows a complete want of judgment. It is my duty to point it out in the proper quarter.' 'Oh,' said I, 'that fellow—what's his name?—the brickmaker, will make a readable report for you.' He appeared confounded for a moment. It seemed to me I had never breathed an atmosphere so vile, and I turned mentally to Kurtz for relief—positively for relief. 'Nevertheless, I think Mr Kurtz is a remarkable man,' I said with emphasis. He started, dropped on me a cold heavy glance, said very quietly, 'He was,' and turned his back on me. My hour of favour was over; I found myself lumped along with Kurtz as a partisan of methods for which the time was not ripe: I was unsound! Ah! but it was something to have at least a choice of nightmares.

"I had turned to the wilderness really, not to Mr Kurtz, who, I was ready to admit, was as good as buried. And for a moment it seemed to me as if I also were buried in a vast grave full of unspeakable secrets. I felt an intolerable weight oppressing my breast, the smell of the damp earth, the unseen presence of victorious corruption, the darkness of an impenetrable night. . . . The Russian tapped me on the shoulder. I heard him mumbling and stammering something about 'brother seaman—couldn't conceal—knowledge of matters that would affect Mr Kurtz's reputation.' I waited. For him evidently Mr Kurtz was not in his grave; I suspect that for him Mr Kurtz was one of the immortals. 'Well!' said I at last, 'speak out. As it happens, I am Mr Kurtz's friend—in a way.'

"He stated with a good deal of formality that had we not been 'of the same profession,' he would have kept the matter to himself without regard to consequences. He suspected 'there was an active ill-will towards him on the part of these white men that—' 'You are right,' I said, remembering a certain conversation I had overheard. 'The manager thinks you ought to be hanged.' He showed a concern at this intelligence which amused me at first. 'I had better get out of the way quietly,' he said, earnestly. 'I can do no more for Kurtz now, and they would soon find some excuse. What's to stop them? There's a military post three hundred miles from here.' 'Well, upon my word,' said I, 'perhaps you had better go if you have any friends amongst the savages near by.' 'Plenty,' he said. 'They are simple people—and I want nothing, you know.' He stood biting his lip, then: 'I don't want any harm to happen to these whites here, but of course I was thinking of Mr Kurtz's reputation—but you are a brother seaman and—' 'All right,' said I, after a time. 'Mr Kurtz's reputation is safe with me.' I did not know how truly I spoke.

"He informed me, lowering his voice, that it was Kurtz who had ordered the attack to be made on the steamer. 'He hated sometimes the idea of being taken away—and then again . . . But I don't understand these matters. I am a simple man. He thought it would scare you away—that you would give it up, thinking him dead. I could not stop him. Oh, I had an awful time of it this last month.' 'Very well,' I said. 'He is all right now.' 'Ye-e-es,' he muttered, not very convinced apparently. 'Thanks,' said I; 'I shall keep my eyes open.' 'But quiet—eh?' he urged, anxiously. 'It would be awful for his reputation if anybody here—' I promised a complete discretion with great gravity. 'I have a canoe and three black fellows waiting not very far. I am off. Could you give me a few Martini-Henry cartridges?' I could, and did, with proper secrecy. He helped himself, with a wink at me, to a handful of my tobacco. 'Between sailors—you know—good English tobacco.' At the door of the pilot-house he turned round—'I say, haven't you a pair of shoes you could spare?' He raised one leg. 'Look.' The soles were tied with knotted strings sandal-wise under his bare feet. I rooted out an old pair, at which he looked with admiration before tucking it under his left arm. One of his pockets (bright red) was bulging with cartridges, from the other (dark blue) peeped 'Towson's Inquiry,' &c., &c. He seemed to think himself excellently well equipped for a renewed encounter with the wilderness. 'Ah! I'll never, never meet such a man again. You ought to have heard him recite poetry—his own too it was, he told me. Poetry!' He rolled his eyes at the recollection of these delights. 'Oh, he enlarged my mind!' 'Good-bye,' said I. He shook hands and vanished in the night. Sometimes I ask myself whether I had ever really seen him—whether it was possible to meet such a phenomenon! . . .

"When I woke up shortly after midnight his warning came to my mind with its hint of danger that seemed, in the starred darkness, real enough to make me get up for the purpose of having a look round. On the hill a big fire burned, illuminating fitfully a crooked corner of the station-house. One of the agents with a picket of a few of our blacks, armed for the purpose, was keeping guard over the ivory; but deep within the forest, red gleams that wavered, that seemed to sink and rise from the ground amongst confused columnar shapes of intense blackness, showed the exact position of the camp where Mr Kurtz's adorers were keeping their uneasy vigil. The monotonous beating of a big drum filled the air with muffled shocks and a lingering vibration. A steady droning sound of many men chanting each to himself some weird incantation came out from the black, flat wall of the woods as the humming of bees comes out of a hive, and had a strange narcotic effect upon my half-awake senses. I believe I dozed off leaning over the rail, till an abrupt burst of yells, an overwhelming outbreak of a pent-up and mysterious frenzy, woke me up in a bewildered wonder. It was cut short all at once, and the low droning went on with an effect of audible and soothing silence. I glanced casually into the little cabin. A light was burning within, but Mr Kurtz was not there.

"I think I would have raised an outcry if I had believed my eyes. But I didn't believe them at first—the thing seemed so impossible. The fact is, I was completely unnerved by a sheer blank fright, pure abstract terror, unconnected with any distinct shape of physical danger. What made this emotion so overpowering was—how shall I define it?—the moral shock I received, as if something altogether monstrous, intolerable to thought and odious to the soul, had been thrust upon me unexpectedly. This lasted of course the merest fraction of a second, and then the usual sense of commonplace, deadly danger, the possibility of a sudden onslaught and massacre, or something of the kind, which I saw impending, was positively welcome and composing. It pacified me, in fact, so much, that I did not raise an alarm.

"There was an agent buttoned up inside an ulster[26] and sleeping on a chair on deck within three feet of me. The yells had not awakened him; he snored very slightly; I left him to his slumbers and leaped ashore. I did not betray Mr Kurtz—it was ordered I should never betray him—it was written I should be loyal to the nightmare of my choice. I was anxious to deal with this shadow by myself alone,—and to this day I don't know why I was so jealous of sharing with any one the peculiar blackness of that experience.

"As soon as I got on the bank I saw a trail—a broad trail through the grass. I remember the exultation with which I said to myself, 'He can't walk—he is crawling on all-fours—I've got him.' The grass was wet with dew. I strode rapidly with clenched fists. I fancy I had some vague notion of falling upon him and giving him a drubbing. I don't know. I had some imbecile thoughts. The knitting old woman with the cat obtruded herself upon my memory as a most improper person to be sitting at the other end of such an affair. I saw a row of pilgrims squirting lead in the air out of Winchesters held to the hip. I thought I would never get back to the steamer, and imagined myself living alone and unarmed in the woods to an advanced age. Such silly things—you know. And I remember I confounded the beat of the drum with the beating of my heart, and was pleased at its calm regularity.

"I kept to the track though—then stopped to listen. The night was very clear: a dark blue space, sparkling with dew and starlight, in which black things stood very still. I thought I could see a kind of motion ahead of me. I was strangely cocksure of everything that night. I actually left the track and ran in a wide semicircle (I verily

[26]Long overcoat.

believe chuckling to myself) so as to get in front of that stir, of that motion I had seen—if indeed I had seen anything. I was circumventing Kurtz as though it had been a boyish game.

"I came upon him, and, if he had not heard me coming, I would have fallen over him too, but he got up in time. He rose, unsteady, long, pale, indistinct, like a vapour exhaled by the earth, and swayed slightly, misty and silent before me; while at my back the fires loomed between the trees, and the murmur of many voices issued from the forest. I had cut him off cleverly; but when actually confronting him I seemed to come to my senses, I saw the danger in its right proportion. It was by no means over yet. Suppose he began to shout? Though he could hardly stand, there was still plenty of vigour in his voice. 'Go away—hide yourself,' he said, in that profound tone. It was very awful. I glanced back. We were within thirty yards from the nearest fire. A black figure stood up, strode on long black legs, waving long black arms, across the glow. It had horns—antelope horns, I think—on its head. Some sorcerer, some witch-man, no doubt: it looked fiend-like enough. 'Do you know what you are doing?' I whispered. 'Perfectly,' he answered, raising his voice for that single word: it sounded to me far off and yet loud, like a hail through a speaking-trumpet. If he makes a row we are lost, I thought to myself. This clearly was not a case for fisticuffs, even apart from the very natural aversion I had to beat that Shadow—this wandering and tormented thing. 'You will be lost,' I said—'utterly lost.' One gets sometimes such a flash of inspiration, you know. I did say the right thing, though indeed he could not have been more irretrievably lost than he was at this very moment, when the foundations of our intimacy were being laid—to endure—to endure—even to the end—even beyond.

"'I had immense plans,' he muttered irresolutely. 'Yes,' said I; 'but if you try to shout I'll smash your head with—' there was not a stick or a stone near. 'I will throttle you for good,' I corrected myself. 'I was on the threshold of great things,' he pleaded, in a voice of longing, with a wistfulness of tone that made my blood run cold. 'And now for this stupid scoundrel—' 'Your success in Europe is assured in any case,' I affirmed, steadily. I did not want to have the throttling of him, you understand—and indeed it would have been very little use for any practical purpose. I tried to break the spell—the heavy, mute spell of the wilderness—that seemed to draw him to its pitiless breast by the awakening of forgotten and brutal instincts, by the memory of gratified and monstrous passions. This alone, I was convinced, had driven him out to the edge of the forest, to the bush, towards the gleam of fires, the throb of drums, the drone of weird incantations; this alone had beguiled his unlawful soul beyond the bounds of permitted aspirations. And, don't you see, the terror of the position was not in being knocked on the head—though I had a very lively sense of that danger too—but in this, that I had to deal with a being to whom I could not appeal in the name of anything high or low. I had, even like the niggers, to invoke him—himself—his own exalted and incredible degradation. There was nothing either above or below him, and I knew it. He had kicked himself loose of the earth. Confound the man! he had kicked the very earth to pieces. He was alone, and I before him did not know whether I stood on the ground or floated in the air. I've been telling you what we said—repeating the phrases we pronounced,—but what's the good? They were common everyday words,—the familiar, vague sounds exchanged on every waking day of life. But what of that? They had behind them, to my mind, the terrific suggestiveness of words heard in dreams, of phrases spoken in nightmares. Soul! If anybody had ever struggled with a soul, I am the man. And I wasn't arguing with a lunatic either. Believe me or not, his intelligence was perfectly clear—concentrated, it is true, upon himself with horrible intensity, yet clear; and therein was my only chance—barring, of course, the killing him there and then, which wasn't so good, on account of unavoidable noise. But his soul was mad. Being alone in the wilderness, it had looked within itself, and, by heavens! I tell you, it had gone mad. I had—for my sins, I suppose—to go through the ordeal of looking into it myself. No eloquence could have been so withering to one's belief in mankind as his final burst of sincerity. He struggled with himself, too. I saw it,—I heard it. I saw the inconceivable mystery of a soul that knew no restraint, no faith, and no fear, yet struggling blindly with itself. I kept my head pretty well; but when I had him at last stretched on the couch, I wiped my forehead, while my legs shook under me as though I had carried half a ton on my back down that hill. And yet I had only supported him, his bony arm clasped round my neck—and he was not much heavier than a child.

"When next day we left at noon, the crowd, of whose presence behind the curtain of trees I had been acutely conscious all the time, flowed out of the woods again, filled the clearing, covered the slope with a mass of naked, breathing, quivering, bronze bodies. I steamed up a bit, then swung down-stream, and two thousand eyes followed the evolutions of the splashing, thumping, fierce river-demon beating the water with its terrible tail and breathing black smoke into the air. In front of the first rank, along the river, three men, plastered with bright red earth from head to foot, strutted to and fro restlessly. When we came abreast again, they faced the river, stamped their feet, nodded their horned heads, swayed their scarlet bodies; they shook towards the fierce river-demon a bunch of black feathers, a mangy skin with a pendent tail—something that looked like a dried gourd; they shouted periodically together strings of amazing words that resembled no sounds of human language; and the deep murmurs of the crowd, interrupted suddenly, were like the responses of some satanic litany.

"We had carried Kurtz into the pilot-house: there was more air there. Lying on the couch, he stared through the open shutter. There was an eddy in the mass of human bodies, and the woman with helmeted head and tawny cheeks rushed out to the very brink of the stream. She put out her hands, shouted something, and all that wild mob took up the shout in a roaring chorus of articulated, rapid, breathless utterance.

"'Do you understand this?' I asked.

"He kept on looking out past me with fiery, longing eyes, with a mingled expression of wistfulness and hate. He made no answer, but I saw a smile, a smile of indefinable meaning, appear on his colourless lips that a moment after twitched convulsively. 'Do I not?' he said slowly, gasping, as if the words had been torn out of him by a supernatural power.

"I pulled the string of the whistle, and I did this because I saw the pilgrims on deck getting out their rifles with an air of anticipating a jolly lark. At the sudden screech there was a movement of abject terror through that wedged mass of bodies. 'Don't! don't! you frighten them away,' cried some one on deck disconsolately. I pulled the string time after time. They broke and ran, they leaped, they crouched, they swerved, they dodged the flying terror of the sound. The three red chaps had fallen flat, face down on the shore, as though they had been shot dead. Only the barbarous and superb woman did not so much as flinch, and stretched tragically her bare arms after us over the sombre and glittering river.

"And then that imbecile crowd down on the deck started their little fun, and I could see nothing more for smoke.

"The brown current ran swiftly out of the heart of darkness, bearing us down towards the sea with twice the speed of our upward progress; and Kurtz's life was running swiftly too, ebbing, ebbing out of his heart into the sea of inexorable time. The manager was very placid, he had no vital anxieties now, he took us both in with a comprehensive and satisfied glance: the 'affair' had come off as well as could be wished. I saw the time approaching when I would be left alone of the party of 'unsound method.' The pilgrims looked upon me with disfavour. I was, so to speak, numbered with the dead. It is strange how I accepted this unforeseen partnership, this choice of nightmares forced upon me in the tenebrous land invaded by these mean and greedy phantoms.

"Kurtz discoursed. A voice! a voice! It rang deep to the very last. It survived his strength to hide in the magnificent folds of eloquence the barren darkness of his heart. Oh, he struggled! he struggled! The wastes of his weary brain were haunted by shadowy images now—images of wealth and fame revolving obsequiously round his unextinguishable gift of noble and lofty expression. My Intended, my station, my career, my ideas—these were the subjects for the occasional utterances of elevated sentiments. The shade of the original Kurtz frequented the bedside of the hollow sham, whose fate it was to be buried presently in the mould of primeval earth. But both the diabolic love and the unearthly hate of the mysteries it had penetrated fought for the possession of that soul satiated with primitive emotions, avid of lying fame, of sham distinction, of all the appearances of success and power.

"Sometimes he was contemptibly childish. He desired to have kings meet him at railway-stations on his return from some ghastly Nowhere, where he intended to accomplish great things. 'You show them you have in you something that is really profitable, and then there will be no limits to the recognition of your ability,' he would say. 'Of course you must take care of the motives—right motives—always.' The long reaches that were like one and the same reach, monotonous bends that were exactly alike, slipped past the steamer with their multitude of secular[27] trees looking patiently after this grimy fragment of another world, the forerunner of change, of conquest, of trade, of massacres, of blessings. I looked ahead—piloting. 'Close the shutter,' said Kurtz suddenly one day; 'I can't bear to look at this.' I did so. There was a silence. 'Oh, but I will wring your heart yet!' he cried at the invisible wilderness.

"We broke down—as I had expected—and had to lie up for repairs at the head of an island. This delay was the first thing that shook Kurtz's confidence. One morning he gave me a packet of papers and a photograph,—the lot tied together with a shoe-string. 'Keep this for me,' he said. 'This noxious fool' (meaning the manager) 'is capable of prying into my boxes when I am not looking.' In the afternoon I saw him. He was lying on his back with closed eyes, and I withdrew quietly, but I heard him mutter, 'Live rightly, die, die . . .' I listened. There was nothing more. Was he rehearsing some speech in his sleep, or was it a fragment of a phrase from some newspaper article? He had been writing for the papers and meant to do so again, 'for the furthering of my ideas. It's a duty.'

"His was an impenetrable darkness. I looked at him as you peer down at a man who is lying at the bottom of a precipice where the sun never shines. But I had not much time to give him, because I was helping the engine-driver to take to pieces the leaky cylinders, to straighten a bent connecting-rod, and in other such matters. I lived in an infernal mess of rust, filings, nuts, bolts, spanners, hammers, ratchet-drills—things I abominate, because I don't get on with them. I tended the little forge we fortunately had aboard; I toiled wearily in a wretched scrap-heap—unless I had the shakes too bad to stand.

"One evening coming in with a candle I was startled to hear him say a little tremulously, 'I am lying here in the dark waiting for death.' The light was within a foot of his eyes. I forced myself to murmur, 'Oh, nonsense!' and stood over him as if transfixed.

"Anything approaching the change that came over his features I have never seen before, and hope never to see again. Oh, I wasn't touched. I was fascinated. It was as though a veil had been rent. I

[27]Ancient.

saw on that ivory face the expression of sombre pride, of ruthless power, of craven terror—of an intense and hopeless despair. Did he live his life again in every detail of desire, temptation, and surrender during that supreme moment of complete knowledge? He cried in a whisper at some image, at some vision,—he cried out twice, a cry that was no more than a breath—

"'The horror! The horror!'

"I blew the candle out and left the cabin. The pilgrims were dining in the mess-room, and I took my place opposite the manager, who lifted his eyes to give me a questioning glance, which I successfully ignored. He leaned back, serene, with that peculiar smile of his sealing the unexpressed depths of his meanness. A continuous shower of small flies streamed upon the lamp, upon the cloth, upon our hands and faces. Suddenly the manager's boy put his insolent black head in the doorway, and said in a tone of scathing contempt—

"'Mistah Kurtz—he dead.'

"All the pilgrims rushed out to see. I remained, and went on with my dinner. I believe I was considered brutally callous. However, I did not eat much. There was a lamp in there—light, don't you know—and outside it was so beastly, beastly dark. I went no more near the remarkable man who had pronounced a judgment upon the adventures of his soul on this earth. The voice was gone. What else had been there? But I am of course aware that next day the pilgrims buried something in a muddy hole.

"And then they very nearly buried me.

"However, as you see, I did not go to join Kurtz there and then. I did not. I remained to dream the nightmare out to the end, and to show my loyalty to Kurtz once more. Destiny. My destiny! Droll thing life is—that mysterious arrangement of merciless logic for a futile purpose. The most you can hope from it is some knowledge of yourself—that comes too late—a crop of unextinguishable regrets. I have wrestled with death. It is the most unexciting contest you can imagine. It takes place in an impalpable greyness, with nothing underfoot, with nothing around, without spectators, without clamour, without glory, without the great desire of victory, without the great fear of defeat, in a sickly atmosphere of tepid scepticism, without much belief in your own right, and still less in that of your adversary. If such is the form of ultimate wisdom, then life is a greater riddle than some of us think it to be. I was within a hair's-breadth of the last opportunity for pronouncement, and I found with humiliation that probably I would have nothing to say. This is the reason why I affirm that Kurtz was a remarkable man. He had something to say. He said it. Since I had peeped over the edge myself, I understand better the meaning of his stare, that could not see the flame of the candle, but was wide enough to embrace the whole universe, piercing enough to penetrate all the hearts that beat in the darkness. He had summed up—he had judged. 'The horror!' He was a remarkable man. After all, this was the expression of some sort of belief; it had candour, it had conviction, it had a vibrating note of revolt in its whisper, it had the appalling face of a glimpsed truth—the strange commingling of desire and hate. And it is not my own extremity I remember best— a vision of greyness without form filled with physical pain, and a careless contempt for the evanescence of all things—even of this pain itself. No! It is his extremity that I seem to have lived through. True, he had made that last stride, he had stepped over the edge, while I had been permitted to draw back my hesitating foot. And perhaps in this is the whole difference; perhaps all the wisdom, and all truth, and all sincerity, are just compressed into that inappreciable moment of time in which we step over the threshold of the invisible. Perhaps! I like to think my summing-up would not have been a word of careless contempt. Better his cry—much better. It was an affirmation, a moral victory paid for by innumerable defeats, by abominable terrors, by abominable satisfactions. But it was a victory! That is why I have remained loyal to Kurtz to the last, and even beyond, when a long time after I heard once more, not his own voice, but the echo of his magnificent eloquence thrown to me from a soul as translucently pure as a cliff of crystal.

"No, they did not bury me, though there is a period of time which I remember mistily, with a shuddering wonder, like a passage through some inconceivable world that had no hope in it and no desire. I found myself back in the sepulchral city resenting the sight of people hurrying through the streets to filch a little money from each other, to devour their infamous cookery, to gulp their unwholesome beer, to dream their insignificant and silly dreams. They trespassed upon my thoughts. They were intruders whose knowledge of life was to me an irritating pretence, because I felt so sure they could not possibly know the things I knew. Their bearing, which was simply the bearing of commonplace individuals going about their business in the assurance of perfect safety, was offensive to me like the outrageous flauntings of folly in the face of a danger it is unable to comprehend. I had no particular desire to enlighten them, but I had some difficulty in restraining myself from laughing in their faces, so full of stupid importance. I daresay I was not very well at that time. I tottered about the streets—there were various affairs to settle—grinning bitterly at perfectly respectable persons. I admit my behaviour was inexcusable, but then my temperature was seldom normal in these days. My dear aunt's endeavours to 'nurse up my strength' seemed altogether beside the mark. It was not my strength that wanted nursing, it was my imagination that wanted soothing. I kept the bundle of papers given me by Kurtz, not knowing exactly what to do with it. His mother had died lately, watched over, as I was told, by his Intended. A clean-shaved man, with an official manner and wearing gold-rimmed spectacles, called on me one day and made inquiries, at first circuitous, afterwards suavely pressing, about what he was pleased to denominate certain 'documents.' I was not surprised, because I had had two rows with the manager on the subject out there. I had refused to give up the smallest scrap out of that package, and I took the same attitude with the spectacled man. He became darkly menacing at last, and with much heat argued that the Company had the right to every bit of information about its 'territories.' And, said he, 'Mr Kurtz's knowledge of unexplored regions must have been necessarily extensive and peculiar—owing to his great abilities and to the deplorable circumstances in which he had been placed: therefore—' I assured him Mr Kurtz's knowledge, however extensive, did not bear upon the problems of commerce or administration. He invoked then the name of science. 'It would be an incalculable loss if,' &c., &c. I offered him the report on the 'Suppression of Savage Customs,' with the postscriptum torn off. He took it up eagerly, but ended by sniffing at it with an air of contempt. 'This is not what we had a right to expect,' he remarked. 'Expect nothing else,' I said. 'There are only private letters.' He withdrew upon some threat of legal proceedings, and I saw him no more; but another fellow, calling himself Kurtz's cousin, appeared two days later, and was anxious to hear all the details about his dear relative's last moments. Incidentally he gave me to understand that Kurtz had been essentially a great musician. 'There was the making of an immense success,' said the man, who was an organist, I believe, with lank grey hair flowing over a greasy coat-collar. I had no reason to doubt his statement; and to this day I am unable to say what was Kurtz's profession, whether he ever had any—which was the greatest of his talents. I had taken him for a painter who wrote for the papers, or else for a journalist who could paint—but even the cousin (who took snuff during the interview) could not tell me what he had been—exactly. He was a universal genius—on that point I agreed with the old chap, who thereupon blew his nose noisily into a large cotton handkerchief and withdrew in senile agitation, bearing off some family letters and memoranda without importance. Ultimately a journalist anxious to know something of the fate of his 'dear colleague' turned up. This visitor informed me Kurtz's proper sphere ought to have been politics 'on the popular side.' He had furry straight eyebrows, bristly hair cropped short, an eye-glass on a broad ribbon, and, becoming expansive, confessed his opinion that Kurtz really couldn't write a bit—'but heavens! how that man could talk! He electrified large meetings. He had faith—don't you see?—he had the faith. He could get himself to believe anything—anything. He would have been a splendid leader of an extreme party.' 'What party?' I asked. 'Any party,' answered the other. 'He was an—an—extremist.' Did I not think so? I assented. Did I know, he asked, with a sudden flash of curiosity, 'what it was that had induced him to go out there?' 'Yes,' said I, and forthwith handed him the famous Report for publication, if he thought fit. He glanced through it hurriedly, mumbling all the time, judged 'it would do,' and took himself off with this plunder.

"Thus I was left at last with a slim packet of letters and the girl's portrait. She struck me as beautiful—I mean she had a beautiful expression. I know that the sunlight can be made to lie too, yet one felt that no manipulation of light and pose could have conveyed the delicate shade of truthfulness upon those features. She seemed ready to listen without mental reservation, without suspicion, without a thought for herself. I concluded I would go and give her back her portrait and those letters myself. Curiosity? Yes; and also some other feeling perhaps. All that had been Kurtz's had passed out of my hands: his soul, his body, his station, his plans, his ivory, his career. There remained only his memory and his Intended—and I wanted to give that up too to the past, in a way,—to surrender personally all that remained of him with me to that oblivion which is the last word of our common fate. I don't defend myself. I had no clear perception of what it was I really wanted. Perhaps it was an impulse of unconscious loyalty, or the fulfilment of one of those ironic necessities that lurk in the facts of human existence. I don't know. I can't tell. But I went.

"I thought his memory was like the other memories of the dead that accumulate in every man's life,—a vague impress on the brain of shadows that had fallen on it in their swift and final passage; but before the high and ponderous door, between the tall houses of a street as still and decorous as a well-kept alley in a cemetery, I had a vision of him on the stretcher, opening his mouth voraciously, as if to devour all the earth with all its mankind. He lived then before me; he lived as much as he had ever lived—a shadow insatiable of splendid appearances, of frightful realities; a shadow darker than the shadow of the night, and draped nobly in the folds of a gorgeous eloquence. The vision seemed to enter the house with me—the stretcher, the phantom-bearers, the wild crowd of obedient worshippers, the gloom of the forests, the glitter of the reach between the murky bends, the beat of the drum, regular and muffled like the beating of a heart—the heart of a conquering darkness. It was a moment of triumph for the wilderness, an invading and vengeful rush which, it seemed to me, I would have to keep back alone for the salvation of another soul. And the memory of what I had heard him say afar there, with the horned shapes stirring at my back, in the glow of fires, within the patient woods, those broken phrases came back to me, were heard again in their ominous and terrifying simplicity. I remembered his abject pleading, his abject threats, the colossal scale of his vile desires, the meanness, the torment, the tempestuous anguish of his soul. And later on I seemed to see his collected languid manner, when he said one day, 'This lot of ivory now is really mine. The Company did not pay for it. I collected it myself at a very great personal risk. I am afraid they will try to claim it as theirs though. H'm. It is a difficult case. What do you think I ought to do—resist? Eh? I want no more than justice.' . . . He wanted no more than justice—no more than justice. I rang the bell before a mahogany door on the first floor, and while I waited he seemed to stare at me out of the glassy panel—stare with that wide and immense stare embracing, condemning, loathing all the universe. I seemed to hear the whispered cry, 'The horror! The horror!'

"The dusk was falling. I had to wait in a lofty drawing-room with three long windows from floor to ceiling that were like three luminous and bedraped columns. The bent gilt legs and backs of the furniture shone in indistinct curves. The tall marble fireplace had a cold and monumental whiteness. A grand piano stood massively in a corner, with dark gleams on the flat surfaces like a sombre and polished sarcophagus. A high door opened—closed. I rose.

"She came forward, all in black, with a pale head, floating towards me in the dusk. She was in mourning. It was more than a year since his death, more than a year since the news came; she seemed as though she would remember and mourn for ever. She took both my hands in hers and murmured, 'I had heard you were coming.' I noticed she was not very young—I mean not girlish. She had a mature capacity for fidelity, for belief, for suffering. The room seemed to have grown darker, as if all the sad light of the cloudy evening had taken refuge on her forehead. This fair hair, this pale visage, this pure brow, seemed surrounded by an ashy halo from which the dark eyes looked out at me. Their glance was guileless, profound, confident, and trustful. She carried her sorrowful head as though she were proud of that sorrow, as though she would say, I—I alone know how to mourn for him as he deserves. But while we were still shaking hands, such a look of awful desolation came upon her face that I perceived she was one of those creatures that are not the playthings of Time. For her he had died only yesterday. And, by Jove! the impression was so powerful that for me too he seemed to have died only yesterday—nay, this very minute. I saw her and him in the same instant of time—his death and her sorrow—I saw her sorrow in the very moment of his death. Do you understand? I saw them together—I heard them together. She had said, with a deep catch of the breath, 'I have survived'; while my strained ears seemed to hear distinctly, mingled with her tone of despairing regret, the summing-up whisper of his eternal condemnation. I asked myself what I was doing there, with a sensation of panic in my heart as though I had blundered into a place of cruel and absurd mysteries not fit for a human being to behold. She motioned me to a chair. We sat down. I laid the packet gently on the little table, and she put her hand over it. . . . 'You knew him well,' she murmured, after a moment of mourning silence.

"'Intimacy grows quickly out there,' I said. 'I knew him as well as it is possible for one man to know another.'

"'And you admired him,' she said. 'It was impossible to know him and not to admire him. Was it?'

"'He was a remarkable man,' I said, unsteadily. Then before the appealing fixity of her gaze, that seemed to watch for more words on my lips, I went on, 'It was impossible not to—'

"'Love him,' she finished eagerly, silencing me into an appalled dumbness. 'How true! how true! But when you think that no one knew him so well as I! I had all his noble confidence. I knew him best.'

"'You knew him best,' I repeated. And perhaps she did. But with every word spoken the room was growing darker, and only her forehead, smooth and white, remained illumined by the unextinguishable light of belief and love.

"'You were his friend,' she went on. 'His friend,' she repeated, a little louder. 'You must have been, if he had given you this, and sent you to me. I feel I can speak to you—and oh! I must speak. I want you—you who have heard his last words—to know I have been worthy of him. . . . It is not pride. . . . Yes! I am proud to know I understood him better than any one on earth—he told me so himself. And since his mother died I have had no one—no one— to—to—'

"I listened. The darkness deepened. I was not even sure whether he had given me the right bundle. I rather suspect he wanted me to take care of another batch of his papers which, after his death, I saw the manager examining under the lamp. And the girl talked, easing her pain in the certitude of my sympathy; she talked as thirsty men drink. I had heard that her engagement with Kurtz had been disapproved by her people. He wasn't rich enough or something. And indeed I don't know whether he had not been a pauper all his life. He had given me some reason to infer that it was his impatience of comparative poverty that drove him out there.

"'. . . Who was not his friend who had heard him speak once?' she was saying. 'He drew men towards him by what was best in them.' She looked at me with intensity. 'It is the gift of the great,' she went on, and the sound of her low voice seemed to have the accompaniment of all the other sounds, full of mystery, desolation, and sorrow, I had ever heard—the ripple of the river, the soughing of the trees swayed by the wind, the murmurs of wild crowds, the faint ring of incomprehensible words cried from afar, the whisper of a voice speaking from beyond the threshold of an eternal darkness. 'But you have heard him! You know!' she cried.

"'Yes, I know,' I said with something like despair in my heart, but bowing my head before the faith that was in her, before that great and saving illusion that shone with an unearthly glow in the darkness, in the triumphant darkness from which I could not have defended her—from which I could not even defend myself.

"'What a loss to me—to us!'—she corrected herself with beautiful generosity; then added in a murmur, 'To the world.' By the last gleams of twilight I could see the glitter of her eyes, full of tears—of tears that would not fall.

"'I have been very happy—very fortunate—very proud,' she went on. 'Too fortunate. Too happy for a little while. And now I am unhappy for— for life.'

"She stood up; her fair hair seemed to catch all the remaining light in a glimmer of gold. I rose too.

"'And of all this,' she went on, mournfully, 'of all his promise, and of all his greatness, of his generous mind, of his noble heart, nothing remains—nothing but a memory. You and I—'

"'We shall always remember him,' I said, hastily.

"'No!' she cried. 'It is impossible that all this should be lost—that such a life should be sacrificed to leave nothing—but sorrow. You know what vast plans he had. I knew of them too—I could not perhaps understand,—but others knew of them. Something must remain. His words, at least, have not died.'

"'His words will remain,' I said.

"'And his example,' she whispered to herself. 'Men looked up to him,—his goodness shone in every act. His example—'

"'True,' I said; 'his example too. Yes, his example. I forgot that.'

"'But I do not. I cannot—I cannot believe—not yet. I cannot believe that I shall never see him again, that nobody will see him again, never, never, never.'

"She put out her arms as if after a retreating figure, stretching them black and with clasped pale hands across the fading and narrow sheen of the window. Never see him! I saw him clearly enough then. I shall see this eloquent phantom as long as I live, and I shall see her too, a tragic and familiar Shade, resembling in this gesture another one, tragic also, and bedecked with powerless charms, stretching bare brown arms over the glitter of the infernal stream, the stream of darkness. She said suddenly very low, 'He died as he lived.'

"'His end,' said I, with dull anger stirring in me, 'was in every way worthy of his life.'

"'And I was not with him,' she murmured. My anger subsided before a feeling of infinite pity.

"'Everything that could be done—' I mumbled.

"'Ah, but I believed in him more than any one on earth—more than his own mother, more than—himself. He needed me! Me! I would have treasured every sigh, every word, every sign, every glance.'

"I felt like a chill grip on my chest. 'Don't,' I said, in a muffled voice.

"'Forgive me. I—I—have mourned so long in silence—in silence. . . . You were with him—to the last? I think of his loneliness. Nobody near to understand him as I would have understood. Perhaps no one to hear. . . .'

"'To the very end,' I said, shakily. 'I heard his very last words. . . .' I stopped in a fright.

"'Repeat them,' she said in a heart-broken tone. 'I want—I want—something—something—to—to live with.'

"I was on the point of crying at her, 'Don't you hear them?' The dusk was repeating them in a persistent whisper all around us, in a whisper that seemed to swell menacingly like the first whisper of a rising wind. 'The horror! the horror!'

"'His last word—to live with,' she murmured. 'Don't you understand I loved him—I loved him—I loved him!'

"I pulled myself together and spoke slowly.

"'The last word he pronounced was—your name.'

"I heard a light sigh, and then my heart stood still, stopped dead short by an exulting and terrible cry, by the cry of inconceivable triumph and of unspeakable pain. 'I knew it—I was sure!' . . . She knew. She was sure. I heard her weeping; she had hidden her face in her hands. It seemed to me that the house would collapse before I could escape, that the heavens would fall upon my head. But nothing happened. The heavens do not fall for such a trifle. Would they have fallen, I wonder, if I had rendered Kurtz that justice which was his due? Hadn't he said he wanted only justice? But I couldn't. I could not tell her. It would have been too dark—too dark altogether. . . ."

Marlow ceased, and sat apart, indistinct and silent, in the pose of a meditating Buddha. Nobody moved for a time. "We have lost the first of the ebb," said the Director, suddenly. I raised my head. The offing was barred by a black bank of clouds, and the tranquil waterway leading to the uttermost ends of the earth flowed sombre under an overcast sky—seemed to lead into the heart of an immense darkness.

CONTEXTS

THE SCRAMBLE FOR AFRICA

IN THE RUBBER COILS.

SCENE—*The Congo "Free" State.*

In the Rubber Coils: Scene—The Congo "Free" State. In this 1906 cartoon from the satiric magazine *Punch*, a Congo native is entrapped in a snake whose head is a portrait of King Leopold of Belgium. Published as Parliament was debating its response to the revelations of Conrad's friend Roger Casement concerning conditions in the Congo, the cartoon emphasizes Leopold's commercial stranglehold on his private colony, whose principal export was rubber.

The Scramble for Africa

From the Renaissance onward, European explorers and traders had ventured along the coasts of Africa, set up outposts, and gradually increased their presence on the continent, together with direct rule over a few regions such as South Africa. Yet most of sub-Saharan Africa long escaped the widespread colonization experienced in India, the Americas, and elsewhere. In the late nineteenth century, however, new developments in transportation, medicine, weaponry, and communications enabled the European powers to assert themselves much more forcefully and systematically. The competition for territorial control between 1880 and 1911 became known as "the scramble for Africa."

Some rules for this scramble were established by a conference held in Berlin in 1884, at which the European powers divided the continent into different spheres of influence and control, agreeing to respect each other's "rights" to their holdings. Prominent among the beneficiaries was King Leopold of Belgium, who was granted the "Congo Free State" as his personal property; he ruled it through a corporation from 1885 to 1908. The ambiguities of Conrad's *Heart of Darkness* come more sharply into focus against the background of the imperialist fictions and travel accounts that were being written and read during those fractious years—from the strained comedy of W. S. Gilbert's "The King of Canoodle-Dum" (p. 92) to the adventure tales of journalist-explorer Henry Morton Stanley. Stanley wrote bestselling books with titles such as *In Darkest Africa* and *Through the Dark Continent*. The first selection from his works here gives dramatic episodes involving dense jungle and raging rivers; next comes an astonishing speech in which Stanley combines high moral rhetoric with pounds-and-shillings calculations of how much money Manchester's weavers will make if they can sell wedding dresses and burial clothes to the Congolese.

"The Scramble for Africa" begins with a prominent earlier account of African life by the ex-slave Olaudah Equiano, who combined a largely sympathetic account of African life with a strong condemnation of the inhumanity of the slave trade. While Equiano's account shows the earlier history of the slave trade, the horrors of King Leopold's late-Victorian operation—a slave trade in all but the name—were revealed to the world a few years after Conrad published *Heart of Darkness*, when his friend Roger Casement undertook a fact-finding expedition up the Congo River and then rendered a chilling report to the British Parliament.

Olaudah Equiano (c. 1745–1797)

Europeans explored and then colonized Africa over a period of centuries. From the Renaissance on into the nineteenth century, accounts of conditions in Africa rarely came from Africans or from people of recent African descent. A striking exception was The Interesting Narrative of the Life of Olaudah Equiano, or Gustavus Vassa, the African, Written by Himself. *Published in 1789, it went through thirty-six editions over the next fifty years. A former slave who had purchased his freedom, become a merchant seaman, and sailed the world—as Conrad was later to do—Equiano eventually settled in England, became a citizen, and married an Englishwoman. He worked with Methodist groups seeking the abolition of slavery, and wrote his* Narrative *to help the cause, promoting it on a book tour that provided a vital spark in the agitation. He began with a vivid story of growing up in Africa, where native Africans as well as Europeans were participating in capturing and deporting slaves. After giving a warm account of his childhood in what is now Nigeria, Equiano then described the horror of his capture and the "middle passage" to Barbados, as well as his long struggle for freedom.*

There have been some recent suggestions that Equiano may have put together the African episodes from the accounts of others, but the question is still open, and readers in his own day and long afterward accepted the whole narrative as an eyewitness account. What caught the public's attention and spurred calls for abolition was Equiano's

*skill in expanding his own life story into a comprehensive account of
the slave trade and a compelling portrait of the humanity of its victims.
His* Narrative *helped shape Victorian readers' image of African life and
of the slave trade. This work stands as a major precursor to* Heart of
Darkness, *going beyond Conrad in giving an insider's view of African
society, while vividly rendering what Equiano often names "the horror" of slavery.*

from *The Interesting Narrative of the Life of Olaudah Equiano, or Gustavus Vassa, the African, Written by Himself*

That part of Africa, known by the name of Guinea, to which the
trade for slaves is carried on, extends along the coast above 3400
miles, from Senegal to Angola, and includes a variety of kingdoms.
Of these the most considerable is the kingdom of Benin, both as to
extent and wealth, the richness and cultivation of the soil, the
power of its king, and the number and warlike disposition of the
inhabitants. It is situated nearly under the line[1] and extends along
the coast about 170 miles, but runs back into the interior part of
Africa to a distance hitherto I believe unexplored by any traveller;
and seems only terminated at length by the empire of Abyssinia,
near 1500 miles from its beginning.

* * *

We are almost a nation of dancers, musicians, and poets. Thus
every great event, such as a triumphant return from battle, or other
cause of public rejoicing, is celebrated in public dances, which are
accompanied with songs and music suited to the occasion. The
assembly is separated into four divisions, which dance either apart
or in succession, and each with a character peculiar to itself. The
first division contains the married men, who in their dances frequently exhibit feats of arms, and the representation of a battle. To
these succeed the married women, who dance in the second division. The young men occupy the third; and the maidens the fourth.
Each represents some interesting scene of real life, such as a great
achievement, domestic employment, a pathetic story, or some rural
sport; and as the subject is generally founded on some recent event,
it is therefore ever new. This gives our dances a spirit and variety
which I have scarcely seen elsewhere. We have many musical instru-

[1]The equator.

ments, particularly drums of different kinds, a piece of music which resembles a guitar, and another much like a stickado.[2] These last are chiefly used by bethrothed virgins, who play on them on all grand festivals.

As our manners are simple, our luxuries are few. The dress of both sexes is nearly the same. It generally consists of a long piece of calico, or muslin,[3] wrapped loosely round the body, somewhat in the form of a Highland plaid. This is usually dyed blue, which is our favourite colour. It is extracted from a berry, and is brighter and richer than any I have seen in Europe. Besides this, our women of distinction wear golden ornaments, which they dispose with some profusion on their arms and legs. When our women are not employed with the men in tillage, their usual occupation is spinning and weaving cotton, which they afterwards dye, and make into garments. They also manufacture earthen vessels, of which we have many kinds. Among the rest tobacco pipes, made after the same fashion, and used in the same manner, as those in Turkey.

* * *

As we live in a country where nature is prodigal of her favours, our wants are few and easily supplied; of course we have few manufactures. They consist for the most part of calicoes, earthen ware, ornaments, and instruments of war and husbandry. But these make no part of our commerce, the principal articles of which, as I have observed, are provisions. In such a state money is of little use; however we have some small pieces of coin, if I may call them such. They are made something like an anchor; but I do not remember either their value or denomination. We have also markets, at which I have been frequently with my mother. These are sometimes visited by stout, mahogany-coloured men from the south west of us: we call them *Oye-Eboe*, which term signifies red men living at a distance. They generally bring us firearms, gun-powder, hats, beads, and dried fish. The last we esteemed a great rarity, as our waters were only brooks and springs. These articles they barter with us for odoriferous woods and earth, and our salt of wood-ashes. They always carry slaves through our land; but the strictest account is exacted of their manner of procuring them before they are suffered

[2]Xylophone.
[3]Cotton cloth.

to pass. Sometimes indeed we sold slaves to them, but they were only prisoners of war, or such among us as had been convicted of kidnapping, or adultery, and some other crimes which we esteemed heinous. This practice of kidnapping induces me to think, that, notwithstanding all our strictness, their principal business among us was to trepan[4] our people. I remember too they carried great sacks along with them, which, not long after, I had an opportunity of fatally seeing applied to that infamous purpose.

* * *

Our tillage is exercised in a large plain or common, some hours walk from our dwellings, and all the neighbours resort thither in a body. They use no beasts of husbandry; and their only instruments are hoes, axes, shovels, and beaks, or pointed iron to dig with. Sometimes we are visited by locusts, which come in large clouds, so as to darken the air, and destroy our harvest. This however happens rarely, but when it does, a famine is produced by it. I remember an instance or two wherein this happened. This common is oftimes the theatre of war; and therefore when our people go out to till their land, they not only go in a body, but generally take their arms with them, for fear of a surprise; and when they apprehend an invasion they guard the avenues to their dwellings, by driving sticks into the ground, which are so sharp at one end as to pierce the foot, and are generally dipt in poison. From what I can recollect of these battles, they appear to have been irruptions of one little state or district on the other, to obtain prisoners or booty. Perhaps they were incited to this by those traders who brought the European goods I mentioned amongst us. Such mode of obtaining slaves in Africa is common; and I believe more are procured this way, and by kidnapping, than any other. When a trader wants slaves, he applies to a chief for them, and tempts him with his wares. It is not extraordinary, if on this occasion he yields to the temptation with as little firmness, and accepts the price of his fellow creature's liberty with as little reluctance, as the enlightened merchant. Accordingly, he falls on his neighbours, and a desperate battle ensues. If he prevails, and takes prisoners, he gratifies his avarice by selling them; but, if his party be vanquished, and he falls into the hands of the enemy, he is put to death: for, as he has been known to foment their quarrels, it is

[4]Trap.

thought dangerous to let him survive, and no ransom can save him, though all other prisoners may be redeemed. We have firearms, bows and arrows, broad two-edged swords and javelins; we have shields also, which cover a man from head to foot. All are taught the use of the weapons. Even our women are warriors, and march boldly out to fight along with the men. Our whole district is a kind of militia: on a certain signal given, such as the firing of a gun at night, they all rise in arms and rush upon their enemy. It is perhaps something remarkable, that when our people march to the field, a red flag or banner is borne before them. I was once a witness to a battle in our common. We had been all at work in it one day as usual when our people were suddenly attacked. I climbed a tree at some distance, from which I beheld the fight. There were many women as well as men on both sides; among others my mother was there and armed with a broad sword. After fighting for a considerable time with great fury, and many had been killed, our people obtained the victory, and took their enemy's Chief prisoner. He was carried off in great triumph, and, though he offered a large ransom for his life, he was put to death. A virgin of note among our enemies had been slain in the battle, and her arm was exposed in our market-place, where our trophies were always exhibited. The spoils were divided according to the merit of the warriors. Those prisoners which were not sold or redeemed we kept as slaves: but how different was their condition from that of the slaves in the West-Indies! With us they do no more work than other members of the community, even their master. Their food, cloathing, and lodging were nearly the same as theirs, except that they were not permitted to eat with those who were free born and there was scarce any other difference between them, than a superior degree of importance which the head of a family possesses in our state, and that authority which, as such, he exercises over every part of his household. Some of these slaves have even slaves under them, as their own property, and for their own use.

As to religion, the natives believe that there is one Creator of all things, and that he lives in the sun, and is girded round with a belt, that he may never eat or drink; but, according to some, he smokes a pipe, which is our own favourite luxury. They believe he governs events, especially our deaths or captivity; but, as for the doctrine of eternity, I do not remember to have ever heard of it: some however believe in the transmigration of souls in a certain degree. Those spirits, which are not transmigrated, such as our dear friends or relations, they believe always attend them, and guard them from the bad spirits of their foes. For this reason, they always, before eating, as I have observed, put some small portion of the meat, and pour some of their drink, on the ground for them; and they often make oblations[5] of the blood of beasts or fowls at their graves. I was very fond of my mother, and almost constantly with her. When she went to make these oblations at her mother's tomb, which was a kind of small solitary thatched house, I sometimes attended her. There she made her libations, and spent most of the night in cries and lamentations. I have been often extremely terrified on these occasions. The loneliness of the place, the darkness of the night, and the ceremony of libation, naturally awful and gloomy, were heightened by my mother's lamentations; and these, concurring with the doleful cries of birds, by which these places were frequented, gave an inexpressible terror to the scene.

* * *

I hope the reader will not think I have trespassed on his patience in introducing myself to him with some account of the manners and customs of my country. They had been implanted in me with great care, and made an impression on my mind, which time could not erase, and which all the adversity and variety of fortune I have since experienced served only to rivet and record: for, whether the love of one's country be real or imaginary, or a lesson of reason, or an instinct of nature, I still look back with pleasure on the first scenes of my life, though that pleasure has been for the most part mingled with sorrow.

I have already acquainted the reader with the time and place of my birth. My father, besides many slaves, had a numerous family, of which seven lived to grow up, including myself and a sister, who was the only daughter. As I was the youngest of the sons, I became, of course, the greatest favourite with my mother, and was always with her; and she used to take particular pains to form my mind. I was trained up from my earliest years in the arts of agriculture and war: my daily exercise was shooting and throwing javelins; and my mother adorned me with emblems, after the manner of our greatest

[5]Sacrificial offerings.

warriors. In this way I grew up till I was turned the age of eleven, when an end was put to my happiness in the following manner:—Generally, when the grown people in the neighbourhood were gone far in the fields to labour, the children assembled together in some of the neighbours' premises to play; and commonly some of us used to get up a tree to look out for any assailant, or kidnapper, that might come upon us; for they sometimes took those opportunities of our parents' absence, to attack and carry off as many as they could seize. One day, as I was watching at the top of a tree in our yard, I saw one of those people come into the yard of our next neighbour but one, to kidnap, there being many stout[6] young people in it. Immediately, on this, I gave the alarm of the rogue, and he was surrounded by the stoutest of them, who entangled him with cords, so that he could not escape till some of the grown people came and secured him. But, alas! ere long it was my fate to be thus attacked, and to be carried off, when none of the grown people were nigh. One day, when all our people were gone out to their works as usual, and only I and my dear sister were left to mind the house, two men and a woman got over our walls, and in a moment seized us both; and, without giving us time to cry out, or make resistance, they stopped our mouths, tied our hands, and ran off with us into the nearest wood: and continued to carry us as far as they could, till night came on, when we reached a small house, where the robbers halted for refreshment, and spent the night. We were then unbound, but were unable to take any food; and, being quite overpowered by fatigue and grief, our only relief was some sleep, which allayed our misfortune for a short time. The next morning we left the house, and continued travelling all the day. For a long time we had kept the woods, but at last we came into a road which I believed I knew. I had now some hopes of being delivered[7]; for we had advanced but a little way before I discovered some people at a distance, on which I began to cry out for their assistance; but my cries had no other effect than to make them tie me faster, and stop my mouth, and then they put me into a large sack. They also stopped my sister's mouth, and tied her hands; and in this manner we proceeded till we were out of the sight of these people.—When we went to rest the following night

[6]Strong.
[7]Rescued.

they offered us some victuals; but we refused them; and the only comfort we had was in being in one another's arms all that night, and bathing each other with our tears. But, alas! we were soon deprived of even the smallest comfort of weeping together. The next day proved a day of greater sorrow than I had yet experienced; for my sister and I were then separated, while we lay clasped in each other's arms. It was in vain that we besought them not to part us: she was torn from me, and immediately carried away, while I was left in a state of distraction not to be described. I cried and grieved continually; and for several days I did not eat any thing but what they forced into my mouth.

* * *

From the time I left my own nation I always found somebody that understood me till I came to the sea coast. The languages of different nations did not totally differ, nor were they so copious[8] as those of the Europeans, particularly the English. They were therefore easily learned; and, while I was journeying thus through Africa, I acquired two or three different tongues. In this manner I had been travelling for a considerable time, when one evening, to my great surprise, whom should I see brought to the house where I was but my dear sister. As soon as she saw me she gave a loud shriek, and ran into my arms.—I was quite overpowered; neither of us could speak, but, for a considerable time, clung to each other in mutual embraces, unable to do any thing but weep. Our meeting affected all who saw us; and indeed I must acknowledge, in honour of those sable destroyers of human rights, that I never met with any ill treatment, or saw any offered to their slaves, except tying them, when necessary, to keep them from running away. When these people knew we were brother and sister they indulged us to be together; and the man, to whom I supposed we belonged, lay with us, he in the middle, while she and I held one another by the hands across his breast all night; and thus for a while we forgot our misfortunes in the joy of being together: but even this small comfort was soon to have an end; for scarcely had the fatal morning appeared, when she was again torn from me for ever! I was now more miserable, if possible, than before.

* * *

[8]Complicated.

Thus, at the very moment I dreamed of the greatest happiness, I found myself most miserable: and it seemed as if fortune wished to give me this taste of joy only to render the reverse more poignant. The change I now experienced was as painful as it was sudden and unexpected. It was a change indeed from a state of bliss to a scene which is inexpressible by me, as it discovered to me an element I had never before beheld, and till then had no idea of, and wherein such instances of hardship and cruelty continually occurred as I can never reflect on but with horror.

All the nations and people I had hitherto passed through resembled our own in their manners, customs and language: but I came at length to a country, the inhabitants of which differed from us in all those particulars. I was very much struck with this difference, especially when I came among a people who did not circumcise, and eat[9] without washing their hands. They cooked also in iron pots, and had European cutlasses and cross bows, which were unknown to us, and fought with their fists among themselves. Their women were not so modest as ours, for they eat, and drank, and slept with their men. But, above all, I was amazed to see no sacrifices or offerings among them. In some of those places the people ornamented themselves with scars, and likewise filed their teeth very sharp. They wanted sometimes to ornament me in the same manner, but I would not suffer them; hoping that I might some time be among a people who did not thus disfigure themselves, as I thought they did. At last, I came to the banks of a large river, which was covered with canoes, in which the people appeared to live with their household utensils and provisions of all kinds. I was beyond measure astonished at this, as I had never before seen any water larger than a pond or a rivulet; and my surprise was mingled with no small fear when I was put into one of these canoes, and we began to paddle and move along the river. We continued going on thus till night; and when we came to land, and made fires on the banks, each family by themselves, some dragged their canoes on shore, others staid and cooked in theirs, and laid in them all night. Those on the land had mats, of which they made tents, some in the shape of little houses: In these we slept; and after the morning meal we embarked again, and proceeded as before. I was often very much astonished to see

[9]Ate.

some of the women, as well as the men, jump into the water, dive to the bottom, come up again, and swim about. Thus I continued to travel, sometimes by land, sometimes by water, through different countries, and various nations, till, at the end of six or seven months after I had been kidnapped, I arrived at the sea coast. It would be tedious and uninteresting to relate all the incidents which befel me during this journey, and which I have not yet forgotten; of the various hands I passed through, and the manners and customs of all the different people among whom I lived: I shall therefore only observe, that, in all the places where I was, the soil was exceedingly rich; the pomkins, eadas, plantains, yams, &c. &c. were in great abundance, and of incredible size. There were also vast quantities of different gums, though not used for any purpose; and every where a great deal of tobacco. The cotton even grew quite wild; and there was plenty of red wood. I saw no mechanics[10] whatever in all the way, except such as I have mentioned. The chief employment in all these countries was agriculture, and both the males and females, as with us, were brought up to it, and trained in the arts of war.

The first object which saluted my eyes when I arrived on the coast was the sea, and a slave-ship, which was then riding at anchor, and waiting for its cargo. These filled me with astonishment, which was soon converted into terror, which I am yet at a loss to describe, nor the then feelings of my mind. When I was carried on board I was immediately handled, and tossed up, to see if I were sound,[11] by some of the crew; and I was now persuaded that I had gotten into a world of bad spirits, and that they were going to kill me. Their complexions too differing so much from ours, their long hair, and the language they spoke, which was very different from any I had ever heard, united to confirm me in this belief. Indeed, such were the horrors of my views and fears at the moment, that, if ten thousand worlds had been my own, I would have freely parted with them all to have exchanged my condition with that of the meanest slave in my own country. When I looked round the ship too, and saw a large furnace of copper boiling, and a multitude of black people of every description chained together, every one of

[10]Craftsmen.
[11]Healthy.

their countenances expressing dejection and sorrow, I no longer doubted of my fate, and, quite overpowered with horror and anguish, I fell motionless on the deck and fainted. When I recovered a little, I found some black people about me, who I believed were some of those who brought me on board, and had been receiving their pay; they talked to me in order to cheer me, but all in vain. I asked them if we were not to be eaten by those white men with horrible looks, red faces, and long hair? They told me I was not; and one of the crew brought me a small portion of spirituous liquor in a wine glass; but, being afraid of him, I would not take it out of his hand. One of the blacks therefore took it from him and gave it to me, and I took a little down my palate, which, instead of reviving me, as they thought it would, threw me into the greatest consternation at the strange feeling it produced, having never tasted any such liquor before. Soon after this, the blacks who brought me on board went off, and left me abandoned to despair. I now saw myself deprived of all chance of returning to my native country, or even the least glimpse of hope of gaining the shore, which I now considered as friendly: and I even wished for my former slavery in preference to my present situation, which was filled with horrors of every kind, still heightened by my ignorance of what I was to undergo. I was not long suffered to indulge my grief; I was soon put down under the decks, and there I received such a salutation in my nostrils as I had never experienced in my life; so that with the loathsomeness of the stench, and crying together, I became so sick and low that I was not able to eat, nor had I the least desire to taste any thing. I now wished for the last friend, Death, to relieve me; but soon, to my grief, two of the white men offered me eatables; and, on my refusing to eat, one of them held me fast by the hands, and laid me across, I think, the windlass,[12] and tied my feet, while the other flogged me severely. I had never experienced any thing of this kind before; and although, not being used to the water, I naturally feared that element the first time I saw it; yet, nevertheless, could I have got over the nettings, I would have jumped over the side, but I could not; and, besides, the crew used to watch us very closely who were not chained down to the decks, lest we should leap into the water; and I have seen some of these poor African prisoners most severely

[12]Large winch used to haul up the anchor.

cut for attempting to do so, and hourly whipped for not eating. This indeed was often the case with myself. In a little time after, amongst the poor chained men, I found some of my own nation, which in a small degree gave ease to my mind. I inquired of these what was to be done with us? they gave me to understand we were to be carried to these white people's country to work for them. I then was a little revived, and thought, if it were no worse than working, my situation was not so desperate: but still I feared I should be put to death, the white people looked and acted, as I thought, in so savage a manner; for I had never seen among any people such instances of brutal cruelty; and this not only shewn towards us blacks, but also to some of the whites themselves. One white man in particular I saw, when we were permitted to be on deck, flogged so unmercifully with a large rope near the foremast, that he died in consequence of it; and they tossed him over the side as they would have done a brute. This made me fear these people the more; and I expected nothing less than to be treated in the same manner. I could not help expressing my fears and apprehensions to some of my countrymen: I asked them if these people had no country, but lived in this hollow place the ship? they told me they did not, but came from a distant one. "Then," said I, "how comes it in all our country we never heard of them?" They told me, because they lived so very far off. I then asked where were their women? had they any like themselves! I was told they had: "And why," said I, "do we not see them?" they answered, because they were left behind. I asked how the vessel could go? they told me they could not tell; but that there were cloths put upon the masts by the help of the ropes I saw, and then the vessel went on; and the white men had some spell or magic they put in the water when they liked in order to stop the vessel. I was exceedingly amazed at this account, and really thought they were spirits. I therefore wished much to be from amongst them, for I expected they would sacrifice me: but my wishes were vain; for we were so quartered that it was impossible for any of us to make our escape. While we staid on the coast I was mostly on deck; and one day, to my great astonishment, I saw one of these vessels coming in with the sails up. As soon as the whites saw it, they gave a great shout, at which we were amazed; and the more so as the vessel appeared larger by approaching nearer. At last she came to an anchor in my sight, and when the anchor was let go,

I and my countrymen who saw it were lost in astonishment to observe the vessel stop; and were now convinced it was done by magic. Soon after this the other ship got her boats[13] out, and they came on board of us, and the people of both ships seemed very glad to see each other. Several of the strangers also shook hands with us black people, and made motions with their hands, signifying, I suppose, we were to go to their country; but we did not understand them. At last, when the ship we were in had got in all her cargo, they made ready with many fearful noises, and we were all put under deck, so that we could not see how they managed the vessel. But this disappointment was the least of my sorrow. The stench of the hold while we were on the coast was so intolerably loathsome, that it was dangerous to remain there for any time, and some of us had been permitted to stay on the deck for the fresh air; but now that the whole ship's cargo were confined together, it became absolutely pestilential. The closeness of the place, and the heat of the climate, added to the number in the ship, which was so crowded that each had scarcely room to turn himself, almost suffocated us. This produced copious perspirations, so that the air soon became unfit for respiration, from a variety of loathsome smells, and brought on a sickness among the slaves, of which many died, thus falling victims to the improvident avarice, as I may call it, of their purchasers. This wretched situation was again aggravated by the galling of the chains, now become insupportable; and the filth of the necessary tubs,[14] into which the children often fell, and were almost suffocated. The shrieks of the women, and the groans of the dying, rendered the whole a scene of horror almost inconceiveable. Happily perhaps for myself I was soon reduced so low here that it was thought necessary to keep me almost always on deck; and from my extreme youth I was not put in fetters. In this situation I expected every hour to share the fate of my companions, some of whom were almost daily brought upon deck at the point of death, which I began to hope would soon put an end to my miseries. Often did I think many of the inhabitants of the deep much more happy than myself; I envied them the freedom they enjoyed, and as often wished I could change my condition for theirs. Every circumstance I

[13]Rowboats.
[14]Tubs used as toilets.

met with served only to render my state more painful, and heighten my apprehensions, and my opinion of the cruelty of the whites.

* * *

[*Finally the ship completes its Atlantic crossing and arrives at Barbados.*]

Many merchants and planters now came on board, though it was in the evening. They put us in separate parcels,[15] and examined us attentively. They also made us jump,[16] and pointed to the land, signifying we were to go there. We thought by this we should be eaten by these ugly men, as they appeared to us; and, when soon after we were all put down under the deck again, there was much dread and trembling among us, and nothing but bitter cries to be heard all the night from these apprehensions, insomuch that at last the white people got some old slaves from the land to pacify us. They told us we were not to be eaten, but to work, and were soon to go on land, where we should see many of our country people. This report eased us much; and sure enough, soon after we were landed, there came to us Africans of all languages. We were conducted immediately to the merchant's yard, where we were all pent up together like so many sheep in a fold, without regard to sex or age. As every object was new to me, every thing I saw filled me with surprise. What struck me first was, that the houses were built with bricks, in stories, and in every other respect different from those I have seen in Africa: but I was still more astonished on seeing people on horseback. I did not know what this could mean; and indeed I thought these people were full of nothing but magical arts. While I was in this astonishment, one of my fellow prisoners spoke to a countryman of his about the horses, who said they were the same kind they had in their country. I understood them, though they were from a distant part of Africa, and I thought it odd I had not seen any horses there; but afterwards, when I came to converse with different Africans, I found they had many horses amongst them, and much larger than those I then saw. We were not many days in the merchant's custody before we were sold after their usual manner, which is this:—On a signal given, (as the beat of a drum), the buyers rush at once into the yard where the slaves are confined, and make choice of

[15]Groups for sale.
[16]To test their strength.

that parcel they like best. The noise and clamour with which this is attended, and the eagerness visible in the countenances of the buyers, serve not a little to increase the apprehensions of the terrified Africans, who may well be supposed to consider them as the ministers of that destruction to which they think themselves devoted. In this manner, without scruple, are relations and friends separated, most of them never to see each other again. I remember in the vessel in which I was brought over, in the men's apartment, there were several brothers, who, in the sale, were sold in different lots; and it was very moving on this occasion to see and hear their cries at parting. O, ye nominal Christians! might not an African ask you, learned you this from your God? who says unto you, Do unto all men as you would men should do unto you? Is it not enough that we are torn from our country and friends to toil for your luxury and lust of gain? Must every tender feeling be likewise sacrificed to your avarice? Are the dearest friends and relations, now rendered more dear by their separation from their kindred, still to be parted from each other, and thus prevented from cheering the gloom of slavery with the small comfort of being together and mingling their sufferings and sorrows? Why are parents to lose their children, brothers their sisters, or husbands their wives? Surely this is a new refinement in cruelty, which, while it has no advantage to atone for it, thus aggravates distress, and adds fresh horrors even to the wretchedness of slavery.

Henry Morton Stanley (1841–1904)

Orphaned at an early age, Henry Morton Stanley was brought up in a workhouse in Wales. He ran away to sea and ended up in America, where he eventually turned to journalism. He became famous when his newspaper sent him to Central Africa in 1871 to seek out the prominent missionary doctor David Livingstone, who hadn't been heard from for some years. Having found the doctor (greeting him in the midst of the jungle with the famous words, "Dr. Livingstone, I presume?"), Stanley went on to make a career as an explorer, writing up his adventures in a series of bestselling books. Through the Dark Continent (1878) gives a breathless account of his struggles against treacherous rivers and natives in the Congo and surrounding regions.

Daylight at Last! The Advance Column of the Emin Pasha Relief Expedition Emerging from the Great Forest. From Henry Morton Stanley, *In Darkest Africa*, 1890. In this bestselling book, Stanley described his near-fatal expedition to rescue Edward Schnitzer, who held office as the Emin Pasha, governor of the British Equitorial Province of Egypt. The governor had been trapped by rebels at a frontier fort on the shore of Lake Albert in east central Africa. Stanley reached the lake after a grueling overland trek from the Congo. Stick in hand, Stanley surveys the scene with heroic sangfroid as his native troops rejoice at his success in guiding them through the hostile wilderness.

Heart of Darkness *is a kind of grim parody of narratives such as this. Stanley was a particularly apt source for Conrad to draw on because Stanley went to work in the 1880s as a negotiator and publicist for King Leopold of Belgium, just a few years before Conrad went to the Congo in 1890. In his 1886 speech to the Manchester Chamber of Commerce, also presented here, Stanley promoted the building of the railroad that is being constructed in Conrad's novella. In all his works, Stanley provided a remarkably clear expression of the goals and methods of "the scramble for Africa."*

from *Through the Dark Continent*

[*By the end of 1876, when Stanley turned his attention to the Congo River—which he called the Livingstone—he had already been exploring Central Africa for two years, and his expedition had been ravaged by disease, hunger, and conflicts with African tribes. But, he wrote, "the object of the desperate journey is to flash a torch of light across the western half of the Dark Continent," so he pushed on toward his goal of finding a passage to the Atlantic Ocean.*]

Dec. 26.— . . . The next day at dawn we embarked all the men, women, and children, 149 souls in all, and the riding-asses of the Expedition, and, telling Tippu-Tib[1] we should on the morrow pull up stream and descend the river close to the village of Vinya-Njara for a last farewell, we pulled across to the islet near the right bank, where we constructed a rude camp for the only night we should remain.

When I ascertained, after arrival, that every soul connected with the Expedition was present, my heart was filled with a sense of confidence and trust such as I had not enjoyed since leaving Zanzibar.[2]

In the evening, while sleep had fallen upon all save the watchful sentries in charge of the boat and canoes, Frank[3] and I spent a serious time.

---

[1]A powerful Arab trader whose men had escorted Stanley's expedition for two months through hostile territory.

[2]Stanley's journey had begun two years earlier in Zanzibar, an island off the eastern coast of Africa.

[3]The cheerful Francis Pocock accompanied Stanley for nearly three years. He later drowned in rapids on June 3, 1877, two months short of their goal. His brother, Edward, died earlier on the expedition.

Frank was at heart as sanguine as I that we should finally emerge somewhere, but, on account of the persistent course of the great river towards the north, a little uneasiness was evident in his remarks.

"Before we finally depart, sir," said he, "do you really believe, in your inmost soul, that we shall succeed? I ask this because there are such odds against us—not that I for a moment think it would be best to return, having proceeded so far."

"Believe? Yes, I do believe that we shall all emerge into light again some time. It is true that our prospects are as dark as this night. Even the Mississippi presented no such obstacles to DeSoto[4] as this river will necessarily present to us. Possibly its islands and its forests possessed much of the same aspect, but here we are at an altitude of sixteen hundred and fifty feet above the sea. What conclusions can we arrive at? Either that this river penetrates a great distance north of the Equator, and taking a mighty sweep round, descends into the Congo—this, by the way, would lessen the chances of there being many cataracts in the river;—or that we shall shortly see it in the neighbourhood of the Equator, take a direct cut towards the Congo, and precipitate itself, like our Colorado river, through a deep cañon, or down great cataracts; or that it is either the Niger or the Nile. I believe it will prove to be the Congo; if the Congo, then there must be many cataracts. Let us only hope that the cataracts are all in a lump, close together.

"Any way, whether the Congo, the Niger, or the Nile, I am prepared, otherwise I should not be so confident. Though I love life as much as you do, or any other man does, yet on the success of this effort I am about to stake my life, my all. To prevent its sacrifice foolishly I have devised numerous expedients with which to defy wild men, wild nature, and unknown terrors. There is an enormous risk, but you know the adage, 'Nothing risked, nothing won.'"

* * *

"Now look at this, the latest chart which Europeans have drawn of this region. It is a blank, perfectly white. We will draw two curves just to illustrate what I mean. One shows the river reaching the Equator and turning westward. Supposing there are no cataracts, we

[4]Hernando de Soto (c. 1500–42), Spanish explorer of North America.

ought to reach 'Tuckey's Furthest' by the 15th of February; but if the river takes that wider sweep from 2° north of the Equator, we may hope to reach by the 15th of March, and, if we allow a month for cataracts or rapids, we have a right to think that we ought to see the ocean by either the middle or the end of April, 1877.[5]

"I assure you, Frank, this enormous void is about to be filled up. Blank as it is, it has a singular fascination for me. Never has white paper possessed such a charm for me as this has, and I have already mentally peopled it, filled it with most wonderful pictures of towns, villages, rivers, countries, and tribes—all in the imagination—and I am burning to see whether I am correct or not. *Believe?* I see us gliding down by tower and town, and my mind will not permit a shadow of doubt. Good-night, my boy! Good-night! and may happy dreams of the sea, and ships and pleasure, and comfort, and success attend you in your sleep! To-morrow, my lad, is the day we shall cry—'Victory or death!'" . . .

Dec. 29.— . . . Below Kaimba Island and its neighbour, the Livingstone assumes a breadth of 1800 yards. The banks are very populous: the villages of the left bank comprise the district of Luavala. We thought for some time we should be permitted to pass by quietly, but soon the great wooden drums, hollowed out of huge trees, thundered the signal along the river that there were strangers. In order to lessen all chances of a rupture between us, we sheered off to the middle of the river, and quietly lay on our paddles. But from both banks at once, in fierce concert, the natives, with their heads gaily feathered, and armed with broad black wooden shields and long spears, dashed out towards us.

Tippu-Tib before our departure had hired to me two young men of Ukusu—cannibals—as interpreters. These were now instructed to cry out the word "Sennenneh!" ("Peace!"), and to say that we were friends.

But they would not reply to our greeting, and in a bold peremptory manner told us to return.

"But we are doing no harm, friends. It is the river that takes us down, and the river will not stop, or go back."

"This is our river."

[5]Stanley did not reach the Atlantic until August 12, 1877.

"Good. Tell it to take us back, and we will go."

"If you do not go back, we will fight you."

"No, don't; we are friends."

"We don't want you for our friends; we will eat you."

But we persisted in talking to them, and as their curiosity was so great they persisted in listening, and the consequence was that the current conveyed us near to the right bank; and in such near neighbourhood to another district, that our discourteous escort had to think of themselves, and began to skurry hastily up river, leaving us unattacked.

The villages on the right bank also maintained a tremendous drumming and blowing of war-horns, and their wild men hurried up with menace towards us, urging their sharp-prowed canoes so swiftly that they seemed to skim over the water like flying-fish. Unlike the Luavala villagers, they did not wait to be addressed, but as soon as they came within fifty or sixty yards they shot out their spears, crying out, "Meat! meat! Ah! ha! We shall have plenty of meat! Bo-bo-bo-bo, Bo-bo-bo-bo-o o!"

Undoubtedly these must be relatives of the terrible "Bo-bo-bo's" above, we thought, as with one mind we rose to respond to this rabid man-eating tribe. Anger we had none for them. It seemed to me so absurd to be angry with people who looked upon one only as an epicure would regard a fat capon. Sometimes also a faint suspicion came to my mind that this was all but a part of a hideous dream. Why was it that I should be haunted with the idea that there were human beings who regarded me and my friends only in the light of meat? Meat! *We?* Heavens! what an atrocious idea!

"Meat! Ah! we shall have meat to day. Meat! meat! meat!"

There was a fat-bodied wretch in a canoe, whom I allowed to crawl within spear-throw of me; who, while he swayed the spear with a vigour far from assuring to one who stood within reach of it, leered with such a clever hideousness of feature that I felt, if only within arm's length of him, I could have bestowed upon him a hearty thump on the back, and cried out applaudingly, "Bravo, old boy! You do it capitally!"

Yet not being able to reach him, I was rapidly being fascinated by him. The rapid movements of the swaying spear, the steady wide-mouthed grin, the big square teeth, the head poised on one side with the confident pose of a practised spear-thrower, the short brow and square face, hair short and thick. Shall I ever forget him? It appeared to me as if the spear partook of the same cruel inexorable look as the grinning savage. Finally, I saw him draw his right arm back, and his body incline backwards, with still that same grin on his face, and I felt myself begin to count, one, two, three, four— and *whizz!* The spear flew over my back, and hissed as it pierced the water. The spell was broken.

It was only five minutes' work clearing the river. . . .

Jan. 4. [1877]— . . . At 4 P.M. we came opposite a river about 200 yards wide, which I have called the Leopold River, in honour of his Majesty Leopold II., King of the Belgians, and which the natives called either the Kankora, Mikonju, or Munduku. Perhaps the natives were misleading me, or perhaps they really possessed a superfluity of names, but I think that whatever name they give it should be mentioned in connection with each stream.

Soon after passing by the confluence, the Livingstone, which above had been 2500 yards wide, perceptibly contracted, and turned sharply to the east-north-east, because of a hill which rose on the left bank about 300 feet above the river. Close to the elbow of the bend on the right bank we passed by some white granite rocks, from one to six feet above the water, and just below these we heard the roar of the First Cataract of the Stanley Falls series.

But louder than the noise of the falls rose the piercing yells of the savage Mwana Ntaba from both sides of the great river. We now found ourselves confronted by the inevitable necessity of putting into practice the resolution which we had formed before setting out on the wild voyage—to conquer or die. What should we do? Shall we turn and face the fierce cannibals, who with hideous noise drown the solemn roar of the cataract, or shall we cry out "Mambu Kwa Mungu"—"Our fate is in the hands of God"—and risk the cataract with its terrors!

Meanwhile, we are sliding smoothly to our destruction, and a decision must therefore be arrived at instantly. God knows, I and my fellows would rather have it not to do, because possibly it is only a choice of deaths, by cruel knives or drowning. If we do not choose the knives, which are already sharpened for our throats, death by drowning is certain. So finding ourselves face to face with the inevitable, we turn to the right bank upon the savages, who are in the woods and on the water. We drop our anchors and begin the fight, but after fifteen minutes of it find that we cannot force them away. We then pull up anchors and ascend stream again, until, arriving at the elbow above mentioned, we strike across the river and divide our forces. Manwa Sera[6] is to take four canoes and to continue up stream a little distance, and, while we occupy the attention of the savages in front, is to lead his men through the woods and set upon them in rear. At 5.30 P.M. we make the attempt, and keep them in play for a few minutes, and on hearing a shot in the woods dash at the shore, and under a shower of spears and arrows effect a landing. From tree to tree the fight is continued until sunset, when, having finally driven the enemy off, we have earned peace for the night.

Until about 10 P.M. we are busy constructing an impenetrable stockade or boma of brushwood, and then at length, we lay our sorely fatigued bodies down to rest, without comforts of any kind and without fires, but (I speak for myself only) with a feeling of gratitude to Him who had watched over us in our trouble, and a humble prayer that His protection may be extended to us, for the terrible days that may yet be to come. . . .

Feb. 1.— . . . We emerge out of the shelter of the deeply wooded banks in presence of a vast affluent, nearly 2000 yards across at the mouth. As soon as we have fairly entered its waters, we see a great concourse of canoes hovering about some islets, which stud the middle of the stream. The canoe-men, standing up, give a loud shout as they discern us, and blow their horns louder than ever. We pull briskly on to gain the right bank, and come in view of the right branch of the affluent, when, looking up stream, we see a sight that sends the blood tingling through every nerve and fibre of the body, arouses not only our most lively interest, but also our most lively apprehensions—a flotilla of gigantic canoes bearing down upon us, which both in size and numbers utterly eclipse anything encountered hitherto! Instead of aiming for the right bank, we form in line, and keep straight down river, the boat taking position behind. Yet after a moment's reflection, as I note the numbers of the savages, and the

---

[6]A distinguished chief who had been with Stanley in 1871 when he went to assist Livingstone; he was one of his seconds-in-command on this expedition.

daring manner of the pursuit, and the desire of our canoes to abandon the steady compact line, I give the order to drop anchor. Four of our canoes affect not to listen, until I chase them, and threaten them with my guns. This compelled them to return to the line, which is formed of eleven double canoes, anchored 10 yards apart. The boat moves up to the front, and takes position 50 yards above them. The shields are next lifted by the non-combatants, men, women, and children, in the bows, and along the outer lines, as well as astern, and from behind these, the muskets and rifles are aimed.

We have sufficient time to take a view of the mighty force bearing down on us, and to count the number of the war-vessels which have been collected from the Livingstone and its great affluent. There are fifty-four of them! A monster canoe leads the way, with two rows of upstanding paddles, forty men on a side, their bodies bending and swaying in unison as with a swelling barbarous chorus they drive her down towards us. In the bow, standing on what appears to be a platform, are ten prime young warriors, their heads gay with feathers of the parrot, crimson and grey: at the stern, eight men, with long paddles, whose tops are decorated with ivory balls, guide the monster vessel; and dancing up and down from stem to stern are ten men, who appear to be chiefs. All the paddles are headed with ivory balls, every head bears a feather crown, every arm shows gleaming white ivory armlets. From the bow of the canoe streams a thick fringe of the long white fibre of the Hyphene palm. The crashing sound of large drums, a hundred blasts from ivory horns, and a thrilling chant from two thousand human throats, do not tend to soothe our nerves or to increase our confidence. However, it is "neck or nothing." We have no time to pray, or to take sentimental looks at the savage world, or even to breathe a sad farewell to it. So many other things have to be done speedily and well.

As the foremost canoe comes rushing down, and its consorts on either side beating the water into foam, and raising their jets of water with their sharp prows, I turn to take a last look at our people, and say to them:—

"Boys, be firm as iron; wait until you see the first spear, and then take good aim. Don't fire all at once. Keep aiming until you are sure of your man. Don't think of running away, for only your guns can save you."

Frank is with the *Ocean* on the right flank, and has a choice crew, and a good bulwark of black wooden shields. Manwa Sera has the *London Town*—which he has taken in charge instead of the *Glasgow*[7]—on the left flank, the sides of the canoe bristling with guns, in the hands of tolerably steady men.

The monster canoe aims straight for my boat, as though it would run us down; but, when within fifty yards off, swerves aside, and, when nearly opposite, the warriors above the manned prow let fly their spears, and on either side there is a noise of rushing bodies. But every sound is soon lost in the ripping, crackling musketry. For five minutes we are so absorbed in firing that we take no note of anything else; but at the end of that time we are made aware that the enemy is reforming about 200 yards above us.

Our blood is up now. It is a murderous world, and we feel for the first time that we hate the filthy, vulturous ghouls who inhabit it. We therefore lift our anchors, and pursue them up-stream along the right bank, until rounding a point we see their villages. We make straight for the banks, and continue the fight in the village streets with those who have landed, hunt them out into the woods, and there only sound the retreat, having returned the daring cannibals the compliment of a visit.

While mustering my people for re-embarkation, one of the men came forward and said that in the principal village there was a "Meskiti," a "pembé"—a church, or temple, of ivory—and that ivory was "as abundant as fuel." In a few moments I stood before the ivory temple, which was merely a large circular roof supported by thirty-three tusks of ivory, erected over an idol 4 feet high, painted with camwood dye, a bright vermilion, with black eyes and beard and hair. The figure was very rude, still it was an unmistakable likeness of a man. The tusks being wanted by the Wangwana, they received permission to convey them into the canoes. One hundred other pieces of ivory were collected, in the shape of log wedges, long ivory war-horns, ivory pestles to pound cassava[8] into meal and herbs for spinach, ivory armlets and balls, and ivory mallets to beat the figbark into cloth.

* * *

[7]The *Ocean*, the *London Town*, and the *Glasgow* were the names of some of the expedition's canoes.

[8]A tropical plant with fleshy edible roots.

Mar. 15.—The wide wild land which, by means of the greatest river of Africa, we have pierced, is now about to be presented in a milder aspect than that which has filled the preceding pages with records of desperate conflicts and furious onslaughts of savage men. The people no longer resist our advance. Trade has tamed their natural ferocity, until they no longer resent our approach with the fury of beasts of prey.

It is the dread river itself of which we shall have now to complain. It is no longer the stately stream whose mystic beauty, noble grandeur, and gentle uninterrupted flow along a course of nearly nine hundred miles, ever fascinated us, despite the savagery of its peopled shores, but a furious river rushing down a steep bed obstructed by reefs of lava, projected barriers of rock, lines of immense boulders, winding in crooked course through deep chasms, and dropping down over terraces in a long series of falls, cataracts, and rapids. Our frequent contests with the savages culminated in tragic struggles with the mighty river as it rushed and roared through the deep, yawning pass that leads from the broad table-land down to the Atlantic Ocean. . . .

Mar. 16.— . . . Itsi of Ntamo[9] had informed us there were only three cataracts, which he called the "Child," the "Mother," and the "Father." The "Child" was a two hundred yards' stretch of broken water; and the "Mother," consisting of half a mile of dangerous rapids, we had succeeded in passing, and had pushed beyond it by crossing the upper branch of the Gordon-Bennett, which was an impetuous stream, 75 yards wide, with big cataracts of its own higher up. But the "Father" is the wildest stretch of river that I have ever seen. Take a strip of sea blown over by a hurricane, four miles in length and half a mile in breadth, and a pretty accurate conception of its leaping waves may be obtained. Some of the troughs were 100 yards in length, and from one to the other the mad river plunged. There was first a rush down into the bottom of an immense trough, and then, by its sheer force, the enormous volume would lift itself upward steeply until, gathering itself into a ridge, it suddenly hurled itself 20 or 30 feet straight upward, before rolling down into another trough. If I looked up or down along this angry

---

[9]Chief of a village near Livingstone Falls.

scene, every interval of 50 or 100 yards of it was marked by wave-towers—their collapse into foam and spray, the mad clash of watery hills, bounding mounds and heaving billows, while the base of either bank, consisting of a long line of piled boulders of massive size, was buried in the tempestuous surf. The roar was tremendous and deafening. I can only compare it to the thunder of an express train through a rock tunnel. To speak to my neighbour, I had to bawl in his ear.

The most powerful ocean steamer, going at full speed on this portion of the river, would be as helpless as a cockle-boat. . . .

Mar. 21.— . . . The seventeen canoes now left to us were manned according to their capacity. As I was about to embark in my boat to lead the way, I turned to the people to give my last instructions—which were, to follow me, clinging to the right bank, and by no means to venture into mid-river into the current. While delivering my instructions, I observed Kalulu[10] in the *Crocodile*, which was made out of the *Bassia Parkii* tree, a hard heavy wood, but admirable for canoes. When I asked him what he wanted in the canoe, he replied, with a deprecating smile and an expostulating tone, "I can pull, sir; see!" "Ah, very well," I answered.

The boat-boys took their seats, and, skirting closely the cliffy shore, we rowed down stream, while I stood in the bow of the boat, guiding the coxswain, Uledi,[11] with my hand. The river was not more than 450 yards wide; but one cast of the sounding-lead close to the bank obtained a depth of 138 feet. The river was rapid, with certainly a 7-knot current, with a smooth greasy surface, now and then an eddy, a gurgle, and gentle heave, but not dangerous to people in possession of their wits. In a very few moments we had descended the mile stretch, and before us, 600 yards off, roared the furious falls since distinguished by the name "Kalulu."

With a little effort we succeeded in rounding the point and entering the bay above the falls, and reaching a pretty camping-place on a sandy beach. The first, second, and third canoes

[10]Stanley was deeply attached to Kalulu, who had been with him since his previous expedition. Treating him as an adopted son, Stanley had taken him to England and the United States and sent him to school in London for 18 months.

[11]Stanley called Uledi, the pilot of his boat, the *Lady Alice*, "the best soldier, sailor, and artisan, and the most faithful servant, of the Expedition."

arrived soon after me, and I was beginning to congratulate myself on having completed a good day's work, when to my horror I saw the *Crocodile* in mid-river far below the point which we had rounded, gliding with the speed of an arrow towards the falls over the treacherous calm water. Human strength availed nothing now, and we watched it in agony, for I had three favorites in her— Kalulu, Mauredi, and Ferajji; and of the others, two, Rehani Makua and Wadi Jumah, were also very good men. It soon reached the island which cleft the falls, and was swept down the left branch. We saw it whirled round three or four times, then plunged down into the depths, out of which the stern presently emerged pointed upward, and we knew then that Kalulu and his canoe-mates were no more.

Fast upon this terrible catastrophe, before we could begin to bewail their loss, another canoe with two men in it darted past the point, borne by irresistibly on the placid but swift current to apparent, nay, almost certain destruction. I despatched my boat's crew up along the cliffs to warn the forgetful people that in mid-stream was certain death, and shouted out commands for the two men to strike for the left shore. The steersman by a strange chance shot his canoe over the falls, and, dexterously edging his canoe towards the left shore a mile below, he and his companion con-trived to spring ashore and were saved. As we observed them clamber over the rocks to approach a point opposite us, and finally sit down, regarding us in silence across the river, our pity and love gushed strong towards them, but we could utter nothing of it. The roar of the falls completely mocked and overpowered the feeble human voice.

Before the boat's crew could well reach the descending canoes, the boulders being very large and offering great obstacles to rapid progress, a third canoe—but a small and light one—with only one man, the brave lad Soudi, who escaped from the spears of the Wanyaturu assassins in 1875, darted by, and cried out, as he perceived himself to be drifting helplessly towards the falls, "La il Allah, il Allah" (There is but one God), "I am lost, Mas-ter?" He was then seen to address himself to what fate had in store for him. We watched him for a few moments, and then saw him drop. Out of the shadow of the fall he presently emerged, dropping from terrace to terrace, precipitated down, then whirled round, caught by great heavy waves, which whisked him to right and left, and struck madly at him, and yet his canoe did not sink, but he and it were swept behind the lower end of the island, and then darkness fell upon the day of horror. Nine men lost in one afternoon!

from *Address to the Manchester Chamber of Commerce*[1]

There is not one manufacturer here present who could not tell me if he had the opportunity how much he personally suffered through the slackness of trade; and I dare say that you have all some vague idea that if things remain as they are the future of the cotton manufacture is not very brilliant. New inventions are continually cropping up, so that your power of producing, if stimulated, is almost incalculable; but new markets for the sale of your products are not of rapid growth, and as other nations, by prohibitive tariffs, are bent upon fostering native manufacturers to the exclusion of your own, such markets as are now open to you are likely to be taken away from you in course of time. Well, then, I come to you with at least one market where there are at present, perhaps, 6,250,000 yards of cheap cottons sold every year on the Congo banks and in the Congo markets.[2]

I was interested the other day in making a curious calculation, which was, supposing that all the inhabitants of the Congo basin were simply to have one Sunday dress each, how many yards of Manchester cloth would be required; and the amazing number was 320,000,000 yards, just for one Sunday dress! (Cheers.) Proceeding still further with these figures I found that two Sunday dresses and four everyday dresses would in one year amount to 3,840,000,000 yards, which at 2d. [two pence] per yard would be of the value of £16,000,000. The more I pondered upon these things I discovered that I could not limit these stores of cotton cloth to day dresses. I would have to provide for night dresses also—(laughter)—and these would consume 160,000,000 yards. (Cheers.) Then the grave

[1]Stanley delivered this address to the textile manufacturers of Manchester, England, in 1886, seeking their support for the commercial exploitation of the Congo.

[2]Stanley's expeditions (from 1876) had been financed by Leopold, and from 1879 Stanley had set up trading stations along the river to facilitate the exploitation of the area's natural resources.

cloths came into mind, and, as a poor lunatic, who burned Bolobo Station,[3] destroyed 30,000 yards of cloth in order that he should not be cheated out of a respectable burial, I really feared for a time that the millions would get beyond measurable calculation. However, putting such accidents aside, I estimate that, if my figures of population are approximately correct, 2,000,000 die every year, and to bury these decently, and according to the custom of those who possess cloth, 16,000,000 yards will be required, while the 40,000 chiefs will require an average of 100 yards each, or 4,000,000 yards. I regarded these figures with great satisfaction, and I was about to close my remarks upon the millions of yards of cloth that Manchester would perhaps be required to produce when I discovered that I had neglected to provide for the family wardrobe or currency chest, for you must know that in the Lower Congo there is scarcely a family that has not a cloth fund of about a dozen pieces of about 24 yards each. This is a very important institution, otherwise how are the family necessities to be provided for? How are the fathers and mothers of families to go to market to buy greens, bread, oil, ground nuts, chickens, fish, and goats, and how is the petty trade to be conducted? How is ivory to be purchased, the gums, rubber, dye powders, gunpowder, copper slugs, guns, trinkets, knives, and swords to be bought without a supply of cloth? Now, 8,000,000 families at 300 yards each will require 2,400,000,000. (Cheers.) You all know how perishable such currency must be; but if you sum up these several millions of yards, and value all of them at the average price of 2d. per yard, you will find that it will be possible for Manchester to create a trade—in the course of time—in cottons in the Congo basin amounting in value to about £26,000,000 annually. (Loud cheers.) I have said nothing about Rochdale savelist, or your own superior prints, your gorgeous handkerchiefs, with their variegated patterns, your checks and striped cloths, your ticking and twills.[4] I must satisfy myself with suggesting them; your own imaginations will no

---

[3]The London *Times* carried frequent reports of disturbances in the Congo at this time; in March 1884, for example, Congolese attacks on foreign trading establishments at Nokki in the Lower Congo had caused the Europeans to "declare war against the natives."

[4]Savelist is cheap fabric; ticking is a strong cotton or linen fabric; twill is a kind of textile weave.

doubt carry you to the limbo of immeasurable and incalculable millions. (Laughter and cheers.)

Now, if your sympathy for yourselves and the fate of Manchester has been excited sufficiently, your next natural question would be as follows: We acknowledge, sir, that you have contrived by an artful array of imposing millions to excite our attention, at least, to this field; but we beg to ask you what Manchester is to do in order that we may begin realising this sale of untold millions of yards of cotton cloth? I answer that the first thing to do is for you to ask the British Government to send a cruiser to the mouth of the Congo to keep watch and ward over that river until the European nations have agreed among themselves as to what shall be done with the river, lest one of these days you will hear that it is too late. (Hear, hear.) Secondly, to study whether, seeing that it will never do to permit Portugal to assume sovereignty over that river[5]—and England publicly disclaims any wish to possess that river for herself—it would not be as well to allow the International Association to act as guardians of international right to free trade and free entrance and exit into and out of the river. (Hear, hear.) The main point, remember, always is a guarantee that the lower river shall be free, that, however the Upper Congo may be developed, no Power, inspired by cupidity, shall seize upon the mouth of the river and build custom houses. (Hear, hear.) The Lower Congo in the future will only be valuable because down its waters will have to be floated the produce of the rich basin above to the ocean steamships. It will always have a fair trade of its own, but it bears no proportion to the almost limitless trade that the Upper Congo could furnish. If the Association could be assured that the road from Europe to Vivi[6] was for ever free, the first steps to realise the sale of those countless millions of yards of cotton cloth would be taken. Over six millions of yards are now used annually; but we have no means of absorbing more, owing to the difficulties of transport. Every man capable and willing to carry a load is employed. When human power was discovered to be not further available we tested animal power and discovered it to be feebler

---

[5]The mouth of the Congo River had been discovered by the Portuguese in 1482.

[6]A town on the Upper Congo River; from 1882 Stanley had been arguing that a railway should be built between the Lower and Upper Congo to facilitate the exploitation of the interior. It was completed in 1898.

and more costly than the other; and we have come to the conclusion that steam power must now assist us or we remain *in statu quo* [as things now stand]. But before having recourse to this steam power, and building the iron road along which your bales of cotton fabrics may roll on to the absorbing markets of the Upper Congo unceasingly, the Association pauses to ask you, and the peoples of other English cities, such as London, Liverpool, Glasgow, Birmingham, Leeds, Preston, Sheffield, who profess to understand the importance of the work we have been doing, and the absorbing power of those markets we have reached, what help you will render us, for your own sakes, to make those markets accessible? (Hear, hear.) The Association will not build that railway to the Upper Congo, nor invest one piece of sterling gold in it, unless they are assured they will not be robbed of it, and the Lower Congo will be placed under some flag that shall be a guarantee to all the world that its waters and banks are absolutely free. (Cheers.)

You will agree with me, I am sure, that trade ought to expand and commerce grow, and if we can coax it into mature growth in this Congo basin that it would be a praiseworthy achievement, honoured by men and gods; for out of this trade, this intercourse caused by peaceful barter, proceed all those blessings which you and I enjoy. The more trade thrives, the more benefits to mankind are multiplied, and nearer to gods do men become. (Hear, hear.) The builders of railroads through wildernesses generally require large concessions of lands; but the proposed builders of this railway to connect the Lower with the Upper Congo do not ask for any landed concessions; but they ask for a concession of authority over the Lower Congo in order that the beneficent policy which directs the civilising work on the Upper Congo may be extended to the Lower River, and that the mode of government and action may be uniform throughout. The beneficent policy referred to is explained in the treaty made and concluded with the United States Government.[7] That treaty says: "That with the object of enabling civilisation and commerce to penetrate into Equatorial Africa the Free States of the Congo have resolved to levy no customs duties whatever. The Free States also guarantee to all men who establish

---

[7]The United States was the first country to recognize the right of the International Association to govern the Congo territories in April 1884.

themselves in their territories the right of purchasing, selling, or leasing any land and buildings, of creating factories and of trade on the sole condition that they conform to the law. The International Association of the Congo is prepared to enter into engagements with other nations who desire to secure the free admission of their products on the same terms as those agreed upon with the United States."

Here you have in brief the whole policy. I might end here, satisfied with having reminded you of these facts, which probably you had forgotten. Obedience to the laws—that is, laws drawn for protection of all—is the common law of all civilised communities, without which men would soon become demoralised. Can anybody object to that condition? Probably many of you here recollect reading those interesting letters from the Congo which were written by an English clerk in charge of an English factory. They ended with the cry of "Let us alone." In few words he meant to say, "We are doing very well as we are, we do not wish to be protected, and least of all taxed—therefore, let us alone. Our customers, the natives, are satisfied with us. The native chiefs are friendly and in accord wtih us; the disturbances, if any occur, are local; they are not general, and they right themselves quickly enough, for the trader cannot exist here if he is not just and kind in his dealings. The obstreperous and violent white is left to himself and ruin. Therefore, let us alone." Most heartily do I echo this cry; but unfortunately the European nations will not heed this cry; they think that some mode of government is necessary to curb those inclined to be refractory, and if there is at present a necessity to exhibit judicial power and to restrict evil-minded and ill-conditioned whites, as the Congo basin becomes more and more populated this necessity will be still more apparent. At the same time, if power appears on the Congo with an arbitrary and unfeeling front—with a disposition to tax and levy burdensome tariffs just as trade begins to be established—the outlook for enterprise becomes dismal and dark indeed. (Hear, hear.) . . .

No part of Africa, look where I might, appeared so promising to me as this neglected tenth part of the continent. I have often fancied myself—when I had nothing to do better than dream—gazing from some lofty height, and looking down upon this square compact patch of 800,000,000 acres, with its 80,000 native towns, its population of 40,000,000 souls, its 17,000 miles of river waters, and its 30,000 square miles of lakes, all lying torpid, lifeless, inert, soaked in brutishness and bestiality, and I have never yet descended from that airy perch in the empyrean and touched earth but I have felt a purpose glow in me to strive to do something to awaken it into life and movement, and I have sometimes half fancied that the face of aged Livingstone, vague and indistinct as it were, shone through the warm, hazy atmosphere, with a benignant smile encouraging me in my purpose. . . .

Yet, though examined from every point of view, a study of the Upper Congo and its capabilities produces these exciting arrays of figures and possibilities, I would not pay a two-shilling piece for it all so long as it remains as it is. It will absorb easily the revenue of the wealthiest nation in Europe without any return. I would personally one hundred times over prefer a snug little freehold in a suburb of Manchester to being the owner of the 1,300,000 English square miles of the Congo basin if it is to remain as inaccessible as it is to-day, or if it is to be blocked by that fearful tariff-loving nation, the Portuguese. (Hear, hear.) But if I were assured that the Lower Congo would remain free, and the flag of the Association guaranteed its freedom, I would if I were able build that railway myself—build it solid and strong—and connect the Lower Congo with the Upper Congo, perfectly satisfied that I should be followed by the traders and colonists of all nations. . . . The Portuguese have had nearly 400 years given them to demonstrate to the world what they could do with the river whose mouth they discovered, and they have been proved to be incapable to do any good with it, and now civilisation is inclined to say to them, "Stand off from this broad highway into the regions beyond—(cheers); let others who are not paralytic strive to do what they can with it to bring it within the number of accessible markets. There are 40,000,000 of naked people beyond that gateway, and the cotton spinners of Manchester are waiting to clothe them. Rochdale and Preston women are waiting for the word to weave them warm blue and crimson savelist. Birmingham foundries are glowing with the red metal that shall presently be made into iron-work in every fashion and shape for them, and the trinkets that shall adorn those dusky bosoms; and the ministers of Christ are zealous to bring them, the poor benighted heathen, into the Christian fold." (Cheers.)

MR JACOB BRIGHT, M. P., who was received with loud cheers, said: I have listened with extreme interest to one of the ablest, one of the most eloquent addresses which have ever been delivered in this city—(cheers); and I have heard with uncommon pleasure the views of a man whose ability, whose splendid force of character, whose remarkable heroism, have given him a world-wide reputation. (Cheers.) . . .

MR GRAFTON, M.P., moved:—

That the best thanks of this meeting be and are hereby given to Mr H. M. Stanley for his address to the members of the Chamber, and for the interesting information conveyed by him respecting the Congo and prospects of international trade on the West Coast and interior of Africa.

He remarked that Mr Stanley's name was already enrolled in the pages of history, and would be handed down to posterity with the names of the greatest benefactors of our species, such as Columbus, who had opened out the pathways of the world. Long might Mr Stanley be spared to witness the benefit of his arduous and beneficient labours. (Cheers.)

Joseph Conrad (1857–1924)

Joseph Conrad's spare, sharply observed diary records his experiences as he traveled up the Congo River in the summer of 1890, where he first met Roger Casement, whom he would later support in exposing the horrors they found in King Leopold's colony. Conrad's jotted notes differ dramatically from the rosy picture painted by Stanley and provided the germ for his vastly elaborated and transformed novella.

from *Joseph Conrad's Congo Diary*

Arrived at Matadi[1] on the 13th of June, 1890.

Mr Gosse, chief of the station (O.K.) retaining us for some reason of his own.

---

[1]Colonial station near the mouth of the Congo River. Conrad arrived there on his way to take up his command of a steamship upriver at Kinshasa.

Made the acquaintance of Mr Roger Casement,[2] which I should consider as a great pleasure under any circumstances and now it becomes a positive piece of luck.

Thinks, speaks well, most intelligent and very sympathetic.

Feel considerably in doubt about the future. Think just now that my life amongst the people (white) around here cannot be very comfortable. Intend avoid acquaintances as much as possible. . . .

24th. Gosse and R. C. gone with a large lot of ivory down to Boma. On G.['s] return to start to up the river. Have been myself busy packing ivory in casks. Idiotic employment. Health good up to now. . . .

Prominent characteristic of the social life here: people speaking ill of each other.

*   *   *

Friday, 4th July.

Left camp at 6h a.m. after a very unpleasant night. Marching across a chain of hills and then in a maze of hills. At 8:15 opened out into an undulating plain. Took bearings of a break in the chain of mountains on the other side. . . .

Saw another dead body lying by the path in an attitude of meditative repose.

In the evening three women of whom one albino passed our camp. Horrid chalky white with pink blotches. Red eyes. Red hair. Features very Negroid and ugly. Mosquitos. At night when the moon rose heard shouts and drumming in distant villages. Passed a bad night.

Saturday, 5th July. go.

Left at 6:15. Morning cool, even cold and very damp. Sky densely overcast. Gentle breeze from NE. Road through a narrow plain up to R. Kwilu. Swift-flowing and deep, 50 yds. wide. Passed in canoes. After[war]ds up and down very steep hills intersected by deep ravines. Main chain of heights running mostly NW-SE or W and E at times. Stopped at Manyamba. Camp[in]g place bad—in hollow—water very indifferent. Tent set at 10:15.

Section of today's road. NNE Distance 12 m. [a drawing].

Today fell into a muddy puddle. Beastly. The fault of the man that carried me. After camp[in]g went to a small stream, bathed and washed clothes. Getting jolly well sick of this fun.

[2]Casement (1864–1916) and Conrad were working for the same company.

Tomorrow expect a long march to get to Nsona, 2 days from Manyanga. No sunshine today.

* * *

Saturday, 26th.

Left very early. Road ascending all the time. Passed villages. Country seems thickly inhabited. At 11h arrived at large market place. Left at noon and camped at 1h p.m.

[section of the day's march with notes]

a camp—a white man died here—market—govt. post—mount—crocodile pond—Mafiesa. . . .

Sunday, 27th.

Left at 8h am. Sent luggage carriers straight on to Luasi and went ourselves round by the Mission of Sutili.

Hospitable reception by Mrs Comber. All the missio[naries] absent.

The looks of the whole establishment eminently civilized and very refreshing to see after the lots of tumble-down hovels in which the State and Company agents are content to live—fine buildings. Position on a hill. Rather breezy.

Left at 3h pm. At the first heavy ascent met Mr Davis, miss[ionary] returning from a preaching trip. Rev. Bentley away in the South with his wife. . . .

Tuesday, 29th.

Left camp at 7h after a good night's rest. Continuous ascent; rather easy at first. Crossed wooded ravines and the river Lunzadi by a very decent bridge.

At 9h met Mr Louette escorting a sick agent of the Comp[an]y back to Matadi. Looking very well. Bad news from up the river. All the steamers disabled. One wrecked. Country wooded. At 10:30 camped at Inkissi. . . .

Today did not set the tent but put up in Gov[ernmen]t shimbek.[3] Zanzibari in charge—very obliging. Met ripe pineapple for the first time. On the road today passed a skeleton tied up to a post. Also white man's grave—no name. Heap of stones in the form of a cross.

Health good now.

---

[3] A group of huts.

Wednesday, 30th.

Left at 6 a.m. intending to camp at Kinfumu. Two hours' sharp walk brought me to Nsona na Nsefe. Market. ½ hour after, Harou arrived very ill with billious [sic] attack and fever. Laid him down in Gov[ernmen]t shimbek. Dose of Ipeca.[4] Vomiting bile in enormous quantities. At 11h gave him 1 gramme of quinine and lots of hot tea. Hot fit ending in heavy perspiration. At 2 p.m. put him in hammock and started for Kinfumu. Row with carriers all the way. Harou suffering much through the jerks of the hammock. Camped at a small stream.

At 4h Harou better. Fever gone. . . .

Up till noon, sky clouded and strong NW wind very chilling. From 1h pm to 4h pm sky clear and very hot day. Expect lots of bother with carriers tomorrow. Had them all called and made a speech which they did not understand. They promise good behaviour. . . .

Friday, 1st of August 1890.

. . . Row between the carriers and a man stating himself in Gov[ernmen]t employ, about a mat. Blows with sticks raining hard. Stopped it. Chief came with a youth about 13 suffering from gunshot wound in the head. Bullet entered about an inch above the right eyebrow and came out a little inside. The roots of the hair, fairly in the middle of the brow in a line with the bridge of the nose. Bone not damaged apparently. Gave him a little glycerine to put on the wound made by the bullet on coming out. Harou not very well. Mosquitos. Frogs. Beastly. Glad to see the end of this stupid tramp. Feel rather seedy. Sun rose red. Very hot day. Wind S[ou]th.

Roger Casement (1864–1916)

Roger Casement first came to the Congo as an employee of the same steamship company that hired Conrad. He later served as British consul in several parts of Africa and returned to the Congo in 1904 on a parliamentary investigation of shocking rumors of abuses by the cor-

---

[4]A medicine.

poration that controlled the Congo on behalf of King Leopold. Though he couched his report in diplomatic language, Casement was unsparing in exposing the conditions he found; he was knighted in 1912. Always a champion of liberty, Casement took part in the 1916 Easter Rising (or, as the British called it, "the Easter Rebellion") against British rule in his native Ireland. He was tried and executed by the British, but agitation continued, leading to the creation of the independent Irish Republic in 1922.

from *Report to Parliament on the Congo*

Mr. Casement to the Marquess of Lansdowne

London, December 11, 1903

My Lord,

I have the honour to submit my Report on my recent journey on the Upper Congo.

I left Matadi on the 5th June, and arriving at Léopoldville on the 6th, remained in the neighbourhood of Stanley Pool until the 2nd July, when I set out for the Upper Congo. My return to Léopoldville was on the 15th of September, so that the period spent in the Upper River was one of only two and a half months, during which time I visited several points on the Congo River itself, up to the junction of the Lulongo River, ascended that river and its principal feeder, the Lopori, as far as Bongandanga, and went round Lake Mantumba.

Although my visit was of such brief duration, and the points touched at nowhere lay far off the beaten tracks of communication, the region visited was one of the most central in the Congo State, and the district in which most of my time was spent, that of the Equator, is probably one of the most productive. Moreover, I was enabled, by visiting this district, to contrast its present day state with the condition in which I had known it some sixteen years ago. Then (in 1887) I had visited most of the places I now revisited, and I was thus able to institute a comparison between a state of affairs I had myself seen when the natives lived their own savage lives in anarchic and disorderly communities, uncontrolled by Europeans, and that created by more than a decade of very energetic European intervention. That very much of this intervention has been called for no one who formerly knew the Upper Congo could doubt, and there are today widespread proofs of the great energy displayed by Belgian officials in introducing their methods of rule over one of the most savage regions of Africa.

Admirably built and admirably kept stations greet the traveller at many points; a fleet of river steamers, numbering, I believe, forty-eight, the property of the Congo Government, navigate the main river and its principal affluents at fixed intervals. Regular means of communication are thus afforded to some of the most inaccessible parts of Central Africa.

A railway, excellently constructed in view of the difficulties to be encountered, now connects the ocean ports with Stanley Pool, over a tract of difficult country, which formerly offered to the weary traveller on foot many obstacles to be overcome and many days of great bodily fatigue. To-day the railway works most efficiently, and I noticed many improvements, both in the permanent way and in the general management, since the date of my last visit to Stanley Pool in January 1901. The cataract region, through which the railway passes, is a generally unproductive and even sterile tract of some 220 miles in breadth. This region is, I believe, the home, or birthplace of the sleeping sickness—a terrible disease, which is, all too rapidly, eating its way into the heart of Africa, and has even traversed the entire continent to well-nigh the shores of the Indian Ocean. The population of the Lower Congo has been gradually reduced by the unchecked ravages of this, as yet, undiagnosed and incurable disease, and as one cause of the seemingly wholesale diminution of human life which I everywhere observed in the regions revisited, a prominent place must be assigned to this malady. The natives certainly attribute their alarming death-rate to this as one of the inducing causes, although they attribute, and I think principally, their rapid decrease in numbers to other causes as well. Perhaps the most striking change observed during my journey into the interior was the great reduction observable everywhere in native life. Communities I had formerly known as large and flourishing centres of population are to-day entirely gone, or now exist in such diminished numbers as to be no longer recognizable. The southern shores of Stanley Pool had formerly a population of fully 5,000 Batekes, distributed through the three towns of Ngaliema's

(Léopoldville), Kinchasa and Ndolo, lying within a few miles of each other. These people, some twelve years ago, decided to abandon their homes, and in one night the great majority of them crossed over into the French territory on the north shores of Stanley Pool. Where formerly had stretched these populous native African villages, I saw to-day only a few scattered European houses, belonging either to Government officials or local traders. In Léopoldville to-day there are not, I should estimate, 100 of the original natives or their descendants now residing. At Kinchasa a few more may be found dwelling around one of the European trading depôts, while at Ndolo none remain, and there is nothing there but a station of the Congo Railway Company and a Government post. These Bateke people were not, perhaps, particularly desirable subjects for an energetic Administration, which desired, above all things, progress and speedy results. They were themselves interlopers from the northern shores of the Congo River, and derived a very profitable existence as trading middlemen, exploiting the less sophisticated population among whom they had established themselves. Their loss to the southern shores of Stanley Pool is none the less to be deplored, I think, for they formed, at any rate, a connecting link between an incoming European commercial element and the background of would-be native suppliers.

* * *

On the whole the Government workmen at Léopoldville struck me as being well cared for, and they were certainly none of them idle. The chief difficulty in dealing with so large a staff arises from the want of a sufficiency of food supply in the surrounding country. The staple food of the entire Upper Congo is a preparation of the root of the cassava plant, steeped and boiled, and made up into loaves or puddings of varying weight. The natives of the districts around Léopoldville are forced to provide a fixed quantity each week of this form of food, which is levied by requisitions on all the surrounding villages. The European Government staff is also mainly dependent upon food supplies obtained from the natives of the neighbourhood in a similar manner. This, however necessary, is not a welcome task to the native suppliers who complain that their numbers are yearly decreasing, while the demands made upon them remain fixed, or tend even to increase.

The Government station at Léopoldville and its extensive staff exist almost solely in connection with the running of Government steamers upon the Upper Congo.

A hospital for Europeans and an establishment designed as a native hospital are in charge of a European doctor. Another doctor also resides in the Government station whose bacteriological studies are unremitting and worthy of much praise. The native hospital—not, I am given to understand, through the fault of the local medical staff—is, however, an unseemly place. When I visited the three mud huts which serve the purpose of the native hospital, all of them dilapidated, and two with the thatched roofs almost gone, I found seventeen sleeping sickness patients, male and female, lying about in the utmost dirt. Most of them were lying on the bare ground—several out on the pathway in front of the houses, and one, a woman, had fallen into the fire just prior to my arrival (while in the final, insensible stage of the disease) and had burned herself very badly. She had since been well bandaged, but was still lying out on the ground with her head almost in the fire, and while I sought to speak to her, in turning she upset a pot of scalding water over her shoulder. All the seventeen people I saw were near their end, and on my second visit two days later, the 19th June, I found one of them lying dead out in the open.

In somewhat striking contrast to the neglected state of these people, I found, within a couple of hundred yards of them, the Government workshop for repairing and fitting the steamers. Here all was brightness, care, order, and activity, and it was impossible not to admire and commend the industry which had created and maintained in constant working order this useful establishment. In conjunction with a local missionary, some effort was made during my stay at Léopoldville to obtain an amelioration of the condition of the sleeping sickness people in the native hospital, but it was stated, in answer to my friend's representations, that nothing could be done in the way of building a proper hospital until plans now under consideration had been matured elsewhere. The structures I had visited, which the local medical staff, I believe, greatly deplored—had endured as the only form of hospital accommodation for several years—provided for the numerous native staff of the district.

* * *

At the first village I touched at up the Lulongo River, a small collection of dwellings named Bolongo, the people complained that there was no rubber left in their district, and yet that the La Lulanga Company required of them each fortnight a fixed quantity they could not supply. Three forest guards of that Company were quartered, it was said, in this village, one of whom I found on duty, the two others, he informed me, having gone to Mampoko to convoy the fortnight's rubber. No livestock of any kind could be seen or purchased in this town, which had only a few years ago been a large and populous community, filled with people and well stocked with sheep, goats, ducks, and fowls. Although I walked through most of it, I could only count ten men with their families. There were said to be others in the part of the town I did not visit, but the entire community I saw were living in wretched houses and in most visible distress. Three months previously (in May, I believe), they said a Government force, commanded by a white man, had occupied their town owing to their failure to send in to the Mampoko head-quarters of the La Lulanga Company a regular supply of india-rubber, and two men, whose names were given, had been killed by the soldiers at that time.

As Bolongo lies upon the main stream of the Lulongo River, and is often touched at by passing steamers, I chose for the next inspection a town lying somewhat off this beaten track, where my coming would be quite unexpected. Steaming up a small tributary of the Lulongo, called the Bosombo, I arrived, unpreceded by any rumour of my coming, at the village of Ifomi, where I spent a part of the 26th and the 27th August. In an open shed built at the landing-place I found two sentries of the La Lulanga Company guarding fifteen native women, five of whom had infants at the breast, and three of whom were about to become mothers. The chief of these sentries, a man called Epinda—who was bearing a double-barrelled shot-gun, for which he had a belt of cartridges—at once volunteered an explanation of the reason for these women's detention. Four of them, he said, were hostages who were being held to insure the peaceful settlement of a dispute between two neighbouring towns, which had already cost the life of a man. His employer, the agent of the La Lulanga Company at Bokakata near by, he said, had ordered these women to be seized and kept until the Chief of the offending town to which they belonged should come in to talk over the palaver.[1] The sentry pointed out that this was evidently a much better way to settle such troubles between native towns than to leave them to be fought out among the people themselves.

The remaining eleven women, whom he indicated, he said he had caught and was detaining as prisoners to compel their husbands to bring in the right amount of india-rubber required of them on next market day. When I asked if it was a woman's work to collect india-rubber, he said, "No; that, of course, it was man's work." "Then why do you catch the women and not the men?" I asked. "Don't you see," was the answer, "if I caught and kept the men, who would work the rubber? But if I catch their wives, the husbands are anxious to have them home again, and so the rubber is brought in quickly and quite up to the mark." When I asked what would become of these women if their husbands failed to bring in the right quantity of rubber on the next market day, he said at once that then they would be kept there until their husbands had redeemed them. Their food, he explained, he made the Chief of Ifomi provide, and he himself saw it given to them daily. They came from more than one village of the neighbourhood, he said, mostly from the Ngombi or inland country, where he often had to catch women to insure the rubber being brought in in sufficient quantity. It was an institution, he explained, that served well and saved much trouble. When his master came each fortnight to Ifomi to take away the rubber so collected, if it was found to be sufficient, the women were released and allowed to return with their husbands, but if not sufficient they would undergo continued detention. The sentry's statements were clear and explicit, as were equally those of the Chief of Ifomi and several of the villagers to whom I spoke. The sentry further explained, in answer to my inquiry, that he caught women in this way by direction of his employers. That it was a custom generally adopted and found to work well; that the people were very lazy, and that this was much the simplest way of making them do what was required of

---

[1]Negotiation.

them. When asked if he had any use for his shot-gun, he answered that it had been given him by the white man "to frighten people and make them bring in rubber," but that he had never otherwise used it. I found that the two sentries at Ifomi were complete masters of the town. Everything I needed in the way of food or firewood they at once ordered the men of the town to bring me. One of them, gun over shoulder, marched a procession of men—the Chief of the village at their head—down to the water side, each carrying a bundle of firewood for my steamer. A few chickens which were brought were only purchased through their intermediary, the native owner in each case handing the fowl over to the sentry, who then brought it on board, bargained for it, and took the price agreed upon. When, in the evening, the Chief of the village was invited to come and talk to me, he came in evident fear of the sentries seeing him or overhearing his remarks, and the leader, Epinda, finding him talking to me, peremptorily broke into the conversation and himself answered each question put to the Chief. When I asked this latter if he and his townsmen did not catch fish in the Bosombo River, in which we learned there was much, the sentry, intervening, said it was not the business of these people to catch fish—"they have no time for that, they have got to get the rubber I tell them to."

At nightfall the fifteen women in the shed were tied together, either neck to neck or ankle to ankle, to secure them for the night, and in this posture I saw them twice during the evening. They were then trying to huddle around a fire. In the morning the leading sentry, before leaving the village, ordered his companion in my hearing to "keep close guard on the prisoners." I subsequently discovered that this sentry, learning that I was not, as he had at first thought, a missionary, had gone or sent to inform his employer at Bokakata that a strange white man was in the town.

An explanation of what I had witnessed at Ifomi was later preferred by the representative of this Company for my information, but was in such direct conflict with what I had myself observed that it could not be accepted either as explaining the detention of the women I had seen tied neck to neck, or as a refutation of the statements of the sentry, made to me at a time when he had no thought that his avowals had any bearing on his employer's interests.

* * *

Other people were waiting, desirous of speaking with me, but so much time was taken in noting the statements already made that I had to leave, if I hoped to reach Ikanzana-Bosunguma at a reasonable hour. Accompanied by two of the missionaries, I proceeded in a canoe across the Lulongo and up a tributary to a landing-place which seemed to be about 8 miles from Bonginda. Here, leaving the canoes, we walked for a couple of miles through a flooded forest to reach the village. I found here a sentry of the La Lulanga Company and a considerable number of natives. After some little delay a boy of about 15 years of age appeared, whose left arm was wrapped up in a dirty rag. Removing this, I found the left hand had been hacked off by the wrist, and that a shot hole appeared in the flesh part of the forearm. The boy, who gave his name as Epondo, in answer to my inquiry, said that a sentry of the La Lulanga Company now in the town had cut off his hand. I proceeded to look for this man, who at first could not be found, the natives to a considerable number gathering behind me as I walked through the town. After some delay the sentry appeared, carrying a cap-gun. The boy Epondo, whom I placed before him, then accused him to his face of having mutilated him. The Chief and Headmen of the town who were questioned in succession, corroborated the boy's statement. The sentry, who gave his name as Mbilu, but who the people said was called Kelengo, could make no answer to the charge. He met it by vaguely saying some other sentry of the Company had mutilated Epondo; his predecessor he said, had cut off several hands, and probably this was one of the victims.

The natives around said that there were two other sentries at present in the town, who were not so bad as Kelengo, but that he was a villain. As the evidence against him was perfectly clear, man after man standing out and declaring he had seen the act committed, I informed him and the people present that I should appeal to the local authorities for his immediate arrest and trial. In the course of my interrogatory several other charges transpired against Kelengo. These were of a minor nature, consisting of the usual characteristic acts of blackmailing, only too commonly reported on all sides. One man, named Cianzo, said that Kelengo had tied up his wife and only released her on payment of 1,000 rods. Another man said that Kelengo had robbed him of two ducks and a dog. These minor offences Kelengo equally demurred to, and again said that Epondo had been mutilated by some other sentry, naming several. I took the boy back with me and later brought him to Coquilhatville, where he formally charged Kelengo with the crime, alleging to the Commandant, who took his statement, that it had been done "on account of rubber." As I was myself unable to return to Bonginda, I sent the boy back by canoe to the missionary in charge of that station, who had undertaken to see him safely back to his home. I have since been informed that, acting on my request, the authorities at Coquilhatville had arrested Kelengo, who presumably will be tried in due course.

It was obviously impossible that I should visit all the villages of the natives who came to beg me to do so at Bonginda or elsewhere during my journey, or to verify on the spot, as in the case of the boy, the statements they made. In that one case the truth of the charges preferred was amply demonstrated, and their significance was not diminished by the fact that, whereas this act of mutilation had been committed within a few miles of Mampoko, the headquarters of a European civilising agency, and the guilty man was still in their midst, armed with the gun with which he had first shot his victim (for which he could produce no licence when I asked for it, saying it was his employers'), no one of the natives of the terrorized town had attempted to report the occurrence. They had in the interval visited Mampoko each fortnight with the india-rubber from their district. There was also in their midst another mutilated boy, (Ikabo), whose hand had been cut off either by this or another sentry.

The main waterway of the Lulongo River lay at their doors, and on it well-nigh every fortnight a Government steamer had passed up and down stream on its way to bring the india-rubber of the A.B.I.R. Company to Coquilhatville. They possessed, too, some canoes; and, if all other agencies of relief were closed, the territorial tribunal at Coquilhatville lay open to them, and the journey to it downstream from their village could have been accomplished in some twelve hours. It was no greater journey, indeed, than many of the towns I had elsewhere visited were forced to undertake each week or fortnight to deliver supplies to their local tax collectors. The fact that no effort had been made by these people to secure relief from their unhappy situation impelled me to believe that a very real fear of reporting such occurrences actually existed among them. That everything asserted by such a people, under such circumstances, is strictly true I should in no wise assert. That discrepancies must be found in much alleged by such rude savages, to one whose sympathies they sought to awaken, must equally be admitted. But the broad fact remained that their previous silence said more than their present speech. In spite of contradictions, and even seeming misstatements, it was clear that these men were stating either what they had actually seen with their eyes or firmly believed in their hearts. No one viewing their unhappy surroundings or hearing their appeals, no one at all cognizant of African native life or character, could doubt that they were speaking, in the main, truly; and the unhappy conviction was forced upon me that in the many forest towns behind the screen of trees, which I could not visit, these people were entitled to expect that a civilized administration should be represented among them by other agents than the savages euphemistically termed "forest guards."

* * *

Statements dealing with the Condition of the Natives in Lake Mantumba during the period of the Rubber Wars which began in 1893

The disturbance consequent on the attempt to levy a rubber tax in this district, a tax which has since been discontinued, appears to have endured up to 1900.

The population during the continuance of these wars diminished, I estimate, by some 60 per cent., and the remnant of the inhabitants are only now, in many cases, returning to their destroyed or abandoned villages. Mr. Clark, the resident missionary at Ikoko, was living on Lake Mantumba during the whole of this period, and his letter to me treats of some of the many cases which came to his personal observation at that time.

He and his wife maintain a large school at Ikoko, chiefly for girls and women. Many of these females were handed to the

Mission as orphans by the local Government officials at various times. On questioning some of these women as to how they came to be orphaned and to be handed to the Mission, I found that in many cases they had been captured during the frequent "wars" waged by the Government upon the natives of the lake, their parents having been killed during the course of these military operations. The statements of the five women appended were made in my presence, carefully translated into English, and then repeated into the Ntomba language, and then certified to as a just rendering of what they had stated. Each one of these women or girls signed her name to the original, they having all learned to read and write in their own tongue since their entry into the Mission.

Many similar statements were made to me during the time I spent in Lake Mantumba, some of those made by native men being unfit for repetition. The five statements appended were made by women of excellent life and character who sought to tell me how their homes came to be broken up and themselves to be handed over as children for training by the Mission. The statements were taken down just as translated to me by their teacher, word for word; I accept them as being, in the main, true.

* * *

Elima's Statement

Elima came from the far back Bwanga. One day the soldiers went to her town to fight; she did not know that the soldiers had come to fight them until she saw the people from the other side of the town running towards their end, then they, too, began to run away. Her father, mother, three brothers, and sister were with her. About four men were killed at this scene. It was at this fight that one of the station girls, Ncongo, was taken prisoner. After several days, during which time they were staying at other villages, they went back to their own town. They were only a few days in their own town when they heard that the soldiers who had been at the other towns were coming their way too, so the men gathered up all their bows and arrows and went out to the next town to wait for the soldiers to fight them. Some of the men stayed behind with all the women and children. After that

Elima and her mother went out to their garden to work; while there Elima told her mother that she had dreamed that Bula Matadi was coming to fight with them, but her mother told her she was trying to tell stories.

After that Elima went back to the house, and left her mother in the garden. After she had been a little while in the house with her little brother and sister she heard the firing of guns. When she heard that she took up her little sister and a big basket with a lot of native money[2] in it, but she could not manage both, so she left the basket behind and ran away with the youngest child; the little boy ran away by himself. The oldest boys had gone away to wait for the soldiers at the other town. As she went past she heard her mother calling to her, but she told her to run away in another direction, and she would go on with the little sister. She found her little sister rather heavy for her, so she could not run very fast, and a great number of people went past her, and she was left alone with the little one. Then she left the main road and went to hide in the bush. When night came on she tried to find the road again and followed the people who had passed her, but she could not find them, so she had to sleep in the bush alone. She wandered about in the bush for six days, then she came upon a town named Bokongo. At this town she found that the soldiers were fighting there too. Before entering the town she dug up some sweet manioc to eat, because she was very, very hungry. She went about looking for a fire to roast her sweet manioc, but she could not find any. Then she heard a noise as of people talking, so she hid her little sister in a deserted house, and went to see those people she had heard talking, thinking they might be those from her own town, but when she got to the house where the noise was coming from she saw one of the soldiers' boys sitting at the door of the house, and then also she could not quite understand their language, so she knew that they were not her people, so she took fright and ran away in another direction from where she had put her sister.

After she had reached the outside of the town she stood still, and remembered that she would be scolded by her father and mother for leaving her sister, so she went back at night. She came

[2]Brass rods [Casement's note].

upon a house where the white man was sleeping; she saw the sentry on a deck chair outside in front of the house, apparently asleep, because he did not see her slip past him. Then she came to the house where her sister was, and took her and she started to run away again. They slept in a deserted house at the very end of the town. Early in the morning the white man sent out the soldiers to go and look for people all over the town and in the houses. Elima was standing outside in front of the house, trying to make her sister walk some, as she was very tired, but the little sister could not run away through weakness. While they were both standing outside the soldiers came upon them and took them both. One of the soldiers said: "We might keep them both, the little one is not bad-looking;" but the others said "No, we are not going to carry her all the way; we must kill the youngest girl." So they put a knife through the child's stomach, and left the body lying there where they had killed it. They took Elima to the next town, where the white man had told them to go and fight. They did not go back to the house where the white man was, but went straight on to the next town. The white man's name was Bonginda (Lieutenant Durieux). The soldiers gave Elima something to eat on the way. When they came to this next town they found that all the people had run away.

In the morning the soldiers wanted Elima to go and look for manioc for them, but she was afraid to go out as they looked to her as if they wanted to kill her. The soldiers thrashed her very much, and began to drag her outside, but the Corporal (Lambola) came and took her by the hand and said, "We must not kill her; we must take her to the white man." Then they went back to the town where Bonginda was, and they showed him Elima. Bonginda handed her over to the care of a soldier. At this town she found that they had caught three people, and among them was a very old woman, and the cannibal soldiers asked Bonginda to give them the old woman to eat, and Bonginda told them to take her. Those soldiers took the woman and cut her throat, and then divided her and ate her. Elima saw all this done. In the morning the soldier who was looking after her was sent on some duty by Bonginda, and before the soldier went out he had told Elima to get some manioc leaves not far from the house and to cook them. After he left she went to do as he had told her, and those cannibal soldiers went to Bonginda and said that Elima was trying to run away, so they wanted to kill her; but he told them to tie her, so the soldiers tied her to a tree, and she had to stand in the sun nearly all day. When the soldier who had charge of her came back he found her tied up. Bonginda called to him to ask about Elima, so he explained to Bonginda what he had told Elima to do, so he was allowed to untie her. They stayed several days at this place, then Bonginda asked Elima if she knew all the towns round about, and she said yes, then he told her to show them the way, so that they could go and catch people.

They came to a town and found only one woman, who was dying of sickness, and the soldiers killed her with a knife. At several towns they found no people, but at last they came to a town where several people had run to, as they did not know where else to go, because the soldiers were fighting everywhere. At this town they killed a lot of people—men, women, and children—and took some as prisoners. They cut the hands off those they had killed, and brought them to Bonginda; they spread out the hands in a row for Bonginda to see. After that they left to return to Bikoro. They took a lot of prisoners with them. The hands which they had cut off they just left lying, because the white man had seen them, so they did not need to take them to Bikoro. Some of the soldiers were sent to Bikoro with the prisoners, but Bonginda himself and the other soldiers went to Bofiji, where there was another white man. The prisoners were sent to Misolo (M. Müller). Elima was about two weeks at Bikoro, and then she ran away into the bush at Bikoro for three days, and when she was found she was brought back to Misolo, and he asked her why she had run away. She said because the soldiers had thrashed her. Mr. Clark happened to be at Bikoro the day that Elima was found and brought back to Misolo. Misolo told her to go and work in the garden, but Mr. Clark asked to take her over to the Mission station at Ikoko. She came here about January of 1896.

Elima's mother was killed by soldiers, and her father died of starvation, or rather he refused to eat because he was bereaved of his wife and all his children.

(Signed) Elima.

Signed by Elima before me, after the foregoing statements had been translated by Miss Lena Clark to her, before me, at Ikoko, this 12th day of August, 1903.

(Signed) ROGER CASEMENT,
His Britannic Majesty's Consul.

Further Reading

Historical and Cultural Background

Anstey, Roger. *Britain and the Congo in the Nineteenth Century.* Clarenden Press, 1962.

Ashcroft, Bill, ed. *The Empire Writes Back: Theory and Practice in Post-Colonial Literatures.* Routledge, 1989.

Ashcroft, Bill, Gareth Griffiths, and Helen Tiffin, eds. *The Post-Colonial Studies Reader.* Routledge, 1995.

Brantlinger, Patrick. *Rule of Darkness: British Literature and Imperialism, 1830–1914.* Cornell Univ. Press, 1988.

Casement, Roger. *The Crime Against Europe: The Writings and Poetry of Roger Casement,* ed. Herbert O. Mackey. C. J. Fallon, 1958.

David, Deirdre. *Rule Britannia: Women, Empire, and Victorian Writing.* Cornell Univ. Press, 1995.

Hobsbawm, E. J. *The Age of Empire, 1875–1914.* Vintage, 1987.

Hochschild, Adam. *King Leopold's Ghost.* Mariner Books, 1999.

McClintock, Anne, Aamir Mufti, Ella Shohat, and Social Text Collective, eds. *Dangerous Liaisons: Gender, Nations, and Postcolonial Perspectives.* Univ. of Minnesota Press, 1997.

Memmi, Albert. *The Colonizer and the Colonized.* Beacon Press, 1991.

Mongia, Padmini. *Contemporary Postcolonial Theory: A Reader.* Oxford Univ. Press, 1996.

Ngugi wa Thiong'o. *Decolonising the Mind: The Politics of Language in African Literature.* J. Currey, 1986.

Pakenham, Thomas. *The Scramble for Africa: The White Man's Conquest of the Dark Continent from 1876 to 1912.* Random House, 1991.

Pratt, Mary Louise. *Imperial Eyes: Travel Writing and Transculturation.* Routledge, 1992.

Said, Edward W. *Culture and Imperialism.* Vintage, 1994.

———. *Orientalism.* Vintage, 1979.

Singleton-Gates, Peter, and Maurice Girodias. *The Black Diaries: An Account of Roger Casement's Life and Times with a Collection of His Diaries and Public Writings.* Grove Press, 1959.

Spurr, David. *The Rhetoric of Empire: Colonial Discourse in Journalism, Travel Writing, and Imperial Administration.* Duke Univ. Press, 1993.

Viswanathan, Gauri. *Masks of Conquest: Literary Study and British Rule in India.* Columbia Univ. Press, 1989.

Rudyard Kipling's Life and Works

Bauer, Helen Pike. *Rudyard Kipling: A Study of the Short Fiction.* Macmillan, 1994.

Carrington, Charles. *Rudyard Kipling: His Life and Work.* Macmillan, 1955; rev. 1978.

Gilbert, Eliot L., ed. *Kipling and the Critics.* New York Univ. Press, 1965.

Keating, Peter. *Kipling the Poet.* Seeker and Warburg, 1994.

Kipling, Rudyard. *Complete Verse.* Anchor Books, 1989.

———. *Kim.* A Longman Cultural Edition, ed. Paula M. Krebs and Patricia Lootens. Pearson Longman, 2006.

———. *Something of Myself: For My Friends Known and Unknown,* ed. Robert Hampson. Penguin, 1987.

———. *Works,* Sussex Edition, 35 vols. Macmillan, 1937–1939.

Paffard, Mark. *Kipling's Indian Fiction.* St. Martin's Press, 1989.

Sullivan, Zohreh T. *Narratives of Empire: The Fictions of Rudyard Kipling.* Cambridge Univ. Press, 1993.

Joseph Conrad's Life and Works

Batchelor, John. *The Life of Joseph Conrad: A Critical Biography.* Blackwell, 1993.

Billy, Ted, ed. *Critical Essays on Joseph Conrad.* G. K. Hall, 1987.

Bloom, Harold, ed. *Joseph Conrad's "Heart of Darkness."* Chelsea House, 1987.

Conrad, Joseph. *The Works of Joseph Conrad*, 19 vols. W. Heinemann, 1921–1926.

GoGwilt, Christopher L. *The Invention of the West: Joseph Conrad and the Double-Mapping of Europe and Empire.* Stanford Univ. Press, 1995.

Moore, Gene M. *Joseph Conrad's "Heart of Darkness": A Casebook.* Oxford Univ. Press, 2004.

Watt, Ian. *Conrad in the Nineteenth Century.* Univ. of California Press, 1979.

Wollaeger, Mark. *Joseph Conrad and the Fictions of Skepticism.* Stanford Univ. Press, 1990.